**Experts from across the country praise
THE COMPLETE BOOK OF HOME BUYING!**

QUANTITY DISCOUNTS AVAILABLE

You can receive a discount when you order 24 or more copies of this title. For information, contact the Direct Response Department, Bantam Books, 666 Fifth Avenue, New York, N.Y. 10103. Phone (212) 765-6500.

THE COMPLETE BOOK OF HOME BUYING

Michael Sumichrast
Chief Economist,
National Association of
Home Builders
and
Ronald G. Shafer
of The Wall Street Journal

Revised and Updated

BANTAM BOOKS
TORONTO · NEW YORK · LONDON · SYDNEY

THE COMPLETE BOOK OF HOME BUYING
*A Bantam Book / published by arrangement with
Dow Jones-Irwin Company, Inc.*

PRINTING HISTORY
Dow Jones-Irwin edition published May 1980
*A Selection of Book-of-the-Month, March 1979
and Better Homes & Garden, May 1979*
Revised and updated Bantam edition / March 1982

ISBN 0-553-20478-5

Published simultaneously in the United States and Canada

*Bantam Books are published by Bantam Books, Inc. Its trade-
mark, consisting of the words "Bantam Books" and the por-
trayal of a rooster, is Registered in U.S. Patent and Trademark
Office and in other countries. Marca Registrada. Bantam
Books, Inc., 666 Fifth Avenue, New York, New York 10103.*

PRINTED IN THE UNITED STATES OF AMERICA

0 9 8 7 6 5 4 3 2 1

Contents

Chapter One
Why Your Home Is an Investment

Chapter Two
Where You Live and Who You Are Does Make a Difference

Chapter Three
Something Old or Something New? Used Homes versus New Homes

Chapter Four
What Makes a Home a Good Investment

Chapter Five
Investment Strategies; Or How to
Mortgage Your Future and Find
Happiness

Chapter Six
A Home Isn't Always a House;
Condominiums and Townhouses

Chapter Seven
Born-Again Homes: Housing
Rehabilitation

Chapter Eight
Financing Factors

Chapter Nine
Gimme Shelter: You and the Tax Man

Chapter Ten
Home Improvements: Protecting Your Investment

Chapter Eleven
Be a FISBO, and Other Ways to Sell Your Home

Chapter Twelve
Where Will Our Children Live? The Future of Housing

Introduction

Michael Sumichrast and Ronald G. Shafer are to be congratulated. They have, in authoring *The Complete Book of Home Buying*, given us a book that is sorely needed, is well documented, and is, above all, very readable. Anybody who lives in a home (or an apartment, for that matter) would be well-advised to examine and to re-examine this excellent guidebook.

The book actually provides more than its title suggests. It offers, to the prospective buyer, a detailed framework for thinking about an investment in housing. There are excellent chapters on what makes a good housing investment and on how to develop an effective strategy for investing. The intricacies of housing finance and real-estate taxation are explained more clearly than I have seen before in a book for the ordinary home buyer. The review of the pros and cons of buying a new house or an existing house, a condominium or a townhouse, or rehabilitating an older house should prove to be invaluable to the person who is weighing the alternatives.

The authors, in addition, provide many useful tips to the person who already owns his home—on how to improve his property and its value, and on how to sell it when the time comes.

In their final chapter, the authors look into their crystal ball, and, while acknowledging the difficulties of forecasting, offer a projection of housing in the future.

As the reader will see, Mr. Shafer and Mr. Sumichrast have succeeded in organizing and presenting a goodly amount of information needed by prospective home buyers, sellers, and anyone else who wants to understand the operation of housing markets. They have, in short, provided something of value for everyone.

Senator William Proxmire

Foreword

These days, when someone says he made a killing in the market, chances are he isn't talking about the stock market, but the housing market.

The values of homes shot up so rapidly in the 1970s you would think the roofs were lined with gold. The other side of the story is that the high cost of housing seems in danger of turning the American dream of home ownership into a national nightmare.

It's true that home prices generally seem to be performing the magical trick of rising right before your eyes. But the dream of a home of your own is still a possible one. Indeed, more and more people are buying more homes than ever before. You, too, can still get the home you want. But you may have to change your ideas about home buying.

Today, a home is more than a place to live. A home has proved to be about the most profitable investment you can make. By making wise housing investments, you can trade up to the home of your dreams. At the same time, you can achieve two other dreams: You can beat inflation, and, with your housing tax-deductions, you can beat the tax man.

Here's how Jay Janis, former Chairman of the Federal Home Loan Bank Board, explains the changing attitude toward housing: A decade or so ago, a young person ready to start a household sought out Uncle Bill, who knew something about money matters, and asked whether it would be better to rent or to buy a home. While Uncle Bill probably leaned toward buying, he had to admit that from a money standpoint there wasn't much difference between renting and buying.

Today, Uncle Bill's advice would be fast and firm, Mr. Janis says: "Buy a home. It's the best investment you can make."

Whereupon, if Uncle Bill is a rich uncle, his nephew or niece would probably hit him for a loan to make the down payment.

The purpose of this book is to be your Uncle Bill. We can't loan you a down payment, but we can offer some advice on how to buy, maintain and sell your home as an investment. And the right investment can not only put a roof over your head, but it can be a solid foundation on which to build towards other dreams, including the home that you really want.

The idea for a book on housing as an investment originated with Everett Groseclose, director of public affairs for Dow Jones and Company, which publishes The Wall Street Journal. His duties also include overseeing Dow Jones Books. So he asked whether I would be interested in writing a housing book, since I had covered housing as a reporter in the Journal's Washington bureau, where I am now an editor.

As a three-time buyer in the wild Washington housing market, the idea sounded appealing. But I was reluctant about handing out advice on home buying. After all, I'm the guy who in 1976 inadvertently ended up paying on two houses and a second mortgage. Ignoring most of the home-buying lessons I had learned, my wife and I signed a contract to buy a house the first day we looked at it.

Actually, we weren't even looking for a house; my wife had gone with a friend who was house-hunting and had fallen in love with a house for us! I had taken the kids to a movie. The name of the movie, by the way, was "Dumbo," a title that seemed appropriate when we ran into trouble selling our old house. Fortunately, though, I hadn't forgotten everything I had learned, and our house has turned out to be the best housing investment we ever made.

Still, giving home-buying advice called for an expert. So I recruited one as a co-author—Michael Sumichrast, chief economist for the National Association of Home Builders.

Mike Sumichrast is quoted in about every housing article you read in magazines and newspapers. There are several reasons why. For one, he is one of the nation's leading housing experts. For another, he has credibility with reporters, who know he will give his honest opinion even at the risk of temporarily raising the wrath of his builder bosses. To top it off, Mike's lively sense of humor makes him one of the most quotable economists in captivity.

For a book like this, Mike Sumichrast brings another quality: As a man who in 1948 escaped from Communist Czechoslovakia in a midnight boat ride across the Danube River to freedom in the West and eventually to the United States, he has a special understanding of the hopes and dreams of average Americans.

Mike and I have tried to write a book that will give a typical consumer an understanding of today's crazy housing market and some guidance on how to cope with it. Our goal is to explain home buying in a fact-filled but readable fashion, with a dash of humor here and there. To aid in our reporting, we were able to draw on the invaluable resource of housing-trend stories from The Wall Street Journal.

The book covers just about all aspects of home ownership. If you are a potential first-time buyer, we'll show you how to get into a home. If you already own a house, we'll give you tips on how to trade up to a better one. If you hate to mow lawns, you'll want to check the chapter on buying condominiums and townhouses. And if you are tired of living in the suburbs, another chapter tells how to invest in a home you can rehabilitate in the city.

A housing unit is only part of your investment. Other chapters tell you how to get the best financing—or how to get the profit out of your home without even moving—and how to make sure you are getting all the tax benefits you have coming as a homeowner. If you are thinking of making home improvements, we'll tell you which are most likely to add to the value of your home and which aren't. We'll also show you the best way to sell your home, including how you can save real-estate fees by selling it yourself.

Yes, today's soaring home prices are crazy, and the price they are asking for that shack of a house down the street is ridiculous. But that's the way it is in these inflationary times. We can't promise you that you can make a killing in the housing market—indeed, that's not the basic purpose of this book. What we want to do is show you ways to protect yourself so that you can keep up—and get a couple of jumps ahead—in today's housing game.

Ronald G. Shafer

My father always dreamed of owning a house. He never did. He was a different country—Czechoslovakia—and a different time—the Great Depression and the Great War.

My sisters never owned a house. One living in Czechoslovakia could not because of the Communist system. There you rent, most likely from the government.

The other sister, living since 1969 in Switzerland, has found it almost impossible to acquire a house there. Prices are even more astronomical than in the United States. Here, just about anybody who really wants to can own a house.

And that is just the point. When I came to this country in 1953 with my wife, Marika, we had $20 between us when we hit New York City. We had no jobs and, it seemed, no future.

Since then we have owned a number of houses. We are not rich. Yet, each time we moved and purchased a house, we were able to add to our assets. This, plus working hard, has made for a more comfortable life than we would have had otherwise. It made it possible for us to send our children to good schools and to enjoy some of the luxuries of life.

Over the years, we have given a lot of real-estate advice. We can see how our friends have benefited by buying homes. But while being directly involved with home building made this advising less difficult, the best exposure to real life in the buying and selling of homes came to me after my wife began to sell real estate four years ago. The daily stories of ordinary people she brought in were crucial to my understanding of the desires, problems and decision-making agonies of home buyers and sellers. Now we hope our experiences will directly benefit you.

The point is that we have not only realized the American dream of home ownership, we have been able to make it pay off. And just about everybody can do the same thing. You can make a house an investment that will pay.

And that is what this book is all about. It is not a textbook; it is simply a personal explanation of how we did it and how other people did it. The goal Ron Shafer and I have in this book is to show you how to do it.

Mike Sumichrast
Washington, D.C.

THE COMPLETE BOOK OF HOME BUYING

ONE

Why Your Home Is an Investment

"House prices are going up so
much that these days you can
live in a more expensive
neighborhood without ever moving."

The first step to the home of your dreams is to ignore all
those reports that say you can never have it because you
aren't likely to have the stuff that dreams are made of—
enough money.

There is no denying that housing prices and mortgage rates
have gone through the roof in recent years. But in many
ways, your chances of buying the home that you want are
better than ever because our ideas about home buying have
changed.

A house used to be just a nice place in which to live. The
man of the household saved up a nest egg (perhaps with the
help of some "pin money" from the Mrs.), the family picked
out a nice little house for a once-in-a-lifetime purchase, and
they made the biggest down payment possible to keep the
monthly payments low. If possible, the family even tried to
pay off the mortgage ahead of time. After all, a big debt was
bad. And all the time there was the concern that if they ever
did have to sell their house they might not get as much as
they had paid for it.

Times have changed. And how. Today a house is no longer
just a home. Instead, it's the most important investment most
of us will ever make. In today's mobile society, you may buy
several homes over a lifetime and never own any of them free

1

and clear. There's a good chance that both spouses in a family are working and jointly shouldering home-ownership costs. More single people, too, are buying, rather than renting. Our ideas about debt also have changed. You don't want to take on more debt than you can handle, but most home buyers today can't avoid a big mortgage that would have frightened their parents. That mortgage, though, can be your ticket to the house that you want and provide you with a hefty tax break to boot. Moreover, if the past is a guide, you can pay off a fixed amount of debt with dollars made less valuable by inflation in the future.

Housing certainly is the biggest investment for most Americans. In 1981, the nation's 54 million owner-occupied houses were valued at $2.5 trillion. That's the largest single category of assets in the country and represents one-fourth of the nation's entire wealth.

More significant to you as a homeowner—or potential homeowner—is that a housing purchase also is the most profitable investment you are likely to make. During the 1970s hardly any investment—not stocks, not bonds— appreciated as rapidly as single-family homes. The realized capital gains on the sales of owner-occupied single-family homes rose to more than $100 billion in 1981 from $33 billion in 1976 and only $19 billion in 1974.

Those are mighty big numbers, but what do they mean to you as a home buyer? On the theory that clarity begins at home, consider the experience of the co-author of this book, Mike Sumichrast, and his wife, Marika. Back in 1967, Marika suggested that the family move from their home in the Bethesda, Maryland, suburb of Washington, D.C., and buy a house in the more distant environs of Potomac, Maryland, for $50,250. Mike—the housing expert—thought that was too much to pay. After all, the $350 payment would be nearly double that on the Bethesda house they had purchased for $27,000 in 1963.

Marika insisted that the Potomac house would be a good investment and that they should buy it. She prevailed, and she was right. In 13 years the value of the home in Potomac went up to about $200,000. The monthly payments rose only to about $450, mostly because of property-tax increases. The $12,000 down payment the Sumichrasts made in 1967 compares with more than a $180,000 equity in the house today.

Not a bad deal, considering they also have lived there all that time.

In short, today a house can provide more than a roof over your head; it also can provide a handsome profit that can keep you one jump ahead of inflation. It also can be the stake that lets you "trade up" to the house that you *really* want.

Of course, housing prices haven't shot up everywhere as sharply as in the Washington area. But the Sumichrasts' experience isn't unusual.

Housing Prices—Up, Up and Away

In the 1970s, housing prices skyrocketed just about everywhere in the U.S. Nationally, the median price for a newly-built, single-family house jumped 176% from $23,400 in 1970 to $64,600 in 1980. Prices for used homes also rose 176%, from a median $22,800 in December, 1970, to a median $63,000 in 1980. The median price means that half of all homes sold were above the price and half below.

Condominiums and townhouses haven't appreciated quite as rapidly. But the median price for those apartment-type homes has gone up substantially too—from $29,400 in 1970 to $62,000 in 1980 an 111% increase.

Is a Crash Coming in Real-Estate Prices?

The combination of soaring housing prices and the prospect of an economic slowdown in the early 1980s prompted theories that the U.S. real-estate market is about to come crashing down. While such theories are provocative, most housing experts believe that anybody who is waiting for home prices to collapse is waiting in vain.

In terms of historical perspective, the record is clear. Except in the Great Depression of the 1930s, home prices have held their own or moved upward during economic hard times. Even during the depression, when the stock market tumbled 89%, the price index for housing dropped only 34%. In the 1974-1975 recession, the worst since the Great Depression, average home prices climbed nearly 10% a year. A crash in home prices is possible only if we have another depression, and—for all our economic woes—that isn't likely.

Chart 1-1

MEDIAN SALES PRICE, NEW AND EXISTING HOMES SOLD, 1966-1980.

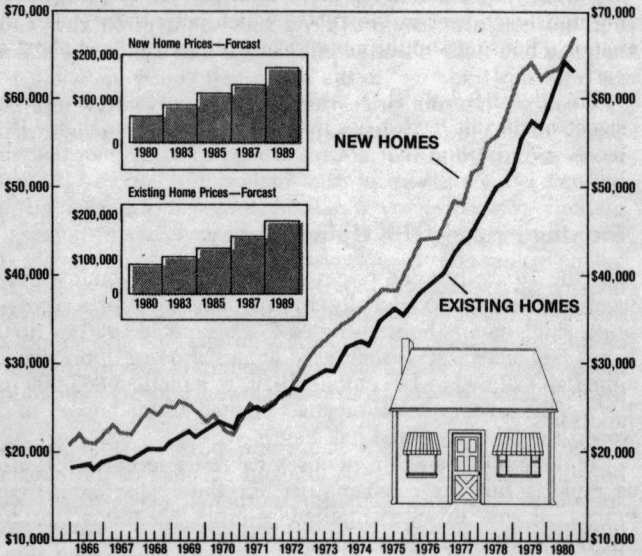

Source: Bureau of the Census;
National Association of Realtors;
NAHB Forcasting Service

Most people who talk about a crash in housing treat buying a real asset—a home—as though it were like speculating in a commodity, such as soy beans or pork bellies. It is true that speculation in housing has helped push up prices in some cities—the speculation involves buying houses not to live in, but to sell later for a profit. The theory is that, during an economic downturn, the speculators will rush to unload their investments and flood the market with houses, thus driving down prices.

Statistics, however, show that speculation has been only a minor factor in the overall housing market. Although home buyers may be gambling on continued appreciation in value, most are really purchasing an asset for their own use. There is not much "speculation" when people buy homes to live in. So housing isn't like soy beans and pork bellies.

Rising home prices mainly reflect, along with inflation, solid demand. That demand will accelerate to record levels in the 1980s as the generation of baby-boom kids born in the 1950s reaches home-buying age. Population studies indicate an underlying demand for more than two million new housing units each year in the 1980s, which potentially leaves the nation's housing supply more than a million homes short as early as 1981.

This doesn't deny that the prices of houses on any given street might not fetch what their owners want for them. It is more an indication that houses are overpriced, than that the bottom is falling out of the real-estate market. Housing markets run hot and cold, and they can be affected by everything from local plant closings to government policies.

One government action that will have a huge impact on housing in the early 1980s is the Federal Reserve Board's decision to fight double-digit inflation by clamping down on credit. An early result was nearly to close off the supply of mortgage money and to send mortgage rates soaring to record levels. Naturally, that drastically slowed housing production and sales.

The Fed's action also had some positive sides for the housing picture. For one, it choked off most of the housing speculation that did exist. For another, it likely means that housing prices in the early 1980s will increase at a slower rate than in the late 1970s. The risk is that, by holding down production and sales at a time of record demand, the action might cause prices to rise faster than ever once mortgage money flows again. Even in 1981, when home sales dropped, average home prices increased 10%.

What should you do when the housing market is uncertain and mortgage money is costly or hard to get at any price? If you can still get a loan, it is a good time to get a home at a bargain price, because sellers are having difficulty finding buyers. Otherwise, whether you are a buyer or a seller, the first thing to do is not to panic. If you can wait, the market eventually will return to normal, mortgage money will become available again, and mortgages rates will ease.

But as a buyer, you can't wait too long; any savings you might get from a lower interest rate will be more than offset by higher costs as prices start moving up again. While increases in prices may slow from time to time, the outlook is that housing will continue to be a solid investment over the long-term. By the mid-1980s, the median home price in the U.S. is expected to climb past the $100,000 mark.

Median Sales Prices of New and Existing Homes, By Quarter, 1966–1980

		New Homes				Existing Homes		
	Q1	Q2	Q3	Q4	Q1	Q2	Q3	Q4
1966	$ 21,000	$22,200	$21,600	$21,400	$ 18,500	$18,500	$18,600	$18,400
1967	22,300	23,300	22,600	22,500	19,000	19,200	19,600	19,300
1968	23,800	25,100	24,900	25,600	19,800	20,300	20,600	20,500
1969	25,600	26,000	25,900	24,800	21,100	21,800	22,400	22,000
1970	23,900	24,600	23,000	22,600	22,500	23,100	23,400	22,900
1971	24,200	25,800	25,300	25,500	24,100	24,900	25,200	24,900
1972	26,200	26,800	27,900	29,200	25,500	26,800	27,300	27,000
1973	30,300	32,600	33,500	34,300	27,900	28,800	29,600	29,400
1974	35,000	35,500	36,200	37,300	30,900	32,200	32,800	32,200
1975	38,000	38,900	38,800	41,300	33,800	35,400	36,200	35,600
1976	42,600	44,300	44,500	45,700	36,600	38,000	39,000	38,800
1977	46,400	48,900	48,700	52,000	40,400	42,500	43,800	44,200
1978	52,900	55,200	56,100	59,000	46,100	48,100	50,000	50,600
1979	60,600	63,200	64,600	62,600	52,600	55,800	57,600	56,100
1980	63,400	63,800	65,400	67,100	58,800	61,700	64,400	63,300
1981 ⎫	69,900				66,500			
1983 ⎬ ANNUAL	87,000				82,700			
1985 ⎬	112,200				105,000			
1987 ⎭	138,100				133,200			
1989	176,800				165,100			

Housing versus Other Investments; Or Keeping up with the Dow Joneses and Doing Better than Average

The only way to keep up with—and ahead of—the steady climb of housing prices is to own a piece of the action. Merely as an illustration, look at the family that bought a $30,000 home in 1974. They put $5,000 down, took out a $25,000 mortgage for 25 years at an annual interest rate of 8%. After seven years, the value of their house more than doubled to, say, at least $70,000. Thus, their equity—the difference between how much they still owe on the mortgage and how much they can sell the house for—grew more than ten-fold to more than $50,000. How many other investments pay off like that?

Chart 1-2

AVERAGE SALES PRICE OF THE
SAME KIND OF HOUSES SOLD SINCE 1963

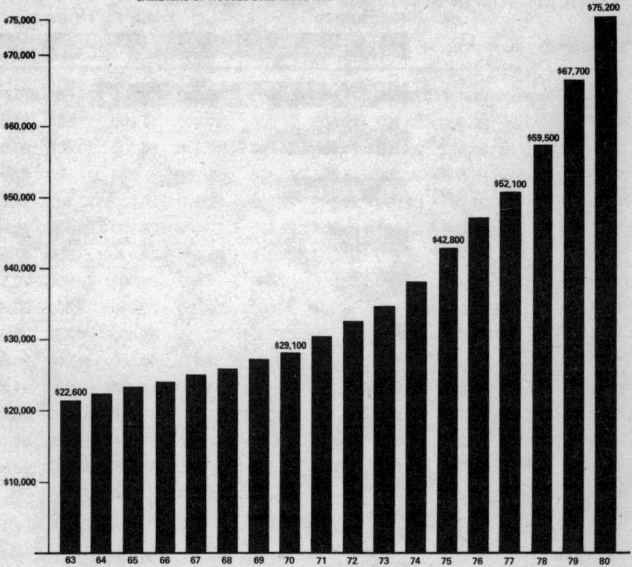

SOURCE: Bureau of Census, C-27 (Price Index).

The answer: not many.

Many buyers have turned their housing into investments. A study by American Standard, Incorporated, entitled "No Place Like Home for Your Money," shows why housing ·is about the best investment around.

The study concludes that the cash growth on home sales between 1966 and 1976 for a new, median-priced home bought in 1966 and sold in 1976 would have yielded an average annual pre-tax gain of 18.5%. This is based on a typical cash outlay for the original down payment and closing costs on a conventionally financed home.

By contrast the average annual pre-tax gains for:

· Stock prices were less than 2%.
· Bond prices were minus 4%.
· Preferred stock yields were 7%.
· Common stock were 2.5%.

Chart 1-3

What are the best hedges against inflation

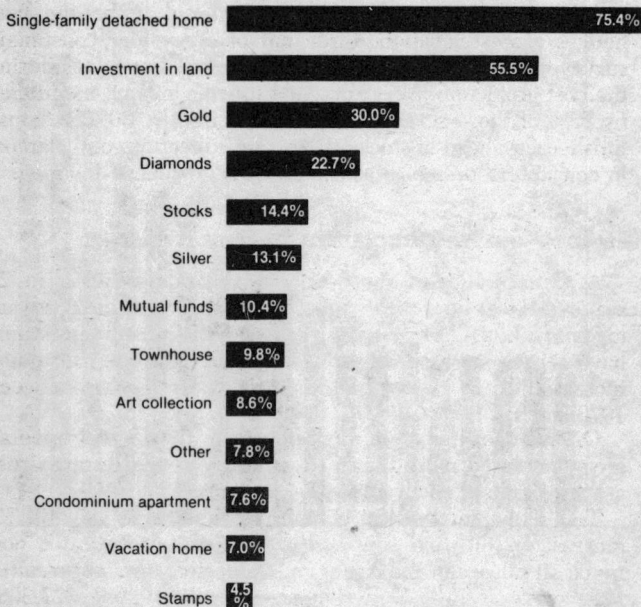

Single-family detached home	75.4%
Investment in land	55.5%
Gold	30.0%
Diamonds	22.7%
Stocks	14.4%
Silver	13.1%
Mutual funds	10.4%
Townhouse	9.8%
Art collection	8.6%
Other	7.8%
Condominium apartment	7.6%
Vacation home	7.0%
Stamps	4.5%

Source: National Association of Home Builders, 1980

- Government bond yields were 6%.
- Corporate bonds were 8%.
- Savings accounts were 5.5%.

There are, of course, other investment alternatives, such as gold, silver, or other precious metals or stones. Then there are antiques, Persian carpets, old cars or the purchase of foreign currencies. None of these, however, provides the combination of appreciation and usage that a house gives.

From 1970 to 1980 home prices rose about 170%, compared to an increase in the inflation rate of 113%. The investment advantage of housing is a major reason why demand hasn't weakened, despite rising prices.

This was clear in the answers to one question in a Consumer Survey conducted in 1980 by the Economics Division of The National Association of Home Builders.

Asked to indicate what they considered to be the best hedges against inflation, three out of every four consumers surveyed cited the single-family detached home as offering the best protection. Next came investments in land, mentioned by 55% of those surveyed, and gold, cited by 30%. A house finished far ahead of stocks, silver, art collections and stamps, in consumers' opinions, as the best hedge against inflation.

Home-Value Appreciation in Major Cities

A Census Bureau survey of housing appreciation in 21 major metropolitan areas underscores the investment advantages of a house. The survey verified what most homeowners have sensed for some time: the value of the average home increased nearly twice as fast as the owners' income between 1970 and 1977.

On average, the value of all houses in the 18 metropolitan areas increased more than 21% annually, while incomes rose at an average of about 10%.

Take a look at the last column in Table 1-1. The 174.7% increase in the first row of the last column indicates how much all houses in the Anaheim, California, area *appreciated* in seven years. In 1970 these houses were worth only $27,300.

The second-highest jump in values was in the Wichita, Kansas, area, where all houses shot up an average of 145.5%. Next came Salt Lake City, with an 138.5% appreciation rate, followed by Spokane, Washington, with 134%; Los Angeles, 129% and Fort Worth, Texas, 122%. The lowest appreciation was in Detroit, where average values increased 58.7% in seven years.

Overall, the numbers are quite startling. All you had to do was own a house in one of these areas and you "earned" anywhere from 10% to 21% a year on your money. On the average, the value of a house more than doubled in seven years in U.S. cities.

The net of all these numbers simply is that the average value of homes increased substantially more than incomes did—meaning that you could take the accumulated equity out and use it for something else—like another house.

Table 1-1

Home Ownership Incomes, Value of Houses—1970 through 1977

Metropolitan area	Income 1977	Income 1970	Home Value 1977	Home Value 1970	% Change '70–77 Income	% Change '70–77 Value
Anaheim, California	$22,400	$13,000	$75,000+	$27,300	72.3%	174.7%
Boston	19,500	12,500	43,600	23,800	56.0	83.2
Dallas	18,600	11,100	32,400	16,600	67.6	95.2
Detroit	19,700	12,300	31,100	19,600	60.2	58.7
Ft. Worth	17,100	10,400	29,300	13,200	64.4	122.0
Los Angeles	19,000	12,200	55,700	24,300	55.7	129.2
Madison, Wisconsin	20,300	11,900	43,600	21,700	70.6	100.9
Memphis	16,200	9,600	31,100	14,300	68.8	117.5
Minneapolis-St. Paul	20,400	12,100	43,900	21,600	68.6	103.2
Newark, N.J.	21,300	13,400	53,300	28,200	59.0	89.0
Orlando	15,000	9,000	32,200	15,400	66.7	109.1
Phoenix	15,900	10,100	36,100	17,400	57.4	107.5
Saginaw, Michigan	17,900	10,900	28,200	16,300	64.2	73.0
Salt Lake City	17,700	10,500	43,400	18,200	68.6	138.5
Spokane	16,400	9,300	33,000	14,100	76.3	134.0
Tacoma	16,600	10,200	34,100	17,600	62.7	93.8
Washington, D.C.	27,300	15,200	61,200	28,300	79.6	116.3
Wichita	17,300	9,700	32,900	13,400	78.4	145.5
U.S. Total	$16,000	$ 9,700	$36,900	$17,100	64.9%	115.8%
Outside metropolitan areas	$12,900	$ 7,500	$30,400	$12,200	72.0%	149.2%

Source: U.S. Department of Housing and Urban Development and the U.S. Department of Commerce, *Annual Housing Survey,* 1977 (Series H-170-77), 1980.

Bigger Prices and Bigger Homes

Why have house prices soared so high so fast? There are several reasons. One, of course, is inflation. Everything has gone up in cost, and housing is no exception. Indeed, a major advantage of housing as an investment is that housing prices have risen at a faster rate than most other prices. Thus, a house is one of the best hedges against inflation, which makes it the best hedge a homeowner can have—unlike the plant kind, it doesn't have to be clipped and it gets more valuable every year.

The rise in home prices also partly reflects sales of bigger

Table 1-2

Characteristics of New Homes, 1940-1979 (Percentage Breakdown)

Characteristics	1940	1950	1970	1980
Average Floor area (S.F.)	1,177	983	1,500	1,658
TYPE OF HOUSE				
Detached	93[1]%	97%		
Semi-detached	2	2	95	94
Row	5	1	5	6
NUMBER OF STORIES				
1 Story	67	86	74	60
Split level	0	0	10	8
Other	33	14	17	32
NUMBER OF BEDROOMS				
2 Bedrooms or Less	50[2]	66	13	17
3 Bedrooms	45	33	63	63
4 Bedrooms or more	5	1	24	20
NUMBER OF BATHROOMS				
1 Bathroom	80	92	26	12
1 Complete, 1 Partial	12	4	21	9
2 Complete	7	3	35	49
More than 2 Complete	1	1	18	30
BASEMENT				
Full or Partial Basement	69	39	37	36
No Basement	31	61	27	19
No Slab	0	4	36	45
GARAGE FACILITIES				
Garage	80	41	58	69
Carport Only	0	6	17	7
No Garage or Carport	20	53	25	24
FIREPLACE				
1 Fireplace	62	22	31	52
2 Fireplaces or more			4	5
No Fireplace	38	78	65	43
INSULATION				
Ceiling	25	83	*	100
Walls	10	34	*	100
HEATING FACILITIES				
Hot Water	22	13	6	4
Warm-Air Furnace	42	43	71	81
Warm-Air Space Heater	34	38	10	6
Other	2	6	13	0

Characteristics	1940	1950	1970	1980
HEATING FUEL				
Gas	47	64	80	41
Oil	13	33	7	3
Electricity	0	1	13	50
Other	40	0	0	6
APPLIANCES				
Range	13	21	89	98
Dishwasher	*	*	38	82
Garbage Disposal	*	5	*	78
Refrigerator	*	10	15	100
Full-home Air Conditioning	*	*	34	63
Clothes Dryer	*	*	*	93
Washing Machine	*	*	*	94
Compactor	*	*	*	8

* + Not Available
1 = Derived from Second Annual Report, Housing and Home Finance
    Agency, 1948, Table 4, page 61.
2 = NAHB Estimate

Source: U.S. Department of Labor, Bureau of Labor Statistics, *New Housing
and its Materials,* 1940–1956; Table 1, U.S. Department of Commerce, Bureau
of the Census, Construction Reports, Series C-25; NAHB Econometric Forecasting Service; NAHB Home Owners Warranty Program; NAHB Survey of New
Home Owners Tools for Planning, Marketing and Development Strategy: Kitchen
Appliances and Other Equipment in New Homes. 1940–1956 data mostly from
BLS; 1966–1980 mostly from Bureau of Census; 1980 some from HOW.

homes. In the 1940s and 1950s, home buyers were happy to
get two bedrooms, one bathroom, a musty basement, and
maybe a driveway. Today, four bedrooms, two or more baths,
a recreation room and a two-car garage, plus amenities like
air-conditioning and a fireplace are minimum requirements
for many buyers.

In 1940 the average floor area of new homes was 1,177
square feet; it dropped to 983 square feet in 1950; increased
to 1,230 in 1956; and reached 1,658 in 1980.

Only 6% of the new homes had storm windows in 1940; 4%
in 1950; 8% in 1956; and more than 81% in 1980.

In the olden days, nearly two-thirds of the new homes had
one or more fireplaces. After World War II, two-thirds of the
homes were built without fireplaces. Now the fireplace is
back again, with 51% of all new homes having one fireplace
and 7% having two or more.

Nowhere is the difference over the years better seen than

in the number of bathrooms: in 1950, 92% of the new homes had only one bathroom, and only 1% had more than two bathrooms. Today only 12% of the units built for sale have one bathroom, while 76% have two bathrooms or more.

Look what happened to the number of bedrooms. In 1950, 66% of the homes had two bedrooms or less, and only 1% had four bedrooms. Today that figure has turned around: 64% of the units built for sale have three bedrooms; 27% have four bedrooms or more; and only 9% have two bedrooms.

But bigger houses aren't the major reason for rapidly rising prices. Houses simply cost more to build today. And costlier new homes eventually mean costlier used homes.

Back in 1969, for example, Edw. R. Carr & Associates, Inc., built a four-bedroom, brick front house in Lake Ridge, Virginia, that sold for $40,950. In 1981 the price of the same model house in the same community had tripled to $129,950 and that included the carport and fireplace— standard features in the 1969 house—as extra-cost options.

Just about everything that goes into the cost of a home— land, financing, lumber and labor—contributed to the rise. But land has been the leader. A quarter-acre lot that cost about $3,000 in 1969 cost $8,500 by 1977 and $12,000 in 1981. Combined land and development costs accounted for

Edward R. Carr & Assoc. Inc. Stewart Bros. Photographers, Inc.

about 23% of the sale price of the Lake Ridge home, up from 18% in 1969.

That is in line with the national trend, as land and land-development costs in the U.S. have risen more than 200% since 1969 and now account for about one-quarter of a new-home price.

Rising Land Costs

One major reason for the increase, of course, is that good sites on which to build houses are harder to come by in many areas simply because so much already has been used up. As Will Rogers once advised: "Buy land. They ain't making any more of that stuff."

Chart 1-4

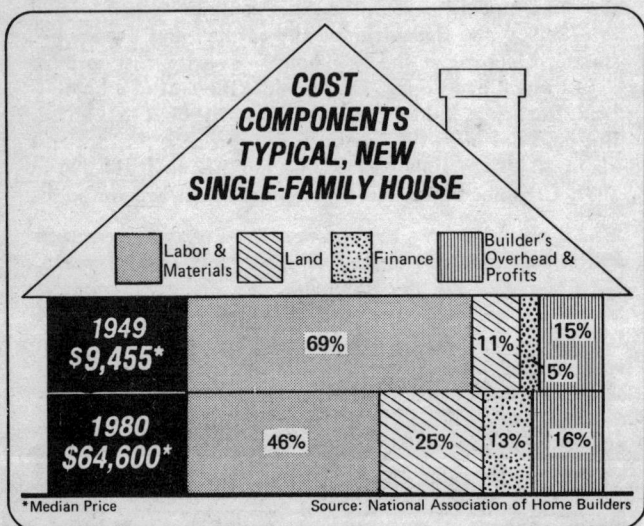

COST COMPONENTS TYPICAL, NEW SINGLE-FAMILY HOUSE

Labor & Materials   Land   Finance   Builder's Overhead & Profits

1949 $9,455*   69%   11%   15% / 5%

1980 $64,600*   46%   25%   13%   16%

*Median Price   Source: National Association of Home Builders

Another reason for rising land costs—and both new and existing home prices—is no-growth policies of some local governments. Fearful of too much development, which in fact has hurt some areas, some communities are closing the doors to new building. One result, however, is to limit the supply of homes and boost housing prices.

That can be good for people who are already there because the homes increase in value. The problem is that it eventually may close out some buyers.

In California, for example, that's happening in Santa Barbara. Only a handful of tract homes have been built recently in this city of 72,000 people. Hundreds of residents are leaving. Plans for redeveloping the downtown area have been put off for years.

A decaying, poverty-stricken little backwater? Far from it. Santa Barbara and vicinity, known collectively as the South Coast, is one of the most attractive places to live and work in California. Thousands of tourists—and potential residents—are drawn to the area by the mild climate, scenic beaches and relaxed way of life.

That is just the way most South Coasters want the place to stay. Revolting against the pressures exerted by rapid growth in the 1960s—the revolt received great impetus from a million-gallon offshore oil spill nine years ago—they have made the area a major proving ground for various measures that have held back residential, commercial and industrial development. Paul Wack, assistant planner of Santa Barbara county, said:

"A lot of people here want to put a big wall across the county line."

As a result the area seems frozen in time, its appearance and style almost unchanged over the past several years. But preserving the status quo has its social and economic price—a price high enough to give pause to other cities and towns that are acting to control growth. In recent years, probably a majority of California's towns have adopted some kind of growth-retarding plan, ranging from low-density zoning ordinances to formal lids on housing starts. Many other places in California and elsewhere are weighing similar moves.[1]

On the South Coast, growth control has produced or contributed to several consequences:

- Construction curbs have sent prices of existing homes rocketing, driving these homes out of the reach of middle-class people with growing families who want more space.

- Many of these people are leaving.
- Also leaving are others who want to stay in the area but can't find career opportunities.
- Limits on business and industrial growth, coupled with the inflated housing values, have pushed property taxes skyward for those who remain.
- Opportunities to bring in more jobs are being lost, both by the curbs on new industries and because of the bloated housing prices.

Fortunately, in many parts of the country many communities are moving toward a sensible compromise between the wasteful extremes of unlimited growth and the drawbridge mentality.

Devilish Red Tape

Driving up costs too is red tape. In some states, merely obtaining required building and environmental permits can take developers more than two years. This process is well described in a tongue-in-cheek rewrite of the story of the earth's creation. It starts:

"In the beginning, God created the heaven and earth. He was then faced with a class-action lawsuit for failing to file an environmental impact statement with HEPA (Heavenly Environmental Protection Agency), an angelically-staffed agency dedicated to keeping the universe pollution free."

The story goes on to report that God eventually was called before a HEPA Council to defend His plan. When He mentioned His idea to "let there be light," one council member immediately demanded to know: "How was the light to be made? Was it to be a coal-fired or nuclear-fired generating plant? Would there be strip mining? What about thermal pollution? Air pollution?"

"God explained that 'the light would come from a huge ball of fire.' Nobody on the Council really understood this, but it was provisionally accepted," the story continues, "assuming 1) there would be no smog or smoke resulting from the ball of fire; 2) a separate burning permit would be required; and 3) since continuous light would be a waste of energy, it should be dark at least one-half of the time."

The story concludes: "It appeared everything was in order

until God stated He wanted to complete the project in six days. At this time He was advised by the Council that His timing was completely out of the question. HEPA would require a minimum of 180 days to review the application and environmental impact statement, then there would be the public hearings. It possibly could take 10 or 12 months before a permit could be granted.

"And God said, 'To Hell with it.'"

The results of excessive red tape, however, aren't funny. A study of the Rutgers University Center for Urban Policy Research estimates that "excessive" local-government regulations add about 20% to the cost of a typical house.

The delays also can add to financing costs, including financing for construction. The share of the price of a single-family house allocated to financing has more than doubled since the end of World War II. 1981 it was estimated at close to 14% of the sales price, compared with about 5% in 1949.

Major Home-Construction Costs

The so-called "hard costs" of a house—the bricks and mortar and labor that it takes to build the house itself—also have jumped substantially in recent years. But these costs have risen more slowly than most other items, climbing over 54% nationally since 1969. As a result, they account for 46% of today's median price, down from 55% eight years ago and 69% in 1949.

Any increase in the share of the total cost of a house that doesn't go towards the structure adversely affects the space the buyer gets for each dollar. What this means is that 46 cents of each dollar for hard costs gives you only 1,212 square feet of house per $50,000 of the sales price, compared to 1,290 square feet at 54 cents, and 1,667 square feet at 69 cents—as was the case in 1949.

Meanwhile, other costs of home-buying have escalated, too. Mortgage costs, to cite one example. The 6% home-mortgage of not too many years ago has gone the way of the dodo. These days, a 15% annual interest rate, or higher, is typical, and mortgage rates are unlikely ever to get below 9% again.

Property taxes and utility bills also have gone up. All these increases add to the homeowner's burden. Consider, for example, the buyers of that Carr home in Lake Ridge,

Virginia, that tripled in price between 1969 and 1981. In 1969, the buyer of that model house obtained a 30-year, conventional loan at an 8% annual interest rate. He made an $8,300 down payment and had monthly payments (including principal, interest, taxes and insurance) of $288. The buyer of the same house in 1981 typically got a 13⅞% mortgage, had to pay $22,700 down and had a monthly payment of $1,450.

To get a mortgage in 1981, the typical home buyer at Lake Ridge needed a family income of at least $60,000, more than four times the amount needed in 1969.

That raises a serious question.

Is Home Ownership Becoming an Impossible Dream?

According to one rule of thumb—that a family's gross income should be at least five times its mortgage payments, including taxes—in 1950 seven out of 10 American families could afford the median-priced new house; by 1975, only four out of 10 could do so; in 1981, because of record interest rates, only two out of ten.

Such calculations raise concern that most Americans are being priced out of the U.S. housing market. The question is more controversial than you might think.

A study by the Harvard University-Massachusetts Institute of Technology Joint Center for Urban Studies and another analysis by the Congressional Budget Office have concluded that a large and growing number of American families are indeed being priced out of the American dream of home ownership.

But other recent studies question that conclusion. American Standard, Incorporated, specifically has sharply challenged the Harvard-MIT study. Although American Standard makes half its sales abroad, it remains the nation's largest manufacturer and distributor of plumbing supplies; consequently, it would like to see you buy a house. And its study, "Study of Single-Family Home Ownership," says the American Dream is alive and well and living in homes still affordable to average Americans.

American Standard, in its study, conceded that the new house you can afford today is likely to be smaller and situated on a smaller lot than you might prefer. But if you will buy it anyway, the company said, you will make an investment that in the past 10 years has outperformed any typical securities investment.

For example, married couples with husbands working full-time who bought a new home in 1965 incurred a cost equal to 28.7% of family income, the study says. It took only three years for ownership costs to fall to 25% of the family's rising income, and by 1975 the cost was below 20%. A similar home-buying couple in 1975 would have incurred a cost equal to 31.5% of family income. By American Standard's projections, it still took only 4½ years, until 1979, for this couple's cost to reach 25% of family income.

Although mortgage lenders in the past often required that a home-buyer's cost shouldn't exceed 25% of family income, American Standard noted that lenders and buyers alike are willing to disregard the 25% rule these days. "Affordability," the study said, "is subjective."

On several points, the Harvard-MIT and the American Standard studies permit unarguable conclusions. For one, to buy a home at any time in past years probably would have been a wise decision. The studies agree that the price of the average home has risen at a greater rate than the broad gauge of inflation, the Consumer Price Index.[2]

Is there an "affordability gap" or not? Are people worse off buying houses today than ever before, or are they actually better off? Or, is the situation about the same as, say, 10 or 20 years ago?

In terms of gross annual income, people today are better off. In 1981 they needed 3.2 years of income to qualify for a new home. In 1940 they needed 5.0 years of income to qualify.

But the problem is not gross income. The problem is disposable income—what is left in our paycheck. Taxes taken out of our gross incomes increased considerably more than incomes since 1955: state taxes increased five times as much as income, social security taxes grew four times as much, real-estate tax rates rose twice as much and federal income taxes increased 1½ times as much as gross income. As a result, net income increased at a considerably lower rate than gross income.

However, all this talk about an "average" house, an "average" family and "average" incomes ignores the fact that, in reality, there are no such things. To attempt to "average" out houses and income is like having one foot in freezing water and the other in boiling water. On the "average" we should be comfortable.

Among other things, most of the studies concentrate on new-home prices, when in fact most home-buyers purchase existing homes, which on "average" are cheaper than new homes. They also don't deal with major market changes, such as the fact that today six out of 10 first-time buyers are families in which both the husband and wife work.

To sum it all up, yes, home ownership probably remains only a dream for America's lowest-income people. But the middle-income people still have the ability to purchase homes, and they do. In that sense they are as well-off as their parents were. There has been little change in the gross income share they pay for housing today compared with the past.

Today's home purchasers have two additional advantages over the "old" ones:

- About 67% of Americans already own homes, compared with only 42% in 1940. Thus, their original nest egg has become a golden egg that gives them a profit that can be put into another and more expensive home.

- In 1981, nearly 16 million households owned their homes free and clear. This also adds to their ability to trade up.

Of course, the profit in a home investment often is, as one owner put it, like play "Monopoly game money" because it has to be put into another house when you move just to keep up your living style. But those who don't have that investment have a hard time even getting into the game.

First-time buyers clearly have the biggest problem. But somehow they seem to be getting a house—if not their dream house at first.

Without a house to trade in, Dennis Sproviero, age 29, of Hercules, California, and his wife "had to scrape" to come up with the 10% down payment they needed to buy a $50,000 house. Although their combined income is $25,000 a year—he is a merchandise manager at a Richmond, California, store and she is a school teacher—they had to borrow from their parents to raise the down payment.

But they did buy, and that's another part of the housing investment story. Despite the soaring prices, Americans are still buying houses.

Still Buying after All These Price Increases

In 1980, despite record-high prices and mortgage rates, Americans purchased nearly 4 million single-family houses. That included 850,000 new houses started and 2.9 million existing homes. In addition, they bought nearly 220,000 mobile homes. And from 1977 through 1980, a record 20.6 million homes were sold—15 million existing and 5.6 million new.

If so many people are priced out of the market, how can this be? The answer is that the desire to own one's own home is as strong as ever, and whether it means using two incomes, getting money from relatives or simply sacrificing other things, somehow Americans seem determined to buy. For one reason, they know that housing prices—however high they may be today—probably will never be lower.

"People are buying because they think they'll never have another chance," said one Denver home-builder.

Many buyers, of course, are using the equity from a previous house.

"People who were going to buy a new house for years now are able to trade up because of the tremendous values they're able to get out of their used homes," said Sandy Krulak, president of Winslow Homes. Added Robert Levenstein, executive vice-president of Kaufman and Broad, Incorporated: In California, for example, "People who bought for $25,000 10 or 15 years ago can sell for $50,000 and put their money into a new house."

The average new-home buyer in 1980 had an annual income of $30,874. But the statistics show that people with more modest incomes are ignoring all those gloomy reports that they can't afford today's housing.

The Wall Street Journal

"Remember when a piece of eight really bought something?"

Rising real-estate prices have caused buyers of both new and used homes to invest larger shares of their incomes in housing. Owners shelled out more than 30% of their take-home pay to own and run a new home in 1980, up from 23% in 1965, according to the National Association of Home Builders. And some experts predict the proportion could approach 35% by 1985.

Initially, at least, until family income increases, that means many middle-income families have to change their spending habits to set aside more of their budgets for housing. "We're going to have to squeeze and start worrying about the things we buy—a new dress and a new suit. We may be hiding our credit cards," said Ira Swadow who, with his wife, Jane, in 1979 bought a townhouse near Baltimore, Maryland, for about $51,000. The mortgage payment was triple the rent that the Swadows had been paying for an apartment.

But like millions of other home buyers, they feel the sacrifice for their housing investment will pay off in the end.

"I guess you either afford it now or it's worse later," sighed Carol Schenderlein, who with her husband, Robert, bought a new $53,000 house in the Denver, Colorado, area after selling their old one for $37,500.

Buying versus Renting

The advantages of owning are so obvious that it hardly needs restating. But we will do it anyway:

ADVANTAGES	DISADVANTAGES
· Pride of ownership	· Non-liquid investment
· Living in own house	· Maintenance and repairs
· Privacy	· Risk
· Benefit from improvements made	· Cash outlay for down payment
· Leverage (Put little down—own a lot)	
· Yield higher than most other investments	
· Tax shelter; deduct interest and property taxes	
· Inflation hedge	
· Stable investment	
· Long-lasting asset	

If you rent a home or an apartment, that means that you don't have the tax advantage—only your landlord gets it (indirectly you get it in a reduced rental rate).

You end up with a bunch of receipts rather than a value which is your own.

This is the way a $60,000 house purchased with 25% down payment looks in terms of "net" payment. The monthly payment of $570.08 is reduced 28% for people in the 30% tax bracket to $407.66 because of tax deductibility. For people in

The Wall Street Journal

"Yes, we have some very nice homes in the $20,000
range - - they're priced at $40,000."

the 20% tax bracket, the deduction for interest and property taxes reduces the monthly payment by 18% to $461.80.

In addition to the tax break, the purchaser of a house is paying off a mortgage, which is like putting money in the bank. In the above example, that adds over $400 in savings the first year and goes up each year thereafter.

What's more, as a buyer you can figure on an appreciation in the value of your house of at least 4% to 15% a year. That's another $2,400 to $9,000 a year. By contrast, a renter making the same payments of $502 a month is paying out over $6,000 a year with nothing in return except a place to live until the lease expires.

This is why Pat Devatz, working as an executive secretary for The National Association of Home Builders in Washington, D.C., finally, in the late part of 1977, at the ripe age of 43, purchased her first house.

For 25 years she has served in the ranks of the employed. During these years her salary seemed never to get to the

**Actual Monthly Payment After
Income Tax Deductions**

Purchase price of home		$60,000.00
Cash Required: $15,000		
Load: $45,000, 30 years at 12%		
interest		
Monthly payments, principal and interest		$ 462.88
Monthly property taxes		$ 91.40
Monthly insurance		$ 15.80
TOTAL		$ 570.08
Expenses for tax purposes:		
First month interest:	$450.00	
Monthly property tax:	$ 91.40	
TOTAL tax deductions	$541.45	
50% tax bracket: savings per month		$ 270.70
40% tax bracket: savings per month		$ 216.56
30% tax bracket: savings per month		$ 162.42
20% tax bracket: savings per month		$ 108.28
(to calculate deduction, multiply tax		
bracket by "total tax deductions")		
Total monthly cost (30% tax bracket)		$ 570.08
Minus tax deduction		$ − 162.42
Actual monthly cost		$ 407.66

point she figured would be necessary to purchase a home—
any home.

At the age of 30 she started seriously considering buying a
home. But a house was always beyond her reach. She was
single, with little savings.

Even with regular increases in her salary, each time she
thought about buying a home, the house price was just one
step ahead of her.

Then, 13 years later, something frightening happened to
her: the realization struck her that she had worked and slaved
all her adult life and had nothing to show for it but a batch of
rumpled receipts. They told her that she had worked very
hard to pay for someone else's property. She was really no
closer to buying that house than she had been 20-odd years

earlier. Rapidly increasing costs in every direction, the impact of skyrocketing inflation, plus the growth of taxes she had to pay as her salary increased all worked to keep her in a static condition from which there seemed to be no escape.

But she did escape and purchased a small house for $30,000, something she should have done a long time before. If she had purchased a house 10 years before, each dollar she invested could have grown 18.5% each year. Compared to almost any other type of investment, she would have done quite well.

The moral: buy a house while you are young. Browbeat your relatives into lending you the money for the down payment, if you don't have enough, and buy something you can barely afford. Believe us, it's never too soon to start.

TWO

Where You Live and Who You Are Does Make a Difference

> "In Omaha, we condemn houses
> that cost $100,000 here."
>
> —Democratic Senator Edward
> Zorinsky of Nebraska, on housing
> prices in Washington, D.C.

To Lana and George, coming from Lansing, Michigan, the high cost of housing in the Washington, D.C., area was mind blowing. George had accepted a teaching position in business administration at George Washington University in the nation's capital, and Lana had several job prospects as a computer analyst. So on their second visit, after spending several days looking for a house, they swallowed hard and, over a weekend, put down a deposit on a $65,000 townhouse in suburban Maryland. In their late 30s, they had no children. This was to be their first house.

George returned to Lansing, leaving Lana behind to fill out the loan application for the townhouse the following Monday. Everything went fine until she arrived at the First Maryland Savings and Loan Association in Silver Spring, Maryland, and saw the lending officer. Minutes after she started to answer questions, she broke down and became hysterical. The thought of buying a $65,000 house was too much for her. "I want to talk to George," she screamed.

On the phone, Lana sobbed hysterically and told George she was not going to buy a house. And she didn't. The purchase was canceled. Less than a year-and-a-half later, the same unit Lana and George had put a deposit on was up for sale again at a price of $80,000.

But while housing in Washington may be costly compared with Lansing, Washington isn't the most expensive city in which to buy houses in the continental U.S. In 1976, San Francisco took over that "honor." And Los Angeles wasn't far behind.

California Dreaming—The Great Land Rush

In 1975 and 1976 a home-buying fever reminiscent of the fever for gold in the Great Gold Rush of 1849 began spreading through California. As a result, housing prices rapidly soared out of sight. Scenes such as the following were typical:

It is late 1976 in Thousand Oaks, California. In a rain-spattered parking lot in the hills outside town, Peggy Giarusso huddles in a car.

She and 25 other people, plus their children, are waiting for morning—and the opening of the newest unit in the Wildflower housing development.

Mrs. Giarusso has been here since 8:30 the previous morning, to secure first place in line, because she knows that most of the 50-unit tract will be sold in hours. She wants a particular house and lot in the San Fernando Valley development, northwest of downtown Los Angeles, and, she says, "I'll do anything to get it."

She and her fellow campers aren't nuts. They are participating in a full-scale home-buying panic in the Southern California housing market, the nation's most active. Pressures accumulating for three years recently exploded into a rush to buy that has real-estate salesmen, builders and lenders goggle-eyed. Demand is so frenzied that putting a new home on the market is like throwing a hunk of meat to a school of sharks.

Hundreds of prospective buyers camp out for days in front of new developments, while thousands of others compete in lotteries for a chance to buy a new home. Prices for houses, new and used, have doubled in some locales within the past two to five years. Low- and medium-priced housing is almost nonexistent as developers cater to the affluent and to current homeowners whose equity in their houses has ballooned. Although as welcomed as cockroaches at most new developments, speculators abound, and they add to the buying frenzy.[3]

Fueled by such frenzy, the average price of all new homes sold in Southern California in 1977 increased 30.6% to $75,100, according to David E. Davies, a Los Angeles housing consultant. This was a staggering 59.1% higher than the average price in 1975. By 1981, average home prices in Los Angeles exceeded $110,000.

The prices of existing homes in California also have skyrocketed, especially in prestigious areas. For example, if you want to live near stars, in Beverly Hills, you will have to pay astronomical prices. The same housing madness that has swept through the entire Southern California market has struck Beverly Hills, a town of 30,000 people and 6,000 homes, but with even greater virulence. Some home prices have escalated 20% a month. A small house that sold for around $35,000 in the 1960s might easily fetch over $225,000 today.

Two houses that sold for $115,000 and $85,000, respectively, as recently as 1975, were on the market again at $395,000 and $197,000 in 1977. So was an estate that changed hands for $850,000 years ago. But the owner wanted $2.6 million. (And in early 1981, singer Kenny Rogers bought a Beverly Hills mansion for $14.1 million, the highest price ever paid for a single-family home in Southern California.)

In addition to the booming demand that hit other areas in Southern California, Beverly Hills has two unusual factors working for it: one is the desire by many wealthy people to live next door to Hollywood stars. The other is a cadre of flamboyant real-estate sellers who cater to that desire. If you're looking for a glamorous Beverly Hills abode, Stan Herman will be glad to show you one. He'll make sure the lights are on, fires are burning slowly in the fireplaces, the gardens are freshly trimmed and sprinkled, and flowers are in the rooms. There will be allusions to celebrities who once lived here, or, failing that, down the street.

You'll be glad to fork over a million or so for the place. It would sell for a fraction of that in Peoria, but Beverly Hills isn't Peoria. It is perhaps the wildest real-estate market in the nation, where a cramped two-bedroom cottage with a single bath sells for $150,000 or more. That's the bottom of the market; the top approaches $4 million.

People with that kind of money are shamelessly coddled and wooed by platoons of real-estate salesmen who can make tens of thousands of dollars on a single sale. "When a person is thinking of buying a million-dollar home," said Mr. Herman, who owns one of the biggest real-estate agencies in town, "he just doesn't walk around and ask how much. There has to be some romance involved."

To Mike Silverman, a rival real-estate man, romancing customers means taking them for a helicopter ride—at $150 an hour—so they can get a bird's-eye view of the property, and having a chilled bottle of Pinot Chardonnay in the house when they alight. Naturally, only clients for expensive houses get such treatment, but Mr. Silverman doesn't handle many economical homes; during one fairly-typical week the cheapest house he had for sale in Beverly Hills was $525,000.[4]

The rapid jumps in housing prices all over California have meant big profits for many home buyers, and real-

Chart 2-1

COMBINED HOUSEHOLD INCOME
NEW HOME BUYERS

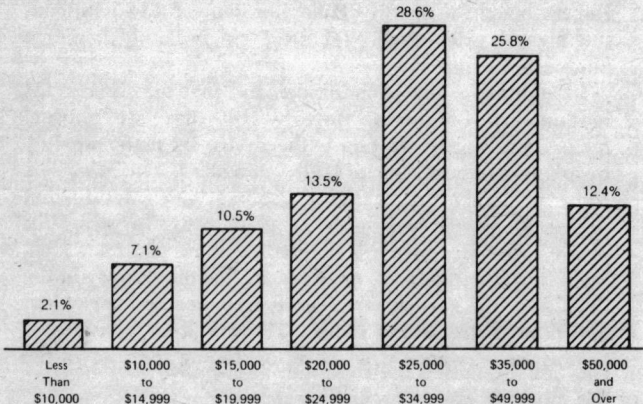

Less Than $10,000	$10,000 to $14,999	$15,000 to $19,999	$20,000 to $24,999	$25,000 to $34,999	$35,000 to $49,999	$50,000 and Over
2.1%	7.1%	10.5%	13.5%	28.6%	25.8%	12.4%

NAHB HOW Survey

estate "investment" is a hot topic of conversation. Some homeowners simply moved up to more expensive houses by selling their appreciated old homes. But others, with little real-estate experience, began getting second mortgages or taking money from the stock market to speculate.

The latter kind of activity became worrisome to real-estate experts, who said that excessive speculation—especially by amateurs—creates instability in the market. If there is a villain in the California housing boom, it is the speculator who buys a house with no intention of living in it. He generally puts up the smallest down payment possible and holds the house for six months or a year, renting it if possible, often for less than his own payments on it. His goal: to sell in a strong upward market for enough to cover any shortfalls in rental plus a fat profit on his money invested.[5]

The Hazards of Speculation

The problem is that the speculation can cause an artificial upward push on prices. Such speculation is based on what is known as the "Greater Fool" theory, with buyers knowingly paying too much for property but hoping to sell it to a "greater fool." Eventually, however, the market can become "overheated"; as rising prices put more people out of the market, greater fools become harder to find, and, as demand goes slack, prices can actually drop with both speculators and regular home-buyers getting burned in the process.

To prevent such artificial price pressures, many mortgage lenders, at the request of the San Francisco Home Loan Bank, which oversees savings and loan associations, cut back on home loans to speculators. And with more houses being built to meet demand, the bloom is somewhat off the boom in California. Prices are continuing to rise in California, but not at the frantic pace of before.

The boom, however, has left its mark on the cost of housing in California's major cities.

High-Priced Housing Cities

The San Francisco metropolitan area has always been one of the most expensive areas for existing houses. But in 1976, San Francisco moved into the Number One spot in the continental U.S. on the housing-cost hit parade. In 1980, prices of homes sold in the San Francisco/Oakland area averaged $120,100, up 18% from $101,700 a year before and up a whopping 171% from only $44,300 in 1973, when the area was the third costliest in the country.

The Los Angeles area was in second place in 1980, with an average price of $110,600, 17% above the year-earlier $94,300. (Honolulu, Hawaii, had the highest average home price of $121,500, up 25% from a year before.)

Rounding out the five most expensive metropolitan areas for used housing in 1980 were San Diego and Washington D.C., followed by New York and Phoenix.

Nationwide, in 1980 the average sales price for all homes was about $79,000, up 13% from 1979. (The "average" price is higher than the median price.)

Table 2-1

Average Sales Price of Homes Sold

Metropolitan area	1980	1979	percent change
Honolulu	$121,500	$97,200	up 25 %
San Francisco/Oakland	120,100	101,700	up 18.1%
Los Angeles	110,600	94,300	up 17.3%
San Diego	106,400	92,200	up 15.4%
Washington, D.C.	100,800	91,600	up 10.0%
New York	94,300	79,100	up 19.2%
Phoenix	93,800	75,900	up 23.6%
Seattle	88,200	74,400	up 18.5%
Dallas	88,000	73,300	up 20.1%
Houston	85,300	72,000	up 18.5%
Milwaukee	85,100	70,100	up 21.4%
Atlanta	81,200	69,900	up 16.2%
Minneapolis	80,300	74,000	up 8.5%
Denver	79,400	75,900	up 4.6%
Chicago	77,000	69,300	up 11.1%

Source: Federal Home Loan Bank Board, compilation by NAHB Economics Division

Of course, housing prices often tend to be cheaper outside metropolitan areas. But there, too, the housing picture is the same as in urban areas. A 1981 Census Bureau report shows that the biggest increase in values of homes between 1970 and 1977 was outside the standard metropolitan statistical areas. In these more rural areas the appreciation was 149.2%, while homes in the central cities appreciated by 115.89%.

Low-Cost Housing Cities

Which raises the question: Are there any "cheap" places to live? As can be seen from the various housing-prices tables, there are.

Table 2-2
Low-Priced Housing Cities—1980

St. Louis	$57,500
Louisville	57,800
Rochester	58,000
Pittsburgh	61,900
Indianapolis	62,200
Philadelphia	62,200
Tampa	63,700
Greensboro	63,800
Cleveland	64,300
Kansas City	65,700
Detroit	67,500

Source: Federal Home Loan Bank Board, Compilation by NAHB Economics Division

Wherever you live, remember that those "median" and "average" prices are just statistics, and that there are plenty of homes for sale below those figures. For example, in 1977 the average new-home price was about $55,000. A survey of 8,500 1977 home buyers by the United States League of Savings Associations found that 62% of the buyers bought homes for $50,000 or less, and 50% purchased homes costing less than $44,000. "In fact, more home buyers bought homes costing less than $30,000 (20%) than bought those priced $70,000 or more (15%)," the study said.

Wide Regional Differences (Or Don't Go to Alaska for a Cheap House)

As we have seen, there are a great many differences among states and cities in the prices of homes, both new and used. There also are a great many differences among regions of the country.

One explanation for these differences lies in the wide range, from one area to another, in the costs of building a new home. The most expensive part of the U.S. in which to build a home is Alaska, followed by Hawaii. The South is generally the cheapest region to build in because of lower land and development costs and a good supply of labor. For instance, in Fairbanks, Alaska, the cost of a house in 1980 was $60.09 a square foot; in Atlanta, Georgia, it was $36.52 a square foot.

In Hawaii, the cost in 1980 was $75.89 per square foot.

Costs generally are higher in the northern U.S. than the South, partly because of construction requirements due to the colder climate. The cost in 1980 was about $47 a square foot in North Dakota; about $41 in Youngstown, Ohio, and about $47 in Olympia, Washington. By contrast, square-foot costs averaged $38 in Tennessee, and $37 in Florida.

As the previous examples indicate, the cheapest area to build new homes in is Florida. The reason is simply that the warm climate eliminates the need to get the footings deep into the ground (below the frost line) because there is no frost, and the structure itself can be of simple concrete block.

Demand Makes a Difference

Prices for both new and used homes also reflect consumer demand, as well as the financial ability of a region's residents to purchase housing. The impact of the California housing boom is evident in regional prices. The prices of homes sold in the western U.S. have risen at a faster clip than the nationwide average.

The smallest degree of change has been registered in the northeast region, in the South, and in the north central region.

The differences in housing prices really hit home to people who are transferred by their employers to high-cost areas

This home in Bethesda, Maryland, sold in 1961
for $37,950. In 1976 comparable houses were selling for
nearly $100,000. In 1981 comparable houses
sold for more than $135,000.
Kettler Brothers & NAHB Journal of Homebuilding

from low-cost areas. The impact is especially noticeable to
people with more expensive houses.

Richard DeAgazio, a 33-year-old brokerage-house executive, felt he was getting a big break when he was transferred from Boston to New York. Then he went house-
hunting in the New York suburbs.

He quickly found that houses equal to his $110,000
nine-room Colonial back in suburban Winchester, Massachusetts, were selling for at least 30% to 50% more.
Alarmed, the aggressive young senior vice-president of
ABD Securities Corp. asked for a larger raise to offset his
higher housing costs. He was turned down. Finally, after a
search that lasted five months and involved going through
60 houses, Mr. DeAgazio and his wife found what they
considered a bargain—a house comparable to their old
one, selling for $135,000 in Westfield, New Jersey.

"And we were lucky to get it," says Ann DeAgazio. "We
won't be putting any money in the bank. And we hope the
cost of living by some miracle won't go any higher."

   The DeAgazios are victims of a growing problem for
executive families: the sharp appreciation in the prices of
homes in the $100,000-plus bracket. These homes have
been shooting up 12% to 15% a year, said Weston Edwards, chairman and chief executive of Merrill Lynch
Relocation Management Inc., a consulting subsidiary of
Merrill Lynch & Company.

   Compounding the problem is the widening divergence of
home values in different areas of the country and in
different communities within the same area, Mr. Edwards
said. That divergence "appears likely to widen further," he
added.

   The highest-priced areas in the country are Los Angeles, San Francisco, Washington, D.C., New York City,
Denver, Chicago and, to a lesser extent, Houston, Dallas
and Boston. Homes in some suburbs of these cities are
appreciating far faster than average, with those in Orange
County, California, and Greenwich, Connecticut, showing
annual gains of 20% to 25%. Among the lower-priced areas
are cities in the Midwest, Southeast and Deep South, Mr.
Edwards said.

   "It's Economics 101—higher demand and lower supply,"
said James Keane, vice-president of Homequity Inc., a
Wilton, Connecticut, relocation concern.

   For their part, executives going to high-cost from low-
cost areas are getting more aggressive about demanding
enough money to cover the big cost-of-living crunch. Failing that, they must dig deeper into their own pockets to
keep up living standards or reluctantly settle for less.

   In the latter case, the executives "stretch for higher value
but give up something in the trade, such as extra land or
central air-conditioning," Mr. Keane said. "They can't
equal their old houses. They have to give up some of the
niceties."

   Some executives believe that they will make up for the
housing-cost crunch when they transfer back to lower-cost
areas. But relocation concerns point out that more dollars
chasing fewer homes can drive up prices in low-cost areas,
too. And they say that variables among different areas can
muddy pure price comparisons.[6]

   The kind of house you can buy clearly depends on where
you live. But it also depends on who you are and what you

can afford to pay. Everybody is different, obviously, but you'll find yourself in one of the following categories.

Previous Homeowners

When it comes to housing investment, current homeowners are sitting pretty. About two-thirds of all U.S. families own their own dwellings, and the proportion has been rising steadily. If you are among them you can use the equity in your house to trade up to a better home, and you won't have to borrow from relatives to do it.

The majority of today's new homes, for example, are being sold to families who are moving up the ladder, using the equity and inflated profit from the sale of their previous homes as a way to move into more expensive ones. Often nowadays families make a profit of $25,000 or more on the

"Hi! I'm handsome Harry Davenport, rising young executive recently transferred here from Birmingham, Michigan, seeking mortgage money for a small place near the country club where we can resume living way beyond our means while attempting to keep up with the Joneses."

sale of homes they purchased only five years ago. And it is a tax-free profit so long as it is invested in another home within 24 months.

In 1979, 82% of home buyers were trading up; only 18% were first-time buyers. Two years before about 36% were first-time buyers, according to the U.S. League of Savings Associations.

Difficulties for First-Time Buyers

In striking contrast to previous homeowners, if you are a first-time buyer you probably will have to juggle with all sorts of financing to come up with the down payment for a home. And, typically, that down payment is very, very low. Typically, also, you are likely to be young—usually 25 years old or younger; only 18% of home buyers in this age group have equity from a previous home.

Dave Miller, president of Miller and Smith, a home builder, said: "We have a condominium project near Crofton, Maryland, with units selling for between $33,000 and $40,000, and we have a great deal of difficulty getting young people to come up with 5% down ($1,650 to $2,000). We pay the closing costs—and they are still hard pressed to get their money together. In most cases they borrow from their parents."

This example, better than anything else, shows the difficulties young people are experiencing in accumulating a sufficient amount of money to purchase a house.

So what do they do? According to an NAHB survey, 8% pay nothing down; 32% pay between 1% and 5% down; 22% pay between 6% and 10% down. The rest, most likely, scrape together between 11% and 20% for the down payment on their dream house.

But all of this is not really their money: 15% borrow the down payment from relatives; another 8% use inheritance funds; and 2% get a second mortgage to finance their down payment. However, about half of the young people under the age of 25 who buy new homes do accumulate enough savings to make the down payment.

Most young people who depend on loans from relatives and borrowing on second mortgages for their down payments are the ones who buy the least expensive homes—those priced either under $30,000 or from $30,000 to $40,000.

Built by Levitt in 1966, this colonial design features
four bedrooms, den and three baths. It originally sold for
$29,990 in Montpelier, Pa.

NAHB Journal of Homebuilding

Young, first-time buyers who use inheritance funds purchase
more expensive homes priced between $40,000 and $50,000.

The strategy for first-time buyers is to get into the housing
game with an investment that can be used to start trading up
to the home that they really want. The prevailing reason why
young people purchase their first homes was well stated by a
24-year-old buyer from Atlanta: "We own it. It's a nice size,
and it's practical. And the price is already up $2,500 since we
bought it nine months ago."

Couples—Two Incomes Are Better than One

If the entry ticket into that first house is higher these
days—and it is—many people still are finding a way to come
up with the price of the ticket thanks, in large measure, to
the women's liberation movement.

One of the most significant social changes of recent times is
the upsurge in the number of working women. Whether the
wife has a full-time career or takes a job to help pay the
family bills, the result is that while two can't live as cheaply
as one, their two incomes can help cover a lot of extra costs.

The change has had a tremendous impact on housing, because the home that may have been out of the financial reach of a family in which only the husband works suddenly becomes a possible dream with two bread-winners to help save for the down payment and to make the mortgage payments. In 1980, more than 56% of all home buyers were couples that included a working wife, and 64% of those who bought their first homes were families in which the wife was employed. A decade before, only 25% of home buyers were couples with two incomes.

Despite the upsurge in the number of working wives, you don't necessarily need two incomes to buy a house, even at today's prices. Many couples still manage to become homeowners in families where the wife decides not to work outside the home. In fact, unlike a decade or so ago, home buying no longer is almost entirely limited to married couples.

Shelter and the Single Person

Should a single person buy a home? More and more do. In some new subdivisions as many as 20% of home buyers are what are now called "nontraditional buyers." This could be a single male or single female or two singles of the opposite sex, or of the same sex, living together.

Although many young unattached individuals would probably prefer to rent—to give them more freedom to travel, for instance—the economics of owning are becoming more and more a determining factor in their decisions to buy or rent. The same is true for older singles, many of whom are divorced or widowed.

This situation is not a rarity, as the following shows.

The 4000 block of Park Lane, 10 miles north of downtown Dallas, was a fairly typical American street a decade ago. Families of four and five people lived in most of the tidy brick homes. Middle-aged couples whose children had married lived in the rest.

Today the couples are still there and so are some of the families, but now there is a difference: someone lives alone in one out of every four houses on the block.

What's happening on Park Lane exemplifies some sweeping changes taking place in the way Americans are living—and spending their money. People who live alone have breathed new life into many housing markets, especially townhouse and condominium markets.

More than 15.5 million people live alone and account for 21% of all the households in the country, up from 17% in 1970. The Census Bureau says that since 1970 the number of people living alone grew by 43%, while the number of households with both husband and wife grew by only 6%.

In 1977 alone, Americans formed 1.3 million new households. Couples, with or without children, accounted for 174,000 of them, singles for 549,000. One-parent families accounted for most of the rest.

Later marriage, higher divorce rates and a widening gap between the life expectancies of men and women are behind the big increase in one-person households. And while there is disagreement as to how pronounced the trend will be in the future, it is expected to continue for a long time.

More Women Buying Homes

The housing industry probably more than any other has felt the impact of single living. Since enactment of the Equal Credit Opportunity Act in 1976 single women have become the fastest-growing segment of the home-buying market and could account for one of every 10 sales by 1980.

Builders even have an abbreviation for their new single, separated, widowed and divorced buyers. "SSWDs are what the townhome market is all about," said Nicholas Schmidts, senior vice-president of Sanford Homes, a Denver builder.

While single buyers tend to favor townhouses and condominiums, buying 70% of them in some developments, many are buying traditional detached homes. Fox and Jacobs, Inc., the Dallas builder, said it sells 10% of its single-family homes to single buyers, up from 5% in 1972.

Many of these singles view living alone as a good transition in their lives. Jack Simunek, an accountant for Florida Gas Company in Orlando, Florida, took his own apartment across town from his parents when he was 22. "I wanted the experience of running a household and managing the bills before I got married," he explains. "That way, I'd be the only one hurt if I made a mistake."

Young singles account for less than 9% of all one-person households, but they're the fastest-growing segment of the household population. The number of young women living alone is up 108% in seven years, and the number of young men is up 174%.

The divorce rate, which doubled in the past decade, also is behind the trend toward single-person households. About 1.1 million marriages ended in divorce in 1976 alone. At that rate, the Census Bureau predicts that one person in three between the ages of 25 and 35 will get a divorce. And while about 80% of them will remarry, the chances of a successful second marriage are even worse.

Widows account for one-third of all one-person households. While the life expectancy of both men and women is rising, a woman now can expect to live to be eight years older than her husband was when he died, compared with 6.7 years in 1960 and two years in 1900.

Because of the gradual aging of the population, the Census bureau says, elderly women will outnumber elderly men by 6.5 million by the end of the century. Widows once moved in with their children, but now they're likely to have fewer children to depend upon; the children are likely to have different attitudes or obligations; and the widows themselves are likely to be more independent than in the past.

Carolyn Taylor of Fort Collins, Colorado, said it never occurred to her to move in with one of her six children when she was widowed in 1973. "I didn't want to burden myself having to consider other people in my plans," she says. In 1977, Mrs. Taylor bought a three-bedroom house and began investing in real estate. She also planned to open an art studio. "It would have been a great sacrifice on both sides," she said, if she had moved in with her children.[7]

For many singles, young or old, the lure of home ownership is the chance to make a solid investment with the money they pay for shelter.

A single 29-year-old man, making $13,000 a year, purchased a $40,000 single-family house in Lincoln, Nebraska, because it was a "better investment than anything else I could find." He had moved to Lincoln from another state—visited seven other subdivisions before purchasing.

He was renting a duplex at $175 per month plus $100 for utilities, and his monthly payment jumped 78% to $350 for the mortgage and $140 for utilities. He was actually paying 45% of his income for the house. That is by any reasonable measure way too high a share—unless he is upwardly mobile and considers this payment to be reasonable in a couple of years. Or, as in his interesting case: only 29 years old, he purchased this house for $40,000 cash. How? He took out a mortgage on another investment and financed his own house.

Obviously, it is unusual for a young person to be able to swing an elaborate financing arrangement like that. For most young buyers, the problem is simply coming up with enough of the green stuff called money to get into a house.

Minority Home Buyers

When Mrs. Sumichrast and I purchased our first house on Olentangy Boulevard in Columbus, Ohio, in 1957, we heard our neighbors complaining: "What is this neighborhood coming to? We already have a Jew living in one house and now a couple of foreigners are moving in"—meaning us, since I am Czech and my wife, Marika, Polish.

The fact that the Jew was a world-renowned psychiatrist, and my wife and I, in addition to working, were enrolled in the Graduate School at Ohio State University, did not make much difference. People simply were afraid of the unknown. "What are we going to do with the property? Will the value of our properties decline as a result of a 'mixed' neighborhood?" they wondered.

Now as it happens we were the first ones on the block to start (immediately—before we moved in) to renovate our house. We put a lot of money into it, probably too much, but we actually upgraded the street. After a while we were accepted by most people, but not by some.

There was probably at that time no way a black family could have purchased on that street.

Looking for an apartment to rent in New York in 1954 showed me for the first time that it does make a difference what color you are. Talking to a landlord on the telephone in response to an ad, his first question was: "Are you black or Puerto Rican?"—M.S.

In many ways, times have changed. Today, housing discrimination because of color or religion is not only morally wrong, it is illegal. And black Americans especially, after being held back by discrimination in both jobs and housing, today are joining the ranks of homeowners at a faster rate than the overall population.

In the 11 years from 1960 to 1970, total home ownership in the U.S. rose to 62.9% from 61.9%, a gain of only one percentage point. At the same time, home ownership by blacks increased 3.1 percentage points to 41.5% from 38.4%. The Census Bureau's latest surveys indicate this trend is continuing; by 1977, 43.6% of the nation's blacks owned their homes, a further gain of 2.1 percentage points. Overall home ownership in those five years advanced only another 1.9 points to 64.8%.

What this means, says a U.S. League of Savings Association study conducted by Andrew F. Brimmer, former Federal Reserve Board Governor, is that mortgage demand among blacks is likely to continue to accelerate faster than among whites. While some lenders have expressed concern over possible extra risk because, in the past, the bulk of black mortgages have been on inner-city houses, Mr. Brimmer said studies show "the percentage of blacks in a neighborhood isn't significant in explaining delinquency rates"—it is the quality of the property that matters.

What's more, many blacks are moving into the suburbs, which often means they also are buying homes there. The number of blacks in U.S. suburbs rose 34% between 1970 and 1977, the Census Bureau reported. The biggest increase was in the Washington, D.C., area, according to a Ford Foundation financed survey by the Washington Center for Metropolitan Studies. And the increase is continuing. As one Fair Housing pioneer in the Washington suburbs put it: "Younger people can scarcely conceive of times when even the idea of blacks in many areas was unthinkable. Tell that to people today and they'll say 'You're kidding me.'"

Of course, that doesn't mean that housing discrimination against blacks, Hispanics and other minorities has ended. Far from it. A $1 million, federally-funded survey released in 1978 by the National Committee against Discrimination in Housing "confirmed the appalling fact that black people still encounter unconscionable racial discrimination," said Patricia Harris, then Secretary of Housing and Urban Development.

The survey involved sending pairs of black and white "customers" to 3,000 real-estate brokers and rental agents in 40 metropolitan areas. Each pair used the same type of income and job information in seeking housing.

When inquiring about buying a home, the white and black shoppers were treated equally only 10.5% of the time in terms of availability. Whites were favored 55.5% of the time and blacks, 34%. Officials who conducted the study said the figures for purchase may be understated, because the results haven't been examined for "steering" of customers to particular neighborhoods—for example, steering blacks to neighborhoods that are predominately black and away from white neighborhoods.

The investigation found that blacks encountered the least housing bias in the Northeast. Prospective black home buyers encountered discrimination most often in the North Central area.

Fighting Discrimination

Combating housing discrimination sometimes is more difficult these days because the bias is more subtle than when sellers simply refused to deal with minorities. When Gloria Toote was an assistant secretary of Housing and Urban Development and one of the highest-ranking blacks in the Nixon-Ford administration, she told this story about a discrimination complaint made to her department: A black couple said they had arranged over the telephone to meet a real-estate agent so that they could inspect a vacant house that was for sale in a predominately white neighborhood. When they arrived at the house at the agreed-on time, the agent was nowhere to be seen. After waiting several minutes, they noticed that the front door was ajar, so they decided to go in and look around the house until the agent arrived. In one room, they opened a closet door. There was the real-estate agent, hiding inside the closet. He apparently hadn't realized the couple was black until, from inside the house, he saw them coming up the front walk.

Both the National Association of Realtors and the National Association of Home Builders have begun Fair Housing programs in conjunction with the U.S. Department of Housing and Urban Development to try to overcome such discrimination. There obviously is a long way to go, but other efforts also are under way.

Discrimination also comes in the form of lending—or not lending—money for housing. Partly at the urging of civil rights groups, the Federal Home Loan Bank Board, which regulates savings and loan associations, in 1978 proposed far-reaching regulations that would seek to monitor any "prescreening" of S&L loan customers that may discourage minorities from seeking loans and help to weed out any discriminatory practices.

Many local areas also have taken steps to encourage housing integration and to avoid "panic peddling" that can damage home values. The community of Oak Park, Illinois, has set up a system of managed integration to encourage whites to stay as minorities move in. In 1979, the village board established an insurance plan that will pay 80% of any loss suffered by an enrolled homeowner who sells a house after five years. If an owner sells at a loss, local tax money will be used to make up the difference.

"The irony of it all is that the program may not be needed because the housing market in Oak Park is strong and continues to get stronger," said the village board president.

As a home buyer, there is a great deal you can do if you feel a seller is discriminating against you because of your race, ethnic background, sex or religion. For one thing, you can complain to the U.S. Department of Housing and Urban Development's Fair Housing Office in Washington, D.C., or phone it on a toll-free number—800-424-8590. The department's authority currently is largely limited to trying to arbitrate complaints, but it also may be able to put you in touch with local authorities.

We hope nothing like that will be necessary. After all, the American goal of home ownership is—or should be—an equal opportunity dream.

THREE

Something Old or Something New? Used Homes versus New Homes

> "What you are talking about is a
> typical tract development: ticky,
> tacky houses in the $300,000 to
> $400,000 range."

Some people, obviously, have strong feelings on the question of new homes vs. old homes. The above remark was made by a homeowner in a wealthy, older Washington, D.C., neighborhood in opposition to plans to build new homes in that area on the former estate of Nelson Rockefeller, Fortunately, in most places housing prices haven't yet soared so high that the prospect of $300,000 homes is likely to cause folks to complain, "Well, there goes the neighborhood."

The question of buying an existing home or a new home is a very private decision that only you can make. Some people prefer older homes. Such homes, they feel, are more likely to be in established neighborhoods near shopping and cultural attractions. Besides, older homes have more "character" than new subdivision homes and also are more solidly built, they argue.

Other people like the idea of living in a brand-new home. They cite the advantages of more modern appliances, more space, often bigger yards, and amenities that may not be available in older homes. And there is another attraction.

47

With today's price trends, the price of a new home likely is the cheapest at which anybody will ever buy that particular house.

No one can tell you which type of home to buy. In terms of appreciation in value, new and used homes average about the same—in recent years, between 10% and 15% a year. Of course, that's only a statistic. The values of some homes, new or used, go up faster than average, some go up slower than average, and some even drop. There are other factors besides age that affect home values, as will be discussed in the next chapter.

To help you decide whether a used or new home is best for you, the authors have prepared a long shopping table that shows the "general" advantages and disadvantages of each. Remember, these are only "general" guides—some of the advantages listed for used homes also may be found in new homes, and vice versa. Actually, the "new" homes category applies to most any home built in the past few years; "older" homes can be anything from 5 to 10 years old, up to a century or more in age.

Advantages of Existing Homes

Used houses have a lot to offer.

- For one thing, there are 50 times as many of them as there are new homes. So the selection is considerably larger among existing homes.

- Second, older homes, as a general rule, are about 15% less costly than new homes.

- A major advantage of older homes over new ones often is location. Older homes tend to be nearer shopping areas, churches, cultural activities, downtown jobs and transportation. Moreover, the neighborhoods often are more attractive because the trees and shrubbery have grown over the years.

- Services also are frequently better in established areas. For instance, if the U.S. Postal Service has its way, letter carriers won't even be delivering mail at the doors of new homes. The Postal Service is pushing rules that would require that mail at new-housing developments be placed in curbside boxes or locked in "cluster boxes" at central delivery points within the developments. Actually, the Postal Service said it already is following that policy in many areas in an effort to hold down costs. Under the policy, however, you would continue to get your mail at your door in an existing home.

· Older houses sometimes offer certain advantages because of the way they are constructed. They often tend to have more individual characteristics than the cookie-cutter styles in some subdivisions. (Of course, many "older" homes on the market are used homes in previously-built subdivisions.) Inside, houses a decade or more older are more likely to have real hardwood floors; many new homes have carpeting over plywood floors. Many older homes, especially those built before the mid-1960s, have "wet" plaster walls that are much thicker than the half-inch "drywall" used in most new homes today. (But today's drywall is thicker than the three-eighth-inch drywall used in many homes in the 1950s and 1960s.)

· On some houses built before the mid-1960s, you may also find construction features that are too costly to be included on most new homes today: long-lasting slate roofs instead of asphalt shingles, steel or copper water lines instead of plastic ones, and solid interior doors instead of hollow ones. Interior wood trim also usually is of a much higher quality.

Table 3-1

**Advantages and Disadvantages of New Versus Existing Homes
(Some Rules of Thumb Applicable in Most Areas,
But Not All)**

Description of Item	New Is Better	Old Is Better	About The Same
Appreciation (annual)			
All houses			X 10-15%
Single-family			X 12-18%
Townhouses			X 8-12%
Condominiums			X 5-10%
[Depends on market conditions]			

Description of Item	New Is Better	Old Is Better	About The Same
Neighborhood			
Schools			X [wide variation]
Established shopping		X	
Available churches		X	
Neighbors			X
Recreation Facilities			
Planned unit development	X		
Satellite city	X		
Large self-contained site	X		
Large subdivisions			X
Small to medium subs.		X	
Transportation			
Bus		X	
Car		X	
Other		X	
Other			
Community facilities			X
Crime	X		
Fire protection	X		
Garbage collection			X
Property taxes	X [probably cheaper]		
Air quality	X		
Proximity to:		X	
Central city		X	
Cultural activity		X	
Hospital		X	
Job		X	
Library		X	
Site			
Drainage	X		
Shade trees	X		
Wildlife			X
Set back	X		
Land compaction		X	

Description of Item	New Is Better	Old Is Better	About The Same
Street			
Paving	X		
Sidewalk	X		
Width	X		
Street parking	X		
Design	X		
[Building codes have forced improved design and quality]			
Utilities			
Underground electric	X	[N.A.]	
Underground telephone	X	[N.A.]	
Sewer	X		
Water			X
Mail delivery		X	
Shopping			
Proximity to:			
Gas stations		X	
Airports		X	
Restaurants		X	
Supermarkets		X	
Theaters	X		
General shopping	X		
Super highway	X		
House Itself			
Land	X [setback is better]		
Land placement	X [designed better]		
Land planning	X		
Land grading	[takes 2-4 years to settle]	X	
Foundation	X [higher basement ceilings, basement walls are poured concrete—stronger than cement block]		

Description of Item	New Is Better	Old Is Better	About The Same
Floors:			
Concrete			X
Hardwood	[carpet over plywood]	X	
Kitchen	X [stronger materials, less maintenance]		
Exterior walls	X [better insulation, less maintenance]		
Interior walls		X [thicker]	
Framing:			
Plaster		X	
Drywall	X		
Amenities	X		
Roof structure			X
Roof material		X [stronger, more durable]	
Windows and doors:			
Windows	X [better insulation, less maintenance]		
Exterior doors	X [better insulation, weather-stripped]		
Interior doors		X [thicker]	
Outside sidings	X		
Gutter and downspouts	X	[consider copper better]	
Heating/Air-Conditioning	X [smaller, more efficient]		
Plumbing			
Pipes	X		
Waste Pipes	X [maintenance free]		
Faucets	X [better design]		
Water closets	X [better design]		
Sinks	X [better design, choice]		

Description of Item	New Is Better	Old Is Better	About The Same
Tubs	X [greater selection]		
Electrical			
Circuit breakers	X [greater capacity]		
Wiring	X [more efficiently wired]	houses wired with aluminum wiring, between 1966 and 1973, have a potential of fire (check with electrician)	
Outlets	X [serves appliance needs]		
Fixtures		X [better quality]	
Insulation			
Ceiling	X		
Attic ducts	X		
Roof deck	X		
Frame walls	X		
Masonry walls	X		
Windows & patio doors	X		
Storm doors	X		
Floors over open space	X		
Floors over crawl space	X		
Ducts in crawl space	X		
Perimeter slab edges	X		
Basement walls	X		
Interior Hardware and Trim			
Door trim		X	
Window trim		X	
Base trim		X	
Closet trim		X	

Description of Item	New Is Better	Old Is Better	About The Same
Stairs		X [generally hardwood]	
Hardware	X [lighter weight]		
Cabinets	X [better selection]		
[Quality of workmanship and materials better in older homes]			
Appliances			
Range/Oven	X [advanced technology]		
Refrigerator	X [advanced technology]		
Dishwasher	X		
Garbage disposals	X		
Trash compactor	X		
Others	X [wide variety of items]		

Disadvantages of Existing Homes

Unless they have been modernized, many older houses have old-fashioned kitchens and bathrooms, smaller rooms and less extra space—such as a recreation room—than newer houses. They also often have poorer insulation and less efficient heating and air-conditioning units than a new home. While locations vary widely, they may be near to areas of poor schools or higher crime-rates.

The major area of concern about an older house, as far as your investment goes, is the problem of things wearing out. Extensive repairs of certain items, or their replacement, could turn your investment into a costly one.

Consider, for example, the experience of a couple in Memphis, Tennessee. In early 1975 they bought a 12-year-old, three-bedroom house in southeast Memphis. A big selling point was the location. It was near the school where the husband taught and the offices of the real-estate concern where his wife worked. The couple, in their early 20s, also were happy with the purchase terms: $1,800 from their savings as the down payment and closing costs, plus monthly payments of $220.

Their pleasure was short-lived. The inexperienced home buyers soon discovered that their new home, acquired from acquaintances, was in sorry shape. They found themselves painting the exterior in the snow to meet Federal Housing Administration requirements (they had an FHA-insured loan) before they sold the house in July of 1975 for $28,500. By then they had leveled the yard, reinforced the foundation, wallpapered the kitchen, repaired the plumbing, refinished the kitchen cabinets, and installed new kitchen sinks and counter tops, a new toilet, new electric outlets, window screens, carpeting and a dishwasher. The couple said they cleared $900 on the sale, after these expenses.

"By the time we got it fixed, we didn't like it," they explained. The husband added: "I hated that house for all the work we had to do." The couple moved back to an apartment.[8]

It doesn't have to happen that way. And it won't, if you thoroughly check an older house before you buy it.

Things That Wear Out and Go "Ouch" in the Pocketbook

If you are considering buying an older house, take a look at the list in this chapter that provides you with the approximate life of most of the major components of a house. This unique list was prepared especially for this book by Dean Crist, an economist for the National Association of Home Builders economics division. Use it to check those houses you look at to see how soon you might expect major repair bills. You'll especially want to check big-ticket items like the furnace, central air-conditioning and the roof, each of which can cost well over $1,000 to replace. Kitchen appliances or laundry equipment also could be on their last legs.

Table 3-2

Life Expectancies of Various Parts of the House

Item	Useful Life	Remarks
Footings and Foundations		
Footings	Life	First four items are likely to last up to 250 yrs. There are homes in the U.S. over 300 yrs. old. Structural defects that do develop are a result of poor soil conditions.
Foundation	Life	
Concrete block	Life	
Water proofing:		
Bituminous coating	5 yrs.	
Parging with Ionite	Life	
Termite proofing	5 yrs.	Maybe earlier in damp climates.
Gravel outside	30-40 yrs.	Depends on usage.
Cement block	Life	Less strong than concrete block.
Rough Structure		
Floor system (basement)	Life	
Framing exterior walls	Life	Usually plaster directly on masonry. Plaster is solid and will last forever. Provides tighter seal than drywall and better insulation.
Framing interior walls	Life	In older homes, usually plaster on wood lath. Lath strips lose resilience, causing waves in ceilings and walls.
Concrete work:		
Slab	Life	(200 yrs)
Pre-cast decks	10-15 yrs.	
Pre-cast porches	10-15 yrs.	
Site-built porches and steps	20 yrs.	
Sheet Metal		
Gutter and downspouts and flashing:		
Aluminum	20-30 yrs.	Never requires painting but dents and pits. May need to be replaced sooner for appearance.
Cooper	Life	Very durable and expensive. Requires regular cleaning and alignment.
Galvanized iron	15-25 yrs.	Rusts easily and must be kept painted every 3-4 yrs.

Item	Useful Life	Remarks
Rough Electrical		
Wiring:		
Copper	Life	
Aluminum	Life	
Romex	Life	
Circuit breaker		
Breaker panel	30-40 yrs.	
Individual breaker	25-30 yrs.	
Rough Plumbing		
Pressure pipes:		
Copper	Life	Strongest and most common. Needs no maintenance.
Galvanized iron	30-50 yrs.	Rusts easily and is major expense in older homes. Most common until 1940.
Plastic	30-40 yrs.	
Waste pipe:		
Concrete	20 yrs.	
Vitreous china	25-30 yrs.	
Plastic	50-70 yrs.	Usage depends upon soil conditions. Acid soils can eat through plastic.
Cast iron	Life	
Lead	Life	A leak cannot be patched. If bathroom is remodeled must be replaced.
Heating and Venting		
Duct work		
Galvanized	50-70 yrs.	
Plastic	40-60 yrs.	Type used depends upon climate.
Fiberglas	40-60 yrs.	
AC rough-in		Same as Duct Work
Roof		
Asphalt shingles	15-25 yrs.	Most common. Deterioration subject to climate. Granules come off shingles. Check downspouts.
Wood shingles & shakes	30-40 yrs.	Expensive. Contracts and expands due to climate.
Tile	30-50 yrs.	Tendency to crack on sides.
Slate	Life	High quality. Maintenance every 2-3 yrs. as nails rust.
Metal	Life	Shorter life if allowed to rust.

Item	Useful Life	Remarks
Built-up asphalt	20-30 yrs.	Maintenance required—especially after winter.
Felt	30-40 yrs.	
Tar-gravel	10-15 yrs.	
Asbestos shingle	30-40 yrs.	Shingles get brittle when walked on. Maintenance every 1-3 yrs.
Composition shingles	12-16 yrs.	
Tin	Life	Will rust easily if not kept painted regularly. Found a lot in inner-city row houses.
4 or 5 built-up ply	15-25 yrs.	Layers of tar paper on tar.
Masonry		
Chimney	Life	
Fireplace	20-30 yrs.	
Fire brick	Life	
Ash dump	Life	
Metal fireplace	Life	
Flue tile	Life	
Brick veneer	Life	Joints must be pointed every 5-6 yrs.
Brick	Life	
Stone	Life	Unless porous grade stone like limestone.
Block wall	Life	
Masonry floors	Life	Must be kept waxed every 1-2 yrs.
Stucco	Life	Requires painting every 8-10 yrs. More susceptible to cracking than brick. Replacement is expensive.
		Maintenance cycles for all types of masonry structures including those found in urban areas subjected to dirt, soot and chemicals: Caulking —every 20 yrs. Pointing —every 35 yrs. Sandblasting—every 35 yrs.
Windows and Doors		
Window glazing	5-6 yrs.	
Storm windows and gaskets	Life	Aluminum and wood.
Screen doors	5-8 yrs.	
Storm doors	10-15 yrs.	

Item	Useful Life	Remarks
Interior doors (Luan)	10 yrs.	
Sliding doors	30-50 yrs.	
Folding doors	30-40 yrs.	
Sliding screens	30 yrs.	
Garage doors	20-25 yrs.	Depends upon initial placement of springs, tracts, and rollers.
Steel casement windows	40-50 yrs.	Have leakage and condensation problems. Installed mostly in 1940s and 1950s.
Wood casement windows	40-50 yrs.	Older types very drafty
Windows and Doors Jalousie	30-40 yrs.	Fair quality available in wood and aluminum. Used mostly for porches.
Wooden double-hung windows	40-50 yrs.	
Insulation Foundation	Life	
Roof, ceiling	Life	
Roof—electric vent—automatic	10-15 yrs.	
Walls	Life	
Floor	Life	
Weatherstripping: Metal	8-9 yrs.	
Plastic gasket	5-8 yrs.	
Exterior Trim Wood siding	Life	Must be kept painted regularly —every 5-7 yrs.
Metal siding	Life	May rust due to climate.
Aluminum siding	Life	Maintenance free if baked-on finish.
Shutters: Wood	20 yrs.	
Metal	20-30 yrs.	
Plastic	Life	
Aluminum	Life	
Posts and columns	Life	
Gable vents: Wood	10-14 yrs.	
Aluminum	Life	
Gable vent screens	Same as gable vents	

Item	Useful Life	Remarks
Cornice and rake trim	Life	
Trellis	20 yrs.	Will rot in back even if painted because of moisture.
Exterior Paint		
Wood	3-4 yrs.	Climate a strong factor.
Brick	3-4 yrs.	
Aluminum	10-12 yrs.	
Gutters, downspouts and flashing:		
Aluminum	10-12 yrs.	
Copper	Life	No painting required.
Stairs		
Stringer	50 yrs.	Usage is a critical factor.
Risers	50 yrs.	
Treads	50 yrs.	
Baluster	50 yrs.	
Rails	30-40 yrs.	
Starting levels	50 yrs.	
Disappearing stairs	30-40 yrs.	
Drywall and Plaster		
Drywall	40-50 yrs.	Lifetime is adequately protected by exterior walls and roof. Cracks must be regularly spackled.
Plaster	Life	Thicker and more durable than drywall. Exterior must be properly maintained.
Ceiling suspension	Life	
Acoustical ceiling	Life	
Luminous ceiling	10-20 yrs.	Discolors easily.
Ceramic Tile		
Tub alcove and shower stall	Life	
Bath wainscote	Life	Proper installment and maintenance required for long life.
Ceramic floor	Life	
Ceramic tile	Life	Cracks appear due to moisture and joints; must be grouted every 3-4 years.
Finish Carpentry		
Baseboard and shoe	40-50 yrs.	
Door and window trim	40-50 yrs.	
Wood paneling	40-50 yrs.	
Closet shelves	40-50 yrs.	
Fireplace mantel	30-40 yrs.	

Item	Useful Life	Remarks
Flooring		
Oak floor	Life	In most older homes, 1st story
Pine floor	Life	floor is oak and 2nd and 3rd
Slate flagstone floor	40-50 yrs.	story floors are hard pine.
Resilient (vinyl)	10-15 yrs.	Because of scuffing may have to be replaced earlier.
Terrazzo	Life	
Carpeting	5-8 yrs.	Standard carpeting.
Cabinets and Vanities		
Kitchen cabinets	18-30 yrs.	
Bath vanities	18-30 yrs.	
Countertop	18-30 yrs.	
Medicine cabinets	15-20 yrs.	
Mirrors	10-15 yrs.	
Tub enclosures	18-25 yrs.	
Shower doors	18-25 yrs.	
Bookshelves	Life	Depends on wood used.
Interior Painting		
Wall paint	3-5 yrs.	
Trim and door	3-5 yrs.	
Wall paper	3-7 yrs.	
Electricial Finish		
Electric range and oven	12-20 yrs.	
Vent hood	15-20 yrs.	
Disposal	5-12 yrs.	
Exhaust fan	8-10 yrs.	
Water heater	10-12 yrs.	
Electric fixtures	20-30 yrs.	
Doorbell and chimes	8-10 yrs.	
Fluorescent bulbs	3-5 yrs.	
Plumbing Finish		
Dishwasher	5-15 yrs.	
Gas water heater	8-12 yrs.	
Gas refrigerator	15-25 yrs.	
Toilet seats	8-10 yrs.	
Commode	15-25 yrs.	
Steel sinks	15-20 yrs.	
China sinks	15-20 yrs.	
Faucets	Life	Washers must be replaced frequently.
Flush valves	18-25 yrs.	
Well and septic system	15-30 yrs.	Depends on soil and rock formations.

Item	Useful Life	Remarks
Hot water boilers	30-50 yrs.	Becomes increasingly inefficient with age and may have to be replaced before it actually breaks down.
Heating Finish		
Wall heaters	12-17 yrs.	
Warm air furnaces	25-30 yrs.	Most common today.
Radiant heating:		
Ceiling	20-30 yrs.	
Baseboard	20-40 yrs.	
AC unit	8-18 yrs.	
AC compressors	10-18 yrs.	Regular maintenance required.
Humidifier	7-8 yrs.	
Electric air cleaners	8-10 yrs.	
Appliances		
Refrigerator	15-25 yrs.	
Washer	8-12 yrs.	
Dryer	8-12 yrs.	
Combo washer and dryer	7-10 yrs.	
Garbage door opener	8-10 yrs.	
Disposal units	8-12 yrs.	
Dishwasher	8-12 yrs.	
Lawn mower	7-10 yrs.	
Vacuum cleaner	6-10 yrs.	
Music system (intercom)	30-40 yrs.	
Appointments		
Closet rods	Life	
Blinds	10-15 yrs.	
Drapes	5-10 yrs.	
Towel bars	10-15 yrs.	
Soap grab	10-12 yrs.	
Others		
Fences and screens	20-30 yrs.	
Splash blocks	6-7 yrs.	
Patios (concrete)	15-50 yrs.	
Gravel walks	3-5 yrs.	
Concrete walks	10-25 yrs.	
Sprinkler system	15-25 yrs.	
Asphalt driveway	5-6 yrs.	With patchwork may last 15-20 yrs.
Tennis court	20-40 yrs.	

Item	Useful Life	Remarks
Swimming pool:		
Pool shell	15-25 yrs.	
Pool filter	3-5 yrs.	Must be cleaned yearly.
Pool heater	4-6 yrs.	

Common Problems Found In Older Homes

Water Problem—a very common problem in older homes. Often it is a result of poor gutter alignment, poor downspout direction, and/or poor surface grading. Water can be detected by discoloration of floor tile, stained paneling at floor level, dark spots on cinderblock and other signs in basement.

Plumbing—In older homes pressure tends to drop substantially because of rusty galvanized pipes. Considered major expense in older homes. Test for leaks and water pressure. A leak in lead waste piping cannot be patched. If bathroom is remodeled, lead pipe must be replaced.

Termite Activity—Combination of wood, dirt, darkness and dampness will bring termites. Particularly acute if there is crawl space with dirt very close to wood floor joists.

Roofs—Older homes may have roofs that have water leaks. Check metal roofs for rust; tile roofs for cracking on sides; slate roofs for rusty nails and tar coming off ridge; tin roofs for rusting; and built-up roof with gravel for spongy spaces and bubbles.

Retaining Walls—Large cracks sometimes form; this usually indicates that the surface water is collecting behind the wall, freezing and causing pressure. Can be demonstrative of poor structure work.

Interior Walls and Ceilings—Most older homes have plaster on wood lath. Over the years wood lath strips lose resilience and pull away from joists and studs, causing waves in walls and ceilings. Wood lath is very sensitive to moisture.

Electrical Wiring—Most homes have inadequate wiring, often only one or two outlets per room, which does not meet many codes. Most newer homes have outlets installed every 12 feet from any doorway to avoid the need for extension cords.

Insulation—Older homes are not as well insulated as newer ones. There may be a lack of insulation between masonry walls and interior walls.

Appliances—Older homes have neither the variety nor the quality of appliances that newer ones do. Technological changes are such that newer and better appliances are available to consumers.

Windows—Older homes usually have windows that readily conduct cold air into the house. Replacement is expensive.

More Items To Think About

Most major industries in the United States have gone through technological revolutions. The building industry, though, still retains many of its construction concepts. The basic components have not changed. Concrete, mortar, brick, block and wood are still primarily used. Foundations are still built with concrete on block, framing is still done with wood or masonry, and wood and shingles are still used for roofs. The changes that have occurred are more cosmetic and/or aesthetic in nature than fundamental.

The advent of consumerism has forced the builder to pay more attention to consumer preferences. This has helped create a trend toward larger and more luxurious homes, more mechanical labor-saving devices, and the use of more maintenance-free materials such as aluminum and plastic. The use of component parts, which is on the increase, has enabled builders to use a greater variety of materials than ever before. Whole sectors of the structure are now mechanically handled and put in place on the site. Today's garbage disposals, dishwashers, washers and dryers, air-conditioning units, and humidifiers, to name a few, are either relatively new products or better-quality improvements on earlier models.

New homes have more and better insulation, and drainage is better today. In the interior of the house, improved fibers and materials have made the job of housekeeping easier. Increased space and new developments in partition design and storage walls provide for more usable interior area. There is also an increased tendency toward the use of maintenance-free materials of both a structural and finish type.

It is wrong to suggest that homes today are built better than older ones. If anything, older homes were built with materials that were more massive and had stress factors greater than those today. Many homes in the United States have lasted for over 300 years. However, newer homes are bigger and provide amenities that simply did not exist years ago.

Finally, there is the question of the maintenance and repair policy of the homeowner—that is, the care he or she puts into the house. Of all the factors relevant to determining the useful life span of a house, this may be the most critical. There can be no lifetime material, regardless of its quality, if it is not properly maintained. Newer and better-quality appliances, for instance, will not provide the long lives suggested by manufacturers and builders if they are not taken care of. Homeowners differ in their attitudes toward their homes, and, because of this, the life expectancies of various parts of the house will also differ.

A major item to check in older houses is the wiring. Sometimes it isn't adequate to meet the needs of today's living with everything from television sets, freezers, and dishwashers to electric tooth brushes and hair dryers. Most houses built before the mid-1950s, unless the wiring has been updated, have only 60 amps of power, which clearly isn't enough for today's uses. A house should have at least 100 amps, and most new homes being built today have 150 to 200 amps or more. The number of amps usually is listed on the service panel of the fuse-box or circuit-breaker box. When you look in there, you also should see something that indicates if you have an extra-heavy 240-volt outlet, for heavy appliances like your washer and dryer. If you have any doubts, have an expert check for you. New wiring could cost you several hundred dollars.

One more thing about wiring. In houses built between 1965 and 1973, the widespread use of aluminum wiring instead of copper wiring has raised questions about possible fire hazards. In 1977, the U.S. Consumer Product Safety Commission said aluminum wiring may be an "imminent hazard" in more than 1.5 million homes built during the 1965–1973 period. Aluminum wiring used after that date isn't in question, but the use of such wiring has steadily declined.

Aluminum wiring came into widespread use during the building boom of the early 1960s when competing copper was in short supply. The danger of fire hazards is said to lurk in pre-1973 connections between aluminum house wire and its termination devices, especially wall sockets. Most of the hundreds of complaints logged by the Consumer Product Safety Commission involve over-heating of outlets, which has led to fires in some cases. Aluminum makers say the problems were caused by improper installation. It doesn't matter to you who is to blame; you just don't want your house to burn down. If you are looking at a home wired with aluminum prior to 1972, "it would be well to have it checked out by a competent electrician," advised one aluminum industry executive.

An older house can be a good buy—if you know what you are buying beneath that seemingly solid exterior.

New Homes—Pros and Cons

All new-home buyers have their own reasons for choosing a newly-built home over an older one. But what are their feelings about the advantages and disadvantages of a new home *after* they buy? Consider some of the praise and complaints from actual new-home buyers. These were contained in unedited reports of new-home buyers' frustrations as well as their delights with their homes, as shown in a survey conducted by the National Association of Home Builders.

Since the raw data runs for 11 pages, we have included only one region, the North Central. The comments are divided between homes in varying price ranges, starting with the lowest, below $50,000, to the most expensive.

On the left side are the comments about "What people like" and on the right side are the comments about "What people did not like" in their new homes. Both comments refer to the same house. So, for instance, the first comments are from a home buyer in Pontiac, Mich.; on the left side he said that "kitchen layout, fireplace" are what he likes about the home. On the opposite side he said that what he does not like about the new house is the "drywall & paint, contractors' workmanship—poor."

If you are looking for most frequent complaints, simply glance down the right side and you will find them.

If you are looking for kudos, look at the left side.

Q. What are some of the things that you particularly like about your new home?

Q. What are some of the things that you particularly dislike about your new home?

$40,000 to $49,999

Kitchen layout, fireplace	Drywall & paint, contractors' workmanship—poor
Quality of builder	None
Style of the house, all rooms on one floor	Location & size of lot
Floor plan, all underground utilities, no wire visible	No storage space; only one car garage
Design of floor plan, general construction quality	Cold floors due to being on slab
Apparent quality of construction	Stairs creak
Roominess	Certain aspects of the construction
Overall size	Quality of workmanship, poor paint job

$50,000 to $59,999

New, clean, excellent working order	Poor, chintzy construction, paper-thin, plastic, synthetic, "built out of match sticks."
All characteristics	Builder's failure to do repair services and inspection items
Fireplace, master bath	Kitchen too small
Master bath, lots of closet space, big kitchen, large foyer, 3 baths	Laundry downstairs, garage too small
It is well constructed, good, good size, and attractive	None

Style, surroundings, park district, schools, the lot	Village government, unfinished repairs
Spaciousness, quiet country life	
Privacy, ownership, style	Finishing construction, phases poorly done, follow-up repairs
Style	Fireplace; the paint is peeling on outside

$50,000 to $59,999

Larger dining room, setting, privacy, family room & laundry on first floor	Property taxes
Built to order, the large kitchen	

$60,000 to $69,999

Large rooms	Poor labor & material in house
Luminous, layout of home	Landscape, tax
Smaller	Water problems, poor job on concrete drive
Size of lot, floor plan, square area	First coat of paint is cheap, inconsistent wood staining
Floor plan	The builder's indifference to repairing items not working correctly

$70,000 to $99,999

Many closets, large bedrooms	Improperly designed heating system
Location, layout	Irritating construction defects, poor workmanship, damp basement

Neighborhood, style, size	Quality of workmanship, and builder repair slow
Floor plan & exterior style	Quality of inside trim, work not as good as expected
Construction	
Neighborhood, style, modern conveniences	Frustration of trying to get builder to resolve construction problems

---

$100,000 AND OVER

Very open	Too little storage space
Location on golf course, convenient floor plan–beauty!	Need insulated windows
Energy efficient design, location	Grading of land surface
Space	Nothing
Floor plan	Workmanship
Energy package, workmanship	Small garage, small bedrooms
Large bedrooms, large kitchen	Poor external weather seal
Energy efficient, excellent trim details	Poor quality sheet rock work, wet basement
Floor plan, big rooms	No backyard to speak of
More space, isolated from neighbors	Large fuel bills, great upkeep
Large rooms	Location
Larger lot, dinning room design, superior bedroom level design & finishing	Distance from shopping & conveniences

Pros and Cons—A Summary

The major advantage of a new home is that it is new; you won't have to worry about major segments of the house wearing out soon. Moreover, new homes are designed with the features many people want these days—bigger rooms, finished basements, recreation rooms and garages. While the walls may be thinner than in many older homes, new homes have better kitchens and bathrooms, more insulation, and heating and cooling units that are smaller yet more efficient than in the homes of yesteryear. Much of the construction is as strong as, or stronger than, existing homes; the basements in most new homes, for instance, are made of poured concrete, which is stronger than previously used cement block.

New homes generally are farther away from center cities than older units. But increasingly, Americans are working and shopping in suburban areas that no longer are only "bedroom" suburbs but self-contained communities. Thus, a new home could be the most convenient location for many people. Some planned communities also offer more recreation facilities than would be available in older neighborhoods, and new homes are likely to be near good schools. And if a new area turns out to be a growth area, you are in on the bottom floor as the house you bought now appreciates in price.

A new house can save you money in a couple of other ways. For one, you probably won't have to pay most closing costs; the builder often pays some costs on a new house. And if you buy a newer house, you can save on home insurance. In 1978 State Farm Fire & Casualty Company began offering a 14% premium discount on new homes and discounts of 12% to 2% on houses between one and six years old. Other companies probably will follow suit, so shop around before buying home insurance.

The "cons" of new homes are pretty much the other side of the coin of the "advantages" we noted for existing homes. A new home usually isn't in an established neighborhood, and transportation can be a problem for those who work in the city.

New subdivision houses also can have a monotonous look of sameness about them. However, the builders increasingly are doing more to vary the styles and placements of homes in subdivisions and also to retain the trees and natural landscape rather than leveling everything in sight. And of course, with a custom-built house you can help design your own home all with a style of your own.

But, as you can see from the list of new-buyer comments, there is one complaint that stands out above all others.

Uncompleted Work—the Biggest New-Home Bugaboo

The most irritating problem people run into when buying new homes is the failure of builders to complete all of the little things—and sometimes the big things—that the buyer was promised. There are defects or items that either aren't completed before the buyer moves in or in a reasonable time afterwards.

Sometimes the house itself isn't completed. At least, not anywhere near the time when the salesman promised it would be.

In December, 1976, Bill and Darlene Hawley signed a contract to buy a new home to be built in a subdivision in Wayne, Michigan, not far from Detroit. The house was supposed to be ready by July, 1977. But construction lagged, the builder went out of business, the developer took over construction, and work in the subdivision fell far behind schedule. Result: The Hawleys weren't able to move into their new home until late March, 1978—a full nine months after the promised occupancy date.

In the meantime they had sold their previous home near Wayne with the expectation that their new house surely would be ready by the end of 1977. But that November, the Hawleys and their four children had to move out of their old home and they had no place to go. Fortunately, a house owned by their church was being vacated by renters at the time, and the Hawleys were able to move there temporarily. Unfortunately, the renters had owned 10 cats and the resulting stench made the house unlivable. The Hawleys spent the Christmas holidays scrubbing the house clean.

When their new home finally was "ready," they moved in to find much of the house still wasn't completed or was done shoddily. Among other things, they discovered that when the toilet in one bathroom was flushed, the bowl filled with steaming hot water due to a misconnected water pipe. Other problems were more serious. For example, there was a dip in the floor of the second-story master bedroom, a problem the developer offered to fix by stuffing the sagging area with shingles before he covered the floor with carpeting. Bill Hawley, envisioning his bed falling through the floor, insisted that the flooring be redone. Then he brought in his wife's uncle, a master carpenter, to inspect other parts of the house. Together they drew up a list of about two dozen items that needed to be redone to bring the house up to, not perfection, but acceptable condition. After looking at the list, the developer agreed the repairs were reasonable.

Bill got the names of the subcontractors and made appointments himself to have the companies complete needed repairs. To make sure the work is completed right on a new house, he said, "You have to be your own contractor." And you have to be persistent.

Choosing a Builder: Protecting Yourself before You Buy

What can you do to protect yourself from such headaches? There is no sure-fire protection. But for one thing, don't sell your current house too soon. The move-in date for your new home probably will be later than the salesman says. And it's not necessarily because he is being deceptive. Bad weather, the shortage of skilled workers, difficulty in scheduling subcontractors, and other unforeseen problems can cause construction delays for even the most conscientious builder. Keep track of the construction progress of your newly-built home. Wait at least until the basement or foundation is poured and the walls go up before selling your current home. Leave leeway in your sales contract for a move-out date. If possible, include a provision allowing you to rent your old house for a time after you sell it.

You also should choose your builder carefully. Check out his reputation, or the reputation of the local unit of the national home building company if you are considering buying a house built by such a company. See if any complaints have been filed against the builder at state and local licensing and housing agencies or at local consumer protection agencies. Your best bet is to talk to people who have bought houses from the same builder. See if they are satisfied with their homes and the builder's handling of any complaints.

With today's rapidly rising costs, some builders may run into financial problems that could delay completion of your home indefinitely. You can't get information on a builder's financial status directly, but your lender can run a credit check on the builder for you. Indeed, a cooperative lender can be very helpful to a new-home buyer. The Hawley family's lender withheld $2,000 of the purchase price on their new home from the builder-developer until specified uncompleted work was finished to their satisfaction.

Other sources to check are the subcontractors that builders hire to do the plumbing, carpentry, roofing and other work. Many home-building delays result from the inability of the builder to obtain the services of such workers, especially if he is slow to pay them. Such subcontractors don't necessarily respond to the builder who pays the most, but are likely to stick with a builder who is a reliable payer—one who pays "like a slot machine," said veteran Michigan carpenter Laurence Wilson.

Finally, when shopping for a new house, look for tell-tale signs of inferior workmanship. A key indicator is carpentry work. There are many things you will never notice in a house, but most people can recognize sloppy carpentry jobs. Things like joints that don't fit, countertop with rough edges, doors that don't close properly and the like. These items, in many cases, indicate sloppy workmanship throughout the house and poor supervision. Beware of this and either look elsewhere or make sure you don't get the same poor work.

Protecting Yourself after Buying a New Home

How do you protect yourself after you've purchased a new home? Before you move in, the builder will provide you with a preinspection list of items in the house that have yet to be completed. This is also called a "punch" list, because the builder's representative punches each listed item when it is completed. (Some buyers call it a punch list because when they see how many items haven't been completed they feel like punching the builder in the nose.) Turn in the list early, before settlement, and don't go to settlement unless (a) all the items are completed, or (b) if they are not, the builder agrees to do the work in 30 to 60 days and a reasonable amount is put aside for completion of the work. This money should be placed in what is called an escrow account, which is held by a third party, usually the title company or settlement attorneys. Both you and the builder should sign the list and mark the date.

Most new homes have at least a one-year warranty, but you sometimes must be persistent to get the builder or his subcontractors to make repairs. (You also can get a longer warranty on many new homes, as will be discussed shortly.) If you purchased from a local builder rather than a large corporate concern, sometimes you can get action on your complaints by writing personally to the builder himself. If you find yourself getting the run-around, and there are enough fellow buyers with serious complaints, an effective strategy is to air your grievances to the local newspapers or TV stations. The press loves such stories, and the builders hate the publicity and may be moved to act on your complaints. Of course, if necessary, you can go to court. If the past, most courts have routinely sided with builders, citing the "buyer beware" doctrine. But the Research Institute of America, a business advisory service in New York, said that courts in at least 19 states have changed, often ruling in favor of homeowners in suits over such things as faulty wiring, poor grading or badly installed ductwork.

Despite such concerns, most builders want to make their customers happy. After all, most of them will be building more houses in the very same area, and nothing sells homes like a good builder reputation. For most new-home buyers, the early aggravation over defects fades away as they see values of their homes rise.

New Homes or Used—What to Look For and What to Look Out For

· Leaky basements. This is probably the most aggravating problem for any new- or old-home buyer.

Look for dampness in walls or signs of water seepage into floor drain. Move any objects obscuring the view of basement walls. Many times this is done to cover up the sights of mildew or water.

An old and useful trick is to go for an inspection right after a good rain. Do not accept the explanation that "we have just washed down the walls and floors." This could or could not be the truth. Investigate.

· Settlement. This could be very irritating and very expensive. Look at the outside ground to make sure that the ground slopes away from the house. The most common cause of many water headaches and settlement problems is improper grading of the ground around the house. It must take the water away from the house. Otherwise it will find its way inside.

Settlement of ground is a long-time proposition. It takes several years for the ground to settle into place firmly. Sewer connections into the house may leave a ditch several inches deep 4 to 6 years after the ditch was filled up.

Steps are one problem area. They seem never to be properly filled and tamped. All of a sudden you will see the whole stoop hanging in the air with holes under it. This is a great potential for water trouble as well as separation of the steps from the house.

- Termites. The favorite food of termites is cellulose, from wood—your wood in your house or your potential house.

One way not to have termites is to build properly. This means that when buying a new house you should make sure that:

- All tree roots, stumps, pieces of wood from construction site are removed before backfilling of the foundation.

- There is no water problem in the house, or moisture to start with.

- The foundation is poured concrete; it is the best protection.

- Termite shields have been placed on top of concrete foundation.

- Exposed wood is high off the ground—at least 6 inches to 12 inches.

After the house is infested, the only thing you can do is to treat it and repair the damage. A reputable firm can give you a written guarantee that the place does not have termites. Do not treat this lightly. Make sure that a termite inspection, paid for by the seller, is included in your purchase contract.

The best advice when it comes to assessing the condition of a house is to get an expert opinion. Hire an independent home inspection service to check the structure and condition of the house you plan to buy. Pay the inspector the $50 to $150 it generally costs for an inspection. It is worth the money, because it could save you a lot more. While an inspection is especially important in an older house, having a new house checked isn't a bad idea. "The biggest surprise is that more than 50% of our business is new-house inspection," said the president of one Washington, D.C., home-inspection service.

When buying a house, especially an older house, you should make your purchase subject to a satisfactory report by an independent inspection. This can be written right into your purchase contract. If the inspector finds major flaws, the purchase can be canceled, or you can negotiate a lower price to take into account the costs of needed repairs.

There are other people you might call on:

- Ask somebody you know who is a professional with experience in housing to look at the home you plan to buy. Let him give you his best advice on what he thinks is wrong with the house.

- Ask a county inspector to give you an appraisal of the house. Some counties do this.

- Finally, with an increasing number of existing and new homes these days, you can get a long-term warranty to protect against major structural or other flaws in the home you buy.

Protecting Yourself with a Warranty Plan

Historically, used homes have been sold without any significant guarantees. It basically was a case of what you bought is what you got. But since 1975, the National Association of Realtors has authorized several insurance or warranty plans for use in various parts of the country for homes sold by its thousands of realtor members. The contracts protect new owners against such things as defective plumbing and wiring and sometimes appliances, roofing or structural defects. And some warranty companies require an inspection of a home before issuing a contract.

The contracts vary, but generally you as buyer purchase a one- to two-year warranty against specified defects. If something goes wrong, the defects are repaired for no further charge, or for a minimum fee. One California warranty company, for example, sells a one-year policy for about $200. It can be worth the extra cost, and sometimes sellers will pay the extra cost as a sales-incentive. A good warranty can be a life-saver, as Gerald Lamberti discovered after he bought a four-bedroom, three bath home in Pleasonton, California, in 1974. The rambling redwood house was just nine years old, but within months after moving in, Mr. Lamberti said, "the furnace stopped working, then the oven broiler went out, and then the dishwasher broke and was unrepairable." Fortunately for him, all were repaired or replaced under a warranty contract that came with the house.

In 1979, the National Association of Realtors began a warranty plan that doesn't require the seller to have his home inspected. The plan warrants four major components—plumbing, electrical system, central heating, and air-conditioning—against repair or replacement for one year. The warranties sell for about $200 to $250. The National Association of Home Builders expects more than 1 million existing homes to be covered by warranties by the early 1980s.

Many new-home builders also offer a warranty developed by the National Association of Home Builders called the Home Owners Warranty (HOW). It provides protection against major structural defects for up to 10 years. Here's how HOW works:

At the time of settlement, both the builder and the buyer sign the HOW Home Warranty Agreement. Application, warranty and insurance documents, explaining the plan are then sent to the home buyer.

- First Year—Builder promises to fix defects caused by faulty workmanship or materials due to noncompliance with HOW's approved standards.
- Second year—HOW backs the builder's warranty if he will not or cannot perform. In this event, a one-time $250 deductible is charged.

For the next 3 through 10 years, the home is directly insured against major structural defects, for a total of 10 years protection. A deductible of 19% of the sales price is charged for each claim.

If a dispute arises over what is or is not covered by the warranty, and it can't be settled by the buyer and the builder, the question is referred to a local HOW Council, which appoints a neutral person to try to resolve the differences, or if that fails, to make an award. During the last 8 years of the warranty, the buyer makes a claim for major structural defects directly to the Local Council, or in a few states, to the insurance company.

Many new-home buyers already have benefited from the HOW warranty. In 1977, HOW's underwriter ended one homeowner's nightmare when it initiated $10,000 of repair work on a structurally damaged home. The builder had gone out of business and the homeowner, a school teacher raising three children by herself, was unable to make needed repairs. An insurance adjustor discovered that because the home's foundation was not built to accommodate a relatively high underground water flow in that area, structural damage appeared in the form of a flooded basement, cracking drywall and buckling walls. "The house was out of kilter—walls were popping loose—which happens whenever there is undue pressure on the basement," the adjustor said.

To solve the problem, half of the basement had to be reworked; the ground had to be re-excavated and the walls repoured to prevent damage by the water. Under the HOW program, thousands of other home-buyer complaints also have been settled, usually before reaching arbitration, without the need of going to court.

In another case in Florida, a newly built home with a cathedral-ceiling-high stone fireplace began to settle. The fireplace separated as much as an inch from the walls, presenting potential danger to the lives of the homeowners.

The builder refused to repair the damage, making the repairs automatically an insurance claim. On investigation, it was discovered that the foundation had been laid without footings and with one of the supporting piers in each row omitted. The building inspector hadn't bothered to check the house. HOW's insurance carrier had the house moved from the foundation so that the old foundation could be bulldozed out and a new one installed. The home then was moved back and the interior damage was repaired. The total cost: about $36,000.

The HOW warranty premium on single-family houses, condominiums and townhouses ranges from $2.60 to $3.90

per thousand dollars of the cost of a house. The cost is paid by the builder, though he usually passes on most of the cost in the purchase price of the home. Not all builders offer the warranty, but the number of those that do is growing. By 1981, nearly 1 million homes were covered by the plan and over 15,000 builders in 46 states and the District of Columbia offered the warranty.

HOW also provides another benefit for your house as an investment. The warranty can be passed on to another buyer, which can increase your home's resale value.

Such things as warranties and the age of homes are only part of the housing-investment picture. Equally important is where the home is located and whether it offers what future buyers may be looking for. That's subject matter for the next chapter.

FOUR

What Makes a Home a Good Investment

> "The highest life-stress events,
> naturally, are things like death
> of a spouse or divorce. But
> ranking not far from these
> events are real estate
> transactions."
>
> —Richard I. Evans,
> University of Houston, Social Psychologist.

There is an old saying in real-estate circles that the three most important features of a house are location, location, and location. And it's true, true, true. Location and the character of the neighborhood largely determine the value of a home.

In every city and town there are certain sections where homes are costlier and appreciate faster simply because those are the areas in which a lot of people want to live. The attraction may be logical—good schools, for example—or it may be psychological or even irrational. It really doesn't matter what the reason is.

For example, it's beyond dispute that many buyers in Beverly Hills are paying far more for houses than they would be worth in other affluent communities. In some areas lots are small and pseudo-mansions squat shoulder to shoulder; other homes haven't been well maintained. "A lot of housing in Beverly Hills just wasn't satisfactory," said Fred Case, professor of real-estate and urban economics at the University of California at Los Angeles. "It had the odor of genteel decay. But then suddenly it became fashionable to live there, and a good market turned into an outrageous market."

"People from back East who look at houses in Beverly Hills are just aghast," said Ed Kelley, a real-estate broker who was once singer Peggy Lee's personal manager. "They're sure we're all crazy."

The key element in the housing boom in Beverly Hills has been the appeal of Beverly Hills itself as a star-studded haven for the super-rich, where wealth can be flaunted. It is a magnet to status-seekers to whom a Beverly Hills address announces to the world: Look at me, I have arrived.

The hunger to be a part of all this, to be a resident, has done queer things to the housing market. In 1976 a house sold for $71,000, which would be an incredible steal by Beverly Hills standards—except that the place had only 22 feet by 26 feet of living space and wasn't even within the city limits. It had a Beverly Hills telephone prefix, however, and by a quirk its mail was delivered through the Beverly Hills post office. "You have to remember that the facade is what's important," said Jane Lewis, a real-estate agent here for 13 years.

Many houses are eccentricities bearing no resemblance whatever to the three-bedroom, two-bath staple of the industry. One, that was priced at $1.3 million, has only two bedrooms, along with five baths, a tennis court, a pool, and an $11,000 annual property-tax bill. There is also a disconcerting jumble of architectural styles. Ersatz French chateaux are snuggled next to houses best described as Hollywood Moorish, which in turn abut columned mansions that look as if they were transplanted from antebellum Virginia. It doesn't seem to matter. If it's in Beverly Hills, it sells.[9]

You don't have to be in Beverly Hills to see a rapid acceleration. It can be anywhere.

"In some parts of Long Island (New York Metro area) one can get a large house for $75,000. The same house in Fairfield County would get $175,000," said Weston E. Edwards, of Merrill Lynch Relocation Management—a company which buys from large corporations about 10,000 units a year and relocates their employees.

And in the Washington, D.C., area, houses are costliest and appreciate the fastest in affluent Montgomery County. Next door, in Prince George's County, the same houses, and bigger ones, are up to 40% cheaper.

The most profitable purchase can be in a neighborhood that is down in prices, but suddenly becomes in demand again.

For example, back in 1961 the late Mortimer Yosk bought a large frame house about a mile from the White House in Washington, D.C. He paid $32,000, which he thought was an outrageous price. But when he died of a heart attack in 1966, his wife was finally able to sell the house for just $25,000. What happened?

The neighborhood had rapidly deteriorated. Just about everybody who moved out lost money on their houses. Those who remained for another 10 years have seen an abrupt turnaround in property values. In 1981, the same house that Yosk's widow sold for $25,000 would have fetched a smart $100,000.

The reason: the whole area has become valuable as speculators started purchasing all the dilapidated units, fixing them, and making a bundle on resale to people looking for rehabilitated homes in the city.

The problem is that there is no way to know which areas are going to be born again and which will continue to decline. So for most home buyers, the best advice is to stay away from deteriorating areas. They usually spell trouble and loss.

As a home buyer, you probably are looking for a home that is both a good place to live and a solid investment. The secret is to find an area that is still on the upswing or one that is going through a rebirth, and to avoid an area that is about to decline.

Finding the Right House in the Right Place—How to Start

Before you start on your house-hunting rounds, take time to consider the alternatives. Do you want:

· A new house?
· An existing older house?
· In the city or in the suburbs?

The Wall Street Journal

"Joey, do you suppose there's life on other blocks?"

- To be close to major roads or farther out?
- To be close to a church or synagogue?

After you have determined in very general terms what kind of community you would like to live in, do the following:

- Sit down with your spouse, if you have one, and make a blueprint of your requirements and needs. People move for many reasons. In a consumer survey conducted by the National Association of Home Builders, the leading reason that people said they decided to move to another house was that they wanted a more energy-efficient home. At the same time, many said they wanted a bigger home with a bigger lot.

The major reasons why home buyers decided to move are shown in a nearby chart (Chart 4-1). You can list your own goals.

· Then figure out what you can reasonably afford. To help you, here is a table provided by NHAB:

What Can You Spend For Monthly Housing?

---

1. Your average monthly income:
(take home pay) (gross pay less taxes) .... $_____
Rents, dividends, interest .... $_____
Other stable income sources _____
Net average monthly
income (add) (1): $_____

2. Your average monthly non-housing expenses:
Food, household supplies .... $_____
Clothing .... _____
Medical costs and insurance .... _____
Life and casualty insurance .... _____
Automobile and insurance .... _____
Education .... _____
Commuting .... _____
Installment payments/interest charges .... _____
Recreation, hobbies (adjust realistically) .... _____
Telephone .... _____
Contributions, dues, fees, etc. .... _____
Personal (cleaning, barber, etc.) .... _____
Savings/Investment program (adjust realistically)............. _____
Other miscellaneous expenses... _____
Total Average Monthly Non-Housing
Expenses: (add) (2) .... $_____

3. Your monthly income available for housing:
Net average Monthly Income (total 1) .... $_____
Subtract Non-Housing Expenses (total 2) .... _____

Average Monthly Income Available for
Housing Expenses (3) .... $_____

4. Average Monthly Housing Expenses:
Condominium Association fee · $_____
Mortgage repayment, principal & interest .... _____
Personal property and liability insurance
  (if not included in mortgage loan repayment) _____
Unit property taxes (if not included in mortgage
  loan repayment) .... _____
Utilities (heat, electricity/gas/oil/water)................................ _____
Other monthly housing expenses
  (decorating, appliances, etc.) .... _____
  Average Monthly Housing Expenses (add)........................ $_____

How Much Down Payment Can You Afford?

---

5. Available funds:
Equity in present home/lot .... $_____
Savings, savings certificates .... _____
Investments/mutual funds (current value) .... _____
Insurance (cash surrender value) .... _____
Other available funds (such as a personal loan) .... _____
  Total Available Funds (add)— .... _____
  Subtract amount you must keep in reserve— .... _____
  Adjusted Total Available Funds (a)...................................... $_____

6. Expected Cash Expenses:
Cash costs for closing and settlement .... $_____
Furniture, furnishings (if any) .... _____
Moving expenses .... _____
Other expected expenses .... _____
  Total Expected Expenses (add) (b) .... $_____

Now subtract total (b) (your expected expenses) from total (a) (your
available funds) to get amount you can afford to spend for your down
payment: (c) $_____
Subtract the down payment from the sales price of the home you wish
to buy and you will know how much of a mortgage you will need to
finance.

Location, Location, Location—What to Look For

Before you even start looking at houses, you should think about what area you want to live in. A good place to start is at your local planning commission. In most cities and counties, the planning commissions have maps that identify areas of homes of various prices. The maps could well be obsolete by several years, but they will give you a good idea of where the various price ranges are and the differences between areas.

As we have shown, not everybody can afford to live in Beverly Hills or would want to. So, look for an area that fits your pocketbook.

Of course, you can also estimate the going prices of certain areas by checking the real-estate advertisements in the newspapers. Get yourself a good map so that you can identify exactly where the advertised homes are. The current prices, however, are only part of the equation. What you want to know: Is the area in demand and on the upswing—or are things leveling off?

How can you tell if an area is growing? Well, one way is to high-tail it off to the library and look up real-estate ads in some old newspapers. See what the houses in the area you are considering were selling for a year ago, two years ago, five years ago. That can give you an idea of what kind of appreciation has taken place and whether values are still on the rise or slowing.

If you have the time and interest, you can check even further. The newspaper ads only show the selling price, not what is actually paid for houses. But also at the library, in most cities you can find a book that lists every house on every street and tells exactly what the owner paid for it and when. In the East, a commonly-used directory is the Lusk's Real Estate Directory Service. In other areas, there are similar services by other names.

A friendly real-estate agent also can show you a directory if the firm subscribes to one. If you are really determined, you can check the house sales records at the local city hall or county office building.

Once you have an idea of where you are interested in buying, grab your map, hop in your car and drive around the area for a visual inspection. Better yet, walk around the

Chart 4-1

Important factors in making a decision to move

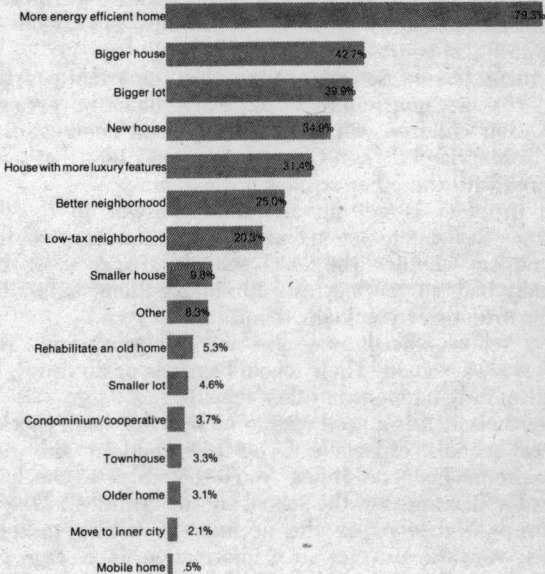

Factor	Percentage
More energy efficient home	79.3%
Bigger house	42.7%
Bigger lot	39.9%
New house	34.9%
House with more luxury features	31.4%
Better neighborhood	25.0%
Low-tax neighborhood	20.3%
Smaller house	9.8%
Other	8.3%
Rehabilitate an old home	5.3%
Smaller lot	4.6%
Condominium/cooperative	3.7%
Townhouse	3.3%
Older home	3.1%
Move to inner city	2.1%
Mobile home	.5%

BUILDER/JANUARY 1, 1981 197

neighborhood and talk to people who live there. A visual inspection generally is sufficient to give you an idea of what an area is like. But it is only a first step. Obviously, if the neighborhood is filled with crummy houses with broken windows and garbage all around, you can figure it's not a good area in which to buy a home. But in most cases, even if the neighborhood looks nice, there are other things to start checking out.

Learn about the Schools

If you have children, start worrying about schools. Even if you don't, you should find out something about how good—or bad—the schools are. Remember, to get the best investment you must think not only about your needs but those of somebody you might want to sell your house to someday—at a nice profit, of course.

For many buyers, schools are the most important consideration. "The first question that prospective home buyers ask is where their children will go to school," said one real-estate agent in Maryland. "Then they want to know how that school compares with the other schools in the county."

The problem is getting an honest answer to that last question. Real-estate agents aren't supposed to give their opinions on whether the local schools are good or bad, especially bad, so you may as well not ask them, unless they are your friends or you know them.

Local school officials may also not level with you. Their school is always good. Their school has little or no drugs, and vandalism only happens in other schools.

Nevertheless, it is a good idea to make a first-hand check on the local schools, especially if you have children who would go to them. For one thing, you'll be able to check the outward appearances of the school and its facilities to see if it seems up to date or on the decline. In talking to school officials, you also can get such information as average class sizes, how students compare with those at other schools on a standardized achievement test, what special courses and counseling may be available, and whether students are being bused to other schools.

But you need to know more. Remember that schools are one of the most important factors in determining the value of the location of your home. If the local schools go to the dogs, you can bet your house will, too.

How else do you find out about schools? The library is a good place to start. Check the index for the local newspapers and look for stories on schools to see what has been happening to them. Librarians also may be good sources of information about local areas.

If you are a church-goer, visit your potential future church and talk to the priest, minister, or rabbi. They are likely to know what the local situation is, and if they won't be honest with you, who will?

Most of all, talk to the parents whose children already attend the local schools—public or private. Find out what they think about the education their children are getting and whether, if they had it all to do over again, they would move into the school district. A good place to find mothers and fathers to whom to put your questions is the school parking lot just before or just after school.

Once you are satisfied with the schools, there are other location factors to consider.

Location and Convenience

The best locations are well-kept neighborhoods that are convenient to things like shopping areas, theaters, and recreational facilities—but where such things are not so close that the commercial building, noise and auto congestion spill over into the neighborhood itself. With a little driving—or walking—around, you can check the convenience of the store where you'll want to go get a loaf of bread, the nearest tennis courts, playgrounds for your kids, hospitals, shopping areas, theaters, museums and other facilities. We've included a checklist entitled "Is the Neighborhood Right for You?" to help you make your evaluation.

While you're checking, take a close look at the streets. They can affect the future saleability of the house you are buying. The best locations are on dead-end streets or streets on which there is no through traffic. That means less worry for parents with small children or people with pets. A busy street with noisy traffic in front of or behind a house can detract from its value.

If the busy street near a house is an interstate highway, approach with special caution. If you live next to such a highway, your house probably is worth less than one farther away—but more than it would be worth if the highway hadn't been built at all.

That, at least, is the conclusion of a study by Pennsylvania State University researchers of "effects of highway noise in highway communities." The Penn State research team studied the effects of noise and pollution on residential property values in four communities bisected by interstate highways:

Bogota, New Jersey; North Springfield, Virginia; Rosedale, Maryland; and Towson, Maryland. In each area, the researchers found a decrease in value, of as much as 15%, for homes abutting the highways.

However, a detailed study of North Springfield showed that although houses less than 150 feet from the highway suffered an average loss in value of $2,100 because of noise and pollution, they also benefitted from a $2,955 gain in value because of accessibility of the community to the highway. All homes in the community shared an identical accessibility benefit, the researchers noted.

The moral of the study seems to be that the prospective home buyer should live close to an interstate highway—but not too close.

Which brings up another subject to consider.

Transportation

How far do you want to travel to work? Most people's limit ends at about 45-50 minutes travel time one way. One full hour or more to get to work and another hour or more to get back is an awful lot of hours to travel. Make sure you are comfortable with the commuting time you will have. And again we stress: remember that future buyers also will want convenient transportation. That's why close-in locations with good access to buses or subways can add value to a home.

Don't rely on what the real-estate agents tell you about travel time. Ask the people who live in the neighborhood. Better yet, take a test commute during rush hour and see for yourself.

After you have checked out the current status of a neighborhood, the next thing you should have a look at is the future of the community. And since you will be investing a lot of money in the area where you buy your house, for you, as a well-known football coach likes to say, The future is now.

Looking at the Present and the Future of a Neighborhood

As a home buyer, you are mainly interested in the near future, say 3 to 10 years. But this may be long enough for the community to change. What kind of change could you expect? Well, on the negative side is the possibility for deterioration. If the community is, say, 30 years old, it could have lost some of the zip it once had. Houses may have reached the zenith of their marketability. A 30-year-old house could need a lot of new things—such as a new roof. The furnace should already have been replaced, the wiring may be out of date and the kitchen hard to sell. If the present owners in the area haven't modernized their houses, future buyers may look elsewhere and the market could decline.

The physical changes concerning the house or the street itself are only part of the puzzle. You also need to be concerned about such questions as whether some master mind at the Planning Commission is plotting to put a freeway right through the middle of the community. Or is there a movement of commercial, industrial properties which would adversely change the neighborhood characteristics?

Some of the changes might strike very close to home. "In discussing residential data with our residential appraisers, we agreed that one of the most overlooked, but important, neighborhood items to consider is the surrounding land use and planning," said Judith Dennis of Wright Realty, Inc., in Manassas, Virginia. "This is particularly important when the property adjoining a house is undeveloped. Far too often a person purchases next to a wooded lot for privacy or buys a home because of an attractive view and is dismayed six months later to find bulldozers clearing trees from surrounding land, or a townhouse project blocking the view he wanted.

"There would be far fewer disappointments if the buyer of a property would take the time to check with public officials for proposed future development surrounding the property," Ms. Dennis said.

And that is what you should do. Go directly to planning commissions (which go under different names in different cities and counties) and ask them for a master plan for the area you are interested in. Find out about any contemplated actions or zoning changes that could change the character of the area, because they could drastically affect the value of homes in the area.

Another source to check for proposed changes, zoning disputes or other developments that could hurt—or boost—the home values in an area is the local newspaper. Not the big metropolitan dailies, but the small area papers that give detailed attention to normally mundane subjects like zoning decisions, local highway plans, proposals for transportation improvements or cutbacks, and a myriad of other community issues that could affect the attractiveness of a community. You can check the papers back a year or so (they are often weekly publications) at the local library or at the newspaper office. Most newspapers have a morgue where they keep back copies of newspapers. It's called a morgue because yesterday's news usually is "dead" news, but as a potential home buyer it also may be a place where you can find where the bodies are buried in a community.

Finding a good location with a good future is only part of the answer to the question, "What makes a home a good investment?" The other part of the answer is the house itself. We have already discussed what to look for in new homes and in existing homes. But there is more to consider.

What Kind of House Should You Buy?

Houses come in all kinds of styles, shapes, sizes and materials. Some people like stately, two-story colonials, others are crazy about easy-living ramblers, still others prefer split-levels, and some go for far-out contemporaries. The question you have to ask yourself is: What is the best style for me and my individual needs, and what difference does it make in my investment?

The basic answer is that style may not make much difference unless you buy an oddball home sitting alone among more conventional ones. You may love it, and it may appeal to an appreciative few, but if you want to make a good housing investment, don't buy the only yellow Spanish villa among two-story red-brick colonials. Remember: most buyers like traditional, conventional-looking homes. They don't go for wild, innovative, screaming-color types of real estate. Neither do builders who know their customers.

"What people like is a hole in the ground and four walls," said a builder in Columbus, Ohio. "They don't buy houses which are unusual in shape or form or style."

As to which styles of houses bring the highest prices or appreciate the fastest, that varies widely in different parts of the country. In casual-living areas like San Diego, ramblers are in biggest demand. In many areas of the country, however, two-story colonials still are the most popular.

Piecing together the ideal house

In giving prospective new home buyers a chance to choose their favorite home designs and features without too much concern for their cost, this survey really allowed those buyers to describe their dream homes. And, in doing that, the survey has shown that what the typical new home buyer wants is really a fairly typical new home.

That is not to say that buyers' preferences and expectations never exceed either their ability to pay for them or the likelihood of builders providing for them. For example, about a third of all the prospective buyers surveyed and about half of those with family incomes more than $50,000 said they would like their next home to have either a hot tub or a whirlpool bath. In this case, there probably will be a big difference between what buyers want and what they actually will get.

However, looked at in total, the survey shows that prospective buy-

ers have neither farfetched expectations nor far-out preferences in housing design. Who are these prospective buyers?

The 1,400 people who completed NAHB's 66-question survey included all types of buyers from all parts of the country. Buyers with incomes of less than $15,000 and those with incomes of more than $70,000. Single buyers and divorced women with children. Empty nesters and young couples.

But the typical survey respondent was a married man with children. He was 36 years old and had a college degree. Both he and his wife worked, and together they earned $29,000 a year. They already owned a home.

According to the survey, the dream home for this typical prospective buyer would be a 2,150-square-foot two-story detached unit. The home would have a brick front and a basement as well as an

attached two-car garage. It would be energy-efficient; storm windows and storm doors would be standard as would extra insulation.

The home would have four bedrooms and two and a half baths, and the bathroom fixtures would be a color other than white. The kitchen would be well-appointed and well-equipped; it would open to a family room, which would have a fireplace and a wet bar. The kitchen would have room enough for a dining area, ample counter space, a walk-in pantry, a double bowl stainless steel sink with a disposer, a double oven with a microwave and a full luminous ceiling.

The home would have a separate living room, dining room and family room and would be carpeted throughout. A deck would overlook a large, private rear yard.

Based on a national average selling price of $40 per square foot, such a home would cost $86,000. ⟁

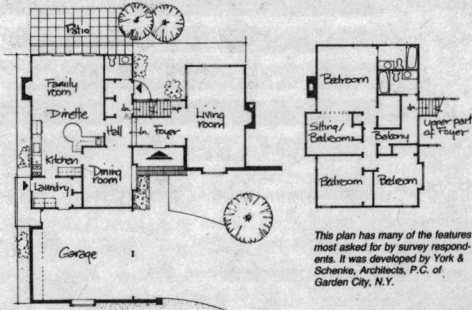

This plan has many of the features most asked for by survey respondents. It was developed by York & Schenke, Architects, P.C. of Garden City, N.Y.

Styles and Costs

In considering styles and prices of homes, it should be remembered that differences in cost of building depend upon the varying styles. In a very general way, the two-story house is the cheapest to build per square foot, measured as the cost

Features important to include in the home's basic purchase price

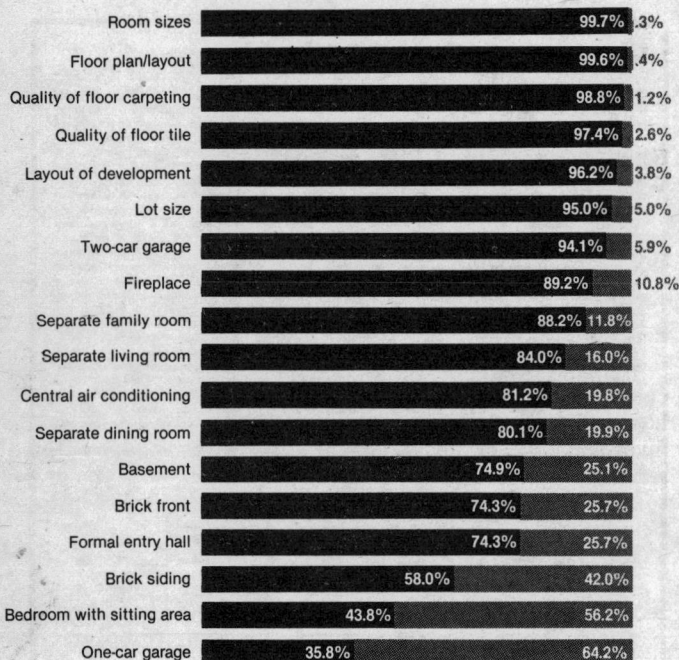

Room sizes	99.7%	.3%
Floor plan/layout	99.6%	.4%
Quality of floor carpeting	98.8%	1.2%
Quality of floor tile	97.4%	2.6%
Layout of development	96.2%	3.8%
Lot size	95.0%	5.0%
Two-car garage	94.1%	5.9%
Fireplace	89.2%	10.8%
Separate family room	88.2%	11.8%
Separate living room	84.0%	16.0%
Central air conditioning	81.2%	19.8%
Separate dining room	80.1%	19.9%
Basement	74.9%	25.1%
Brick front	74.3%	25.7%
Formal entry hall	74.3%	25.7%
Brick siding	58.0%	42.0%
Bedroom with sitting area	43.8%	56.2%
One-car garage	35.8%	64.2%

Source: National Association of Home Builders, 1980

of living area. (This could be a two-story slab, basement or split foyer.)

This is because that kind of design gives double the space of a ranch unit for the same amount of land, and also because a ceiling is cheaper to build than a floor and foundation.

There are really no "rules or thumb," but one can say that to achieve the same amount of living space per $100 spent in a typical two-story would require:

- about \$125 in a ranch,
- about \$120 in a split level,
- about \$115 in a split foyer (not finished),
- about \$98 in a split foyer (with finished lower level).

But whatever the type, the main thing—to repeat it again—is to think of the use and the investment.

Substance is More Important than Style; What Features to Look for

What makes the difference is:

- What shape the house is in.
- What is inside the house.

We have already discussed in the previous chapter how to check out the condition of a home. But how the inside of the house is designed is just as important. In terms of a good investment, some rooms are more important than others. The seller or the real-estate agent may want to show you the spacious living room and the fancy dining room. The wise buyer knows those aren't the rooms that count.

The best-selling houses have:

- Up-to-date kitchens. This may be the most important room in the house in terms of selling future buyers. Look for modern appliances, good layout and work place, modern flooring, a dishwasher that works, chopping blocks, good *outside* ventilation, lots of cupboards, and a sizeable pantry. Make sure the kitchen is big enough to fit in a table and chairs.

A good kitchen must be bright, sunny, easy to clean, close to the garage so you can get groceries in, next to the dining room—and with no traffic through the kitchen.

- Bathrooms. They are the next most important item in the house. Why? Because they shine so well, show so beautifully, and have fancy basins, tubs, colorful drapes and shower curtains. They are considered very, very

sexy, not necessarily because they are all around the
master bedroom (his and hers bathrooms presently are
the in-thing) but because they are the utmost expres-
sion of privacy.

But old-fashioned bathrooms—with plain sinks instead of
modern-looking basins and vanities, for instance—stand out
like a sore thumb. And in housing the rule of sore thumbs is
that they turn off potential buyers. Unless you are prepared
to sink a couple of thousand dollars into updating them, stay
away from homes with outdated bathrooms.

One more thing about bathrooms. One is not enough. In
terms of resaleability, your home should have at least two, and
three is even better.

- Bedrooms. You need as many as you can get—at least
  three, and four if possible in a detached, single-family
  house. Even if you don't have children, a lot of buyers
  still do. Look for privacy, privacy, privacy. Find a house
  with the master bedroom separated by a Chinese Wall,
  if possible. If not, at least by a corridor or a sitting
  room. This really sells and re-sells.

There are a few other "must" items for a house if it is to be
a good investment. Most buyers these days expect a family
room, either as a separate room or a finished basement. The
same is true of garages or carports. Fireplaces are provided in
about 60% of all new units being built these days, compared
with 22% back in 1950, an indication that they are in greater
demand. They do help sell houses, new or used.

According to the National Association of Home Builders
consumer survey, the dream home for a typical prospective
home buyer would be a 2,150-square-foot, two-story detached
unit. The home would have a brick front and a basement as
well as an attached two-car garage. It would be energy-
efficient; storm windows and storm doors would be standard,
as would extra insulation.

The home would have four bedrooms and two-and-a-half
baths, and the bathroom fixtures would be a color other than
white. The kitchen would be well-appointed and well-equipped;
it would open to a family room, which would have a fireplace
and a wet bar. The kitchen would have enough room for a

dining area, ample counter space, a walk-in pantry, a double-bowl stainless steel sink with a disposer, a double oven with a microwave and a full luminous ceiling.

The home would have a separate living room, dining room and family room and would be carpeted throughout. A deck would overlook a large, private rear yard.

Based on a national average selling price of $40 per square foot, such a home would cost $86,000.

Below are a floor plan of this "dream" house and a chart showing the features that home buyers consider important.

Go down the list and compare what you are getting in the house you would like to live in with what the buying public wants. Make sure your house, in addition to meeting your needs, will have many of the features other people will want when it comes time to sell.

Still More Costs to Consider

· Energy: There was a near riot when the people of Poolsville, Maryland, received their electric heating bills for the January/February, 1978, payment period. Some individual bills ran over $880, most were $650—for two months! "This is more than we pay for the mortgage," screamed one woman at a local meeting called to protest the high bills.

Such anguish isn't uncommon these days, as rising energy costs send utility bills soaring. This points up an energy problem (in addition to the big one) for home buyers to consider: you will want to make sure that you can pay the heating and cooling bills.

First you should know how the home you are considering purchasing is heated and cooled. Natural gas is still the cheapest energy source. Oil is second, although heating-oil prices more than doubled in the late 1970s. Electric heating and cooling is the most expensive.

Be cautious about buying an all-electric home, not only because of the electrifying utility bills, but because it might be harder to sell than a home using cheaper energy. On the other hand, new all-electric homes usually have more insulation and energy-saving features, such as heat pumps, than other houses. And in some areas, electric heating may be all that is available in new or recently-built homes.

Whatever kind of home you are considering buying, ask to see the utility bills, especially the heating bills if you live where the weather gets cold. If it is an existing home, insist on seeing all the bills for the past year or two—heating, cooling, electricity and water bills. If it is a new home, check with the local utilities and with buyers who already are living in similar models.

You also will want to check the insulation, whether the house has storm windows, and what energy-saving improvements have been made. Or you can have it checked by a home-inspection service if you sign a contract to buy the home.

· Insulation and energy savings: How much insulation you need depends pretty much on the area you live in. The National Association of Home Builders developed the *Thermal Performance Guidelines* in which they make it possible for builders to select the best cost-effective total energy package for their new homes.

In this publication, NAHB shows the degree days and cooling hours for 150 cities. We always knew that it was cold in Alaska and warm in Miami, but now we can compare these two extremes and use this information in a total energy package.

For instance, the table shows:

City	Heating Degree Days	Cooling-Annual Hours
Fairbanks, Alaska	14,290	190
Fargo, North Dakota	9,250	560
Miami, Florida	200	3,250
San Diego, California	920	1,500
San Juan, Puerto Rico	0	630

The short comparison table above clearly shows that the best place, energy-wise, is Puerto Rico, where you don't need heat at all, and air-conditioning is required at about the same level as for folks in Fargo, North Dakota.

In the continental U.S., the San Diego area needs a minimum of heating (920 heating degree days) but only half as much air-conditioning (1,500 cooling hours) as that needed in Miami.

The whole energy problem becomes quite complex and technical. However, you should have at least some understanding of the problem.

Most of the heat loss occurs through openings such as windows and doors (two-thirds). Most homes today have some insulation in the ceilings. The question is: how much?

You would need, in most cases, in the Midwest, what is called R-19 or 4-inch or 4½-inch ceiling insulation.

A storm window or insulated glass doubles the protection compared to a single glass. Thus, for most of the Midwest and the North you almost have to have storm windows.

Storm doors are another matter. A well-fitted, weather-stripped door provides enough protection without the need for storm doors for all areas with less than 4,000 heating-degree days (such as the area south of Richmond, Virginia).

· What about solar energy? You still are likely to have a hard time finding a house with solar energy to buy. But a growing number of homes, especially newly built homes, are available with solar-energy systems, and the outlook for solar is getting brighter all the time. In California, San Diego County already requires that solar water heaters be installed in houses built in certain areas. And in many places, you can buy homes that use the sun to heat the entire house at great savings on the heating bills.

A major drawback to wider use of solar heating and cooling systems has been their cost and the need to install bulky collectors to store the sun's warmth. But these problems are being overcome by such developments as the use of "passive" systems that collect the sun's energy in the windows, walls or structure of the house itself, without the need for elaborate hardware.

Almost any house lends itself to adaptation to solar energy. The problem is that the cost still will usually wipe out any savings you might realize. You must think in terms of $5,000 to $8,000 for a hot-water system, and as much as $12,000 to $20,000 for the entire home. A Presidential panel concluded that to heat water, gas heaters are a better bargain than solar heaters. The gas heaters cost about $150 and carry monthly bills of $10 to $15. Solar mechanisms cost $2,700 and provide only about 60% to 80% of a home's needs.

Still, as one San Diego builder noted, "If solar saves $10 to $15 a month, that's a substantial savings. And it's got to grow because natural gas prices are going up." Moreover, the federal government and more than 30 states offer homeowners tax incentives to help pay for the cost of installing solar-energy devices. Future developments involving solar energy could have a substantial impact on the economics of homeownership.

- Property Taxes: There's one more expense to check when buying a house. We left it for last because polls show it is the most unpopular tax in the country. Yes, it's the property tax, which in most places is adding an ever-growing amount to housing costs, usually as part of the monthly mortgage payment.

Ask for the property tax receipts for the past several years. This way you will get some idea of how fast they are increasing. Be sure to ask also for the latest reassessment, which may have been made since the last tax payment. That will show you how much more in property taxes you can expect to pay the next time if you buy a house.

Property taxes vary widely across the land. Troubled cities and counties usually spell rapid increases in property taxes. Central cities nearly always have heavier tax burdens than areas located outside of central areas. Homeowners in southern cities generally pay substantially lower property taxes than those in northern states. One Census Bureau study of 21 major metropolitan areas found that the highest taxes for the average homeowner—more than $1,000 a year—were in Hartford, Connecticut; Paterson, New Jersey; and Rochester, N.Y. The lowest annual taxes, averaging under $100, were in New Orleans, La.

There is one very good thing about property taxes. They are tax deductible, and that helps a lot.

We'll take a closer look at the whole property-tax issue in a later chapter. Now it's time to wrap up the question of how to make a solid housing investment by arming you with some weapons to take house-hunting with you.

Be Your Own Appraiser

When a lender makes a loan on a home purchase, he hires an appraiser to determine the long-term value of the home and the area in which it is located. The lender wants to know if he is making a good investment with his mortgage money. The appraiser looks at many of the same things that we have discussed—the location of the home, its age and condition, property taxes, and the future prospects of the neighborhood. Obviously, you can't become an expert appraiser overnight. But, by checking exactly what the appraiser will, you can get an idea of whether the home you are considering is a good investment.

To help you be your own appraiser, we are including on the following pages a standardized appraisal sheet now being used by most appraisers and lending institutions. The form calls for more details than you probably will be able to obtain, but you can use it to make your own list of items to be checked when shopping for a home.

Location, the features of a home, its age and condition all are important factors to consider in your housing investment. To help you keep track of all these things while you are house hunting, reprinted below are two lists of checkpoints—one for outside and the other for inside the home. You can use them when you go house hunting, or as a basis to draw up your own list that meets your specific needs.

Checkpoints for Outside the Home

Make your own personal observations, but also consult your builder, local government, real-estate agent, and friends. As you explore various homes and neighborhoods, use these checkpoints to compare them and see whether the housing environment matches up with your wants and needs.

Borrower/Client		Census Tract	Map Reference
Property Address			
City	County	State	Zip Code
Legal Description			
Sale Price $	Date of Sale	Property Rights Appraised ☐ Fee ☐ Leasehold ☐ De Minimus PUD(FNMA only) ☐ Condo ☐ PUD	
Actual Real Estate Taxes $	(yr) Loan charges to be paid by seller $	Other sales concessions	
Lender		Lender's Address	
Occupant	Appraiser	Instructions to Appraiser	

NEIGHBORHOOD (Completed by Lender)

			Good	Avg	Fair	Poor
Location	☐ Urban ☐ Suburban ☐ Rural	Employment Stability	☐	☐	☐	☐
Built Up	☐ Over 75% ☐ 25% to 75% ☐ Under 25%	Convenience to Employment	☐	☐	☐	☐
Growth Rate ☐ Fully Dev.	☐ Rapid ☐ Steady ☐ Slow	Convenience to Shopping	☐	☐	☐	☐
Property Values	☐ Increasing ☐ Stable ☐ Declining	Convenience to Schools	☐	☐	☐	☐
Demand/Supply	☐ Shortage ☐ In Balance ☐ Over Supply	Quality of Schools	☐	☐	☐	☐
Marketing Time	☐ Under 3 Mos. ☐ 4-6 Mos. ☐ Over 6 Mos.	Recreational Facilities	☐	☐	☐	☐
Present Land Use ___% 1 Family ___% 2-4 Family ___% Apts ___% Condo ___% Commercial		Adequacy of Utilities	☐	☐	☐	☐
___% Industrial ___% Vacant ___%		Property Compatibility	☐	☐	☐	☐
Change in Present Land Use ☐ Not Likely ☐ Likely (*) ☐ Taking Place (*)		Protection from Detrimental Conditions	☐	☐	☐	☐
(*) From ___ To ___		Police and Fire Protection	☐	☐	☐	☐
Predominant Occupancy	☐ Owner ☐ Tenant ___% Vacant	General Appearance of Properties	☐	☐	☐	☐
Single Family Price Range $ ___ to $ ___	Predominant Value $ ___	Appeal to Market	☐	☐	☐	☐
Single Family Age ___ yrs to ___ yrs	Predominant Age ___ yrs					

Note: FHLMC/FNMA do not consider the racial composition of the neighborhood to be a relevant factor and it must not be considered in the appraisal.

Comments (including those factors adversely affecting marketability) _____

SITE

Dimensions		Sq Ft or Acres	☐ Corner Lot
Zoning classification	☐ Present use	☐ do ☐ do not conform to zoning regulations	
Highest and best use ☐ Present use ☐ Other (Describe)		Present improvements	

	Public	Other (Describe)	OFF SITE IMPROVEMENTS		Topo	
Elec	☐		Street Access ☐ Public ☐ Private		Size	
Gas	☐		Surface		Shape	
Water	☐		Maintenance ☐ Public ☐ Private		View	
San Sewer	☐		☐ Storm Sewer ☐ Curb/Gutter		Drainage	
	☐ Underground Elect & Tel		☐ Sidewalk ☐ Street Lights		Is the property located in a HUD identified Flood Hazard Area? ☐ No ☐ Yes	

Comments (favorable or unfavorable including any apparent adverse easements, encroachments or other adverse conditions) _____

IMPROVEMENTS

☐ Existing (approx. yr. blt.) 19____	No. Units ____
☐ Proposed ☐ Under Construction	No. Stories ____

Type (det., duplex, semi/det, etc.) ____ Design (rambler, split level, etc.) ____ Exterior Walls ____

Roof Material	Gutters & Downspouts ☐ None	Window (Type)	Insulation ☐ None ☐ Floor
		☐ Storm Sash	☐ Ceiling ☐ Walls
			☐ Roof

Foundation Walls
- ☐ % Basement
- ☐ Outside Entrance
- ☐ Concrete Floor
- ☐ Crawl Space
- ☐ Slab on Grade
- Evidence of ☐ Dampness ☐ Termites ☐ Settlement

☐ Floor Drain ☐ Finished Ceiling
☐ Sump Pump ☐ Finished Walls
____ % Finished ☐ Finished Floor

Comments ____

ROOM LIST

Room List	Foyer	Living	Dining	Kitchen	Den	Family Rm.	Rec. Rm.	Bedrooms	No. Baths	Laundry	Other
Basement											
1st Level											
2nd Level											

Total ____ Rooms ____ Bedrooms ____ Baths in finished area above grade

INTERIOR FINISH & EQUIPMENT

Kitchen Equipment: ☐ Refrigerator ☐ Range/Oven ☐ Disposal ☐ Dishwasher ☐ Fan/Hood ☐ Compactor ☐ Washer ☐ Dryer

HEAT Type ____ Fuel ____ Cond. ____ AIR COND. ☐ Central ☐ Other ____ ☐ Adequate ☐ Inadequate

Floors	☐ Hardwood ☐ Carpet Over ____		
Walls	☐ Drywall ☐ Plaster ____		
Trim/Finish	☐ Good ☐ Average ☐ Fair ☐ Poor		
Bath Floor	☐ Ceramic		
Bath Wainscot	☐ Ceramic		

Special Features (including fireplaces): ____

ATTIC ☐ Yes ☐ No ☐ Stairway ☐ Drop-stair ☐ Scuttle ☐ Floored
Finished (Describe) ____ ☐ Heated

CAR STORAGE ☐ Garage ☐ Built-in ☐ Attached ☐ Detached ☐ Car Port
No. Cars ____ ☐ Adequate ☐ Inadequate Condition ____

PORCHES, PATIOS, POOL, FENCES, etc. (describe) ____

COMMENTS (including functional or physical inadequacies, repairs needed, modernization, etc.) ____

PROPERTY RATING

	Good	Avg.	Fair	Poor
Quality of Construction (Materials & Finish)	☐	☐	☐	☐
Condition of Improvements	☐	☐	☐	☐
Rooms size and layout	☐	☐	☐	☐
Closets and Storage	☐	☐	☐	☐
Plumbing—adequacy and condition	☐	☐	☐	☐
Electrical—adequacy and condition	☐	☐	☐	☐
Kitchen Cabinets—adequacy and condition	☐	☐	☐	☐
Compatibility to Neighborhood	☐	☐	☐	☐
Overall Livability	☐	☐	☐	☐
Appeal and Marketability	☐	☐	☐	☐

Effective Age ____ Yrs. Est. Remaining Economic Life ____ Yrs.

ATTACH DESCRIPTIVE PHOTOGRAPHS OF SUBJECT PROPERTY AND STREET SCENE

FHLMC Form 70 Rev. 9/75   FNMA Form 1004 Rev 9/75

	Home 1	Home 2	Home 3
Shopping Are there adequate facilities close by?	☐	☐	☐
Churches Are they available and convenient?	☐	☐	☐
Community Is the community well-planned?	☐	☐	☐
Neighbors Are they likely to be compatible with your tastes and lifestyle?	☐	☐	☐
Police and Fire Protection Are they adequate for the area?	☐	☐	☐
Schools Are the schools your children will attend located to suit you?	☐	☐	☐
Hospital Is there a hospital or medical center nearby?	☐	☐	☐
Hazards Are hazards such as gas or oil tanks and streams that might overflow at a considerable distance?	☐	☐	☐
Recreation Are there suitable facilities within walking distance for young and old alike?	☐	☐	☐
Trash and Garbage Disposal Are the arrangements adequate and frequent enough?	☐	☐	☐
Traffic Are streets likely to be busy or quiet? Does the speed limit suit you?	☐	☐	☐
Car Parking Are there adequate car parking spaces and garage facilities for your needs?	☐	☐	☐
Transportation Is public transportation adequate and handy?	☐	☐	☐
Lay of the Land Is land well-drained?	☐	☐	☐

	Home 1	Home 2	Home 3

And do you like the "micro climate"? For example, in a valley you may have a great deal of fog; on a hill, it may be windy!

Landscaping
Has proper landscaping been done to prevent erosion?   ☐   ☐   ☐

Water
Is there a reliable and drinkable source of water with adequate pressure to fit present and future community needs?   ☐   ☐   ☐

Sewerage
Is the sanitary sewerage disposal system reliable and adequate and does it meet present and anticipated future community needs?   ☐   ☐   ☐

Privacy
Are lots or units arranged to suit your family lifestyle?   ☐   ☐   ☐

Nuisance
Are there nearby sources of excessive noise, smoke, soot, dust or odors that will degrade your housing environment or endanger members of your household?   ☐   ☐   ☐

Assessments
Are there special assessments covering a portion of the lot, street, or community development costs which will mean added monthly charges to you for a specified number of years?   ☐   ☐   ☐

Checkpoints for Inside the Home

What you should look for inside the house depends on what you personally need and want, so it's a good idea to compile your own list of features to check. Here are some questions to start you off, but you should add checkpoints according to your personal concerns. Rate the houses you're comparing as good, fair or poor.

	Good	Fair	Poor
Is the roof leakproof?	☐	☐	☐
Do walls seem sound and smooth, floors firm and level, carpentry well-fitted and joined?	☐	☐	☐
Is the basement clean and dry?	☐	☐	☐
Is lighting good, in daylight and at night?	☐	☐	☐
Are rooms large enough to take your furniture and is there sufficient wall space for arranging furniture?	☐	☐	☐
Is the floor plan well laid out with separate areas for living, working and sleeping?	☐	☐	☐
Do bedrooms and baths provide quiet and privacy away from the living area?	☐	☐	☐
Can you get from entry doors to other parts of the house without crossing the living room?	☐	☐	☐
Does the kitchen suit you: does it allow for good light and ventilation and are there enough outlets for plugging in all your kitchen appliances?	☐	☐	☐
Are there ample cabinets and counter work space for your family needs?	☐	☐	☐
Have all interior wall, ceiling and floor surfaces been properly finished?	☐	☐	☐
Is there adequate and convenient closet room and storage space for linens and equipment?	☐	☐	☐
Do doors, windows, and drawers work easily and safely?	☐	☐	☐
Does plumbing work well and quietly, with adequate water pressure and free-flowing drains?	☐	☐	☐
Is heating, cooling and ventilating equipment satisfactory, convenient?	☐	☐	☐
Are there enough electrical outlets well arranged and sufficient amperage for your electrical equipment?	☐	☐	☐
Are bathrooms and lavatories conveniently located?	☐	☐	☐

	Good	Fair	Poor
Are wall spaces useable for attractive furniture arrangement, and not too chopped up by windows and doors?	☐	☐	☐
Are the rooms located to take advantage of sun and shade?	☐	☐	☐
Are the views from the windows to your liking?	☐	☐	☐
Are the temperature controls located in safe and convenient places?	☐	☐	☐
If there are stairs, are there landings and adequate handrails?	☐	☐	☐
Does the home have full roof gutters and an adequate number of downspouts and splash blocks?	☐	☐	☐

FIVE

Investment Strategies: Or How to Mortgage Your Future and Find Happiness

"People always say, 'Wait until
you can afford it'; but if you
wait, you can never afford it."

—Suellen Lewis,
a young home buyer
in Burke, Virginia

*I'll never forget the first house we bought. It was in Columbus,
Ohio. I suggested to the seller that we pay him $15,000. "But
the house has an FHA approval of $16,500," he said.*

"So what," I replied.

"$15,000 is the only price I will pay you for it," I told him.

*Both my wife and I were attending Ohio State University,
and I had just taken a "full-time" job for the summer. This
gave me enough income to qualify for a house.*

*The seller couldn't find another buyer, so we bought our
first house for $15,000 and without making a down payment.
It was pretty much like many other houses with little or no
down payment. We practically redid the house in the next
three years, and we sold it at a reasonable profit.*

*Moral: We purchased a house with no down payment. We
stretched our budget. But we knew that we would be able to
match the payments with our increased incomes—we had the
potential upper mobility.*

Since that time, hundreds of families have purchased homes from the E.G. Fritsche Company I was working for in Columbus for $9.95 down—under the FHA "sweat" equity program (which means doing part of the finishing jobs yourself—like painting).

Actually, the purchase of our house was a "sweat equity"—and more so, since we did most of the upgrading with the purchase of kitchen cabinets, new plumbing fixtures, and so forth—plus our labor.

—Mike Sumichrast

How to Get Going

Save. Save. Save. The best thing you can do is to get into a regular habit of saving. Save $5, $10, $25 a week, or whatever—but Save.

- Save regularly from each paycheck.
- Save any extra money you happen to make.
- Save all or part of your spouse's income.
- Make a bonfire of most or all credit cards if you are tempted to "charge" all of the items you don't really need or cannot afford.
- Make a budget and try to stick with it.
- Ask your employer to deduct from your weekly (or monthly) check a small portion of your net income—and forget it!
- Establish an account at your friendly neighborhood savings and loan association. Chances are that you will have to use their money to finance your home. You need all the brownie points you can get.
- Don't get into a fancy Certificate of Deposit—at least not at the beginning. Establish your regular passbook account and see what will-power you have to save.
- If you do decide to go with Certificates of Deposit—remember that although they pay more interest than passbook savings, the penalties for early withdrawal are quite steep.

When interest rates are high, short-term Certificates of Deposit or Money Market Certificates can be a good way to save your nest egg and earn a good return on it at the same time.

Force yourself to save by renting and putting away the difference. It works like a charm, but you must be strong enough to force yourself to save the difference between what you are paying now for rent and what the monthly payment would be if you purchased a home. You will be surprised at how much it adds up to, and how fast you can accumulate enough for a down payment.

You will also know how large a mortgage you really can carry once you decide to go after a house.

Beg or Borrow the Down Payment—If You Have To

If you think that you don't have enough for a down payment, think hard and find a way to get it—if nothing else, try hard to spend less and save more.

- Borrow from your parents. Don't be bashful. Sign a note and deposit it with your bank to make your parents sleep better. Even agree to pay current interest rates on this loan—if they feel very strongly about the issue.
- Borrow from your friends. You may not find this very easy to do, but try. If needed, sign a second-mortgage note to be repaid in, say, 2 to 4 years.
- Borrow on your life insurance to get the down payment.
- Cash in your savings bonds.
- Sell stocks, bonds, or securities you have.
- Sell the second car, not just because of the payments but because it looks bad on your financial statement (after all, you still owe $3,400, don't you?).
- Get another job. Maybe what you make just is not enough. Find yourself something else where you or your spouse can make more money. As Mrs. Sumichrast told her husband after looking at their recent income-tax statement: "I don't ever remember having only one income since we were married. I guess that's the only way to make it." It's one of the ways.

Start Small

Don't let those high housing prices you read about intimidate you. There are still plenty of homes around that don't cost a small fortune. They may not be the homes of your dreams, but they can be the first step on the way to getting the home that you really want. Sometimes you can buy them almost as cheaply as you can rent them, and that means that your monthly payments are going into your future instead of your landlord's pocket.

Joyce Rhodes, who bought the townhouse she once rented in Loudoun County, Virginia, put it very simply: "I paid $200 to rent a two-bedroom townhouse. Now I pay $238, including a $30 condominium fee. But, I can deduct the interest from my taxes. In my tax bracket, that means a deduction of $44 per month. So I actually pay only $194 per month—and the townhouse is all mine!"

This townhouse section of converted rental units—Pembrooke of Loudoun—sold out in the first three weeks in February, 1977, at an unbelievable rate of over 100 units per week.

Reason: the best units for the price. As a starter unit, a one-bedroom unit sold "as is" for $16,200, a two-bedroom unit for $23,900, and a three-bedroom unit for $26,900.

Completely renovated units sold for $19,200, $27,900 and $30,900.

The choice of housing types is nearly unlimited. But, when it comes to borrowing money, they can only stretch so far.

Therefore, new starters should remember:

- Condominium and townhouse conversions could be *the cheapest* available for-sale homes.
- Small, new condominiums would be second in line.
- Small, new townhouses would follow next in price ranges.
- Single-family houses (cape cod, or rambler with no basement) built after World War II would be next.
- Split-levels built in the 1950s follow.
- After that it is a toss-up among all single-family used homes.

Merrill Buttler (left) and H. Douglas Hoon display
the original sign they used to sell homes in Long Beach Park, CA.
Built in 1955 and sold for $9,095, this house contained
960 square feet with three bedrooms and one bath, situated
on a 6,000 square foot lot. In 1981 the same house
was re-selling at more than $80,000!

· Then come single-family new homes in nearby suburbs.
· The most expensive are the new single-family units
  built close to the center of metropolitan areas.

Buy an Old House to Start With

It is usually cheaper to buy an older home than a new one.
How much cheaper? Between 10% and 25%—although in
some cities the difference is much larger. For instance, in St.
Louis the difference between new and existing homes sold in
the fall of 1979 was $28,900; new homes sold at an average
price of $77,900 and existing homes at $59,000.

For a first-time buyer an older home is nearly always the
best "starter."

Buy an "Affordable" New Home

While older homes usually are cheaper, sometimes a new home can be the best buy for a first-time or a second-time buyer.

In many areas of the country, builders are responding to the booming demand by offering "affordable" homes built to sell at more moderate prices than most new homes. Michael Robinson, a builder in Oregon, is squeezing more homes onto each acre of his developments to hold down prices. "Although houses will be smaller, they will have the same amenities," he said. "It's going to be like having a compact car instead of a gas guzzler."

In some communities, builders are required to build a certain number of "affordable" homes in expensive subdivisions. So don't drive by those high-priced developments too quickly. You just might find an affordable investment in a high-priced neighborhood.

Buy a Duplex and Rent One Side Out

But two units and live in one. Rent the other half. This could be an older duplex or a new one. Also look for townhouses with a twist—the upper two levels are where you will be living; the lower part can be rented to another household, preferably a couple or a single individual.

In most cases the entry is from the side or back. But you have your address and your renter has his own (two separate numbers). All the utilities are separate. The unit is built so that it could be used either as one unit or two, with enough quiet features so that you don't disturb your renter and your renter does not (hopefully) disturb you. And you don't have too far to go to collect the rent.

Look into a Leasing/Buying Agreement

About 20% of the single-family homes in many metropolitan areas are rented. Try this: rent the unit with an option to buy later on.

This may give you a predetermined amount of money (purchase price) you will pay, say one or two years hence, without being stuck paying a higher price. It will also give you a chance to see whether you really like the house and whether the house is any good. After living in it for a year, you should have a pretty good idea of whether it's worth buying.

Buy a Mobile Home

One of the cheapest ways to get started as a homeowner is to get a mobile home. That is exactly what the co-author of this book, Ron Shafer, and his wife, Barbara, did in a housing story that could be called:

Upward Mobility from Woodpecker Way

Her friends thought it was the craziest thing she had done since she kept a boa constrictor for a house pet. It was late 1967, and as a young, single working woman in Detroit, Michigan, Barbara Lucas decided she was tired of paying rent to someone else. She wanted a place of her own. So she took out a $2,900 bank loan and bought the only place she could afford—a two-year-old, blue-and-white house trailer (that's what they called mobile homes back then) in a rather seedy-looking trailer park in a Detroit suburb. The trailer was 10 feet wide and 50 feet long, and attached to the outside was an ugly, black tank that held the heating oil. It wasn't until her first night in the trailer, when she was awakened by what sounded like an artillery barrage in her bedroom, that she realized that her new home was located about 50 yards from a railroad coupling station, where trains were coupled by crashing them into each other. Still, the mobile home was all hers, and that's what counted.

The next month, Barbara made another big decision. I proposed, and she said, "yes". Within a few weeks, I was scheduled to move from the Detroit bureau of The Wall Street Journal to the Journal's Washington bureau. When Barb phoned her friends and relatives to spread the news of our engagement, I could guess from her side of the conversation what were the first two things everyone wanted to know. Invariably, she said:

"January sixth."

"We're taking it with us."

Sure enough, we took it with us. The day after our wedding in January, 1968, we drove to Washington, D.C.;

later that week, a truck pulled our mobile home, filled with all our belongings, across the Pennsylvania Turnpike to a mobile home park named Audubon Estates that I had previously picked out near Alexandria, Virginia.

Audubon Estates is nothing like the stereotype, trashy-looking trailer parks of yesteryear. Looking like a subdivision with mobile homes instead of houses, it has wide, paved streets and sidewalks. Each home has its own grassy yard, a driveway and a storage shed. The wheels that make mobile homes mobile are hidden behind metal skirting, and hook-ups for heating oil also are out of sight beneath each home. Each street is named after a bird. We were assigned a lot on Woodpecker Way—an address that got second glances every place we filled out credit applications.

Life on Woodpecker Way erased any doubts we had about mobile-home living. Certainly, two people living in a 10-foot-wide home have to make certain adjustments—like learning to walk sideways a lot. And there are sure to be plenty of jokes from friends. Like the time Barb was talking on the phone in the bedroom at the back of the trailer and told a friend to hang on while she walked to the living room in the front to get a recipe: the friend, who had never known anyone who lived in a mobile home, said, "Gee, I figured you could reach everywhere in the trailer from where you're sitting."

But our home—with two bedrooms, a bath with double sinks, a big and modern kitchen and a living room—had as much living space as apartments of many of our friends. The difference was that our housing money wasn't going for rent, and we were able to put more aside for our goal of buying a house.

It was our home on wheels that enabled us to move up to a house. I had used my bachelor savings to pay off the $2,900 loan (after discovering that my bride hadn't made her first payment yet), so our basic housing cost was only a $55-a-month lot payment. Barb found a job working for a Texas congressman, and we were able to bank her entire pay plus much of mine toward a down payment. In late 1968, we sold our mobile home for $3,000, or $100 more than we paid for it. With that money and our savings we were able to put $6,000 down on a new, four-bedroom house that we bought for $32,000. We since have traded up to our third house. But

*some months as I mail off the sizeable mortgage payment, I
fondly recall those days on Woodpecker Way—and those
$55-a-month housing payments.*

—*Ron Shafer*

Mobile homes are still a good way to get rolling as a
homeowner. One obvious attraction is that they are just about
the only homes available today for under $20,000. In 1978,
the average price of new mobile homes was $15,925, accord-
ing to Manufactured Housing Institute. Used mobile homes
are even cheaper. And mobile homes come furnished.

A mobile-home buyer today can forget about those old
images of tin-can trailers and run-down trailer camps. Today
the typical mobile home is 14 feet wide by 69 feet long; or
you can buy double-wide homes, at a higher price, that
contain more living space than many conventional houses.
Though mobile homes still have wheels—so they can be
delivered to home-sites—only about 2% of all homes sold
today are ever moved from their original sites. Trailer parks
also have changed; today the modern, subdivision types like
Audubon Estates are the rule.

More and more people are turning to mobile homes to try
to beat the high cost of housing. Nearly 11 million people lived
in about 5 million such homes in 1981, the Manufactured
Housing Institute said. About 42.5% of mobile-home residents are 34 years of age or younger, nearly 75% are married
and have an average family size of 2.3 persons. About 44% of
all mobile-home owners earn $10,000 a year or more.

Mobile Homes—What to Watch Out For

The first thing to remember about mobile homes is that
they usually don't appreciate in value like houses. In fact,
historically they have tended to depreciate like automobiles—the
average depreciation for mobile homes being 12% to 50%
over the first five years. But that is changing. As mobile
homes have gained respectability and acceptability, some
models are actually appreciating in value. A mobile home
located in an attractive park is especially likely to gain in
value. While you can't count on a mobile home giving you
the big profit that you might make on a house, it can be a
home that you can afford to buy now and live in while you
save for a bigger and costlier one later.

Mobile homes also are financed differently from conventional houses. Again, historically they tended to be financed like cars. Instead of a long mortgage, the buyer got a 10- to 12-year loan after paying 20% to 25% down. Interest rates also were higher than mortgage rates. But this too is changing. Lenders now are able to offer 10% down payments and 20-year loans. The longer loans are especially available on double-wide mobile homes and other modern manufactured houses. More favorable terms also may be available with 15-year loans insured by the FHA or, if you are a veteran, the Veterans Administration. Those agencies don't make loans themselves, but their local offices can direct you to lenders who offer such government-backed financing.

Most new mobile homes are purchased from independent dealers. Check out the reputation of a dealer before you buy from him. Be sure to ask if his price includes delivery and set-up expenses. Also find out exactly what the warranty covers. Since 1976 the federal government has required that all mobile homes have at least a one-year warranty, but some producers offer longer warranties. However, the Federal Trade Commission has been highly critical of the warranty work of some manufacturers. Dealers also usually offer financing, but check local lenders or your credit union to make sure you get the best deal.

Often your best buy can be a used mobile home—like cars, the sharpest depreciation for mobile homes that still depreciate is in the early years. Look for homes being sold in well-kept and desirable mobile-home parks. You also might check local lenders, who sometimes are looking for reliable buyers to take over the payments on repossessed mobile homes.

One caution on used mobile homes: poor construction and even fire hazards have been frequent problems in the past. Those problems haven't all been solved, but since June, 1976, new mobile homes have had to meet quality and safety standards established by the U.S. Department of Housing and Urban Development (HUD). Look for homes that are certified to have met those standards. The HUD seal of approval also could enhance the long-term value of a used mobile home that you buy.

As important as your choice of a mobile home is where you park it. A good mobile home park can add to the value of your home, or at least slow its depreciation. Lot fees generally range from $45 to $500 or more a month. Again, make sure there are no excessive move-in or hook-up fees. Also, get a one-year written lease so that you can't be evicted at the whim of the park owners. You should make sure there are no prohibitions against selling your mobile home at its location in the park; beware of the park that requires you to buy a new mobile home from them or from an affiliated dealer in order to move into the park. And like any home buyer, be sure to check utility costs and other expenses in advance.

In some parts of the country you can buy a manufactured house and the lot it sits on in a subdivision just as you can buy conventional housing. Not only do the manufactured homes look like conventional homes, but they are on permanent foundations and the owners pay property taxes like any other home buyer. The difference is that the factory-built homes cost about half as much to produce as conventional homes; even adding the cost of the land, they are far cheaper than conventional homes. Manufactured homes could be one way of satisfying the housing needs of America's low- and moderate-income families in the future.

Get a Subsidy

Don't rule out any help you can get from local, state or federal government. For instance, many localities provide help to people by requiring builders (to whom they usually give something in return, like a favorable zoning, which costs the county nothing) to build some units priced lower than most others in a subdivision.

In April, 1978, 600 potential buyers came to bid for 12 homes in Montgomery County, Maryland. The lucky ones got the privilege of purchasing new units with a maximum price of $35,490. This is in a county where the average price of a new home is over $70,000.

The federal government provides a homeownership subsidy to low- and medium-income people under a program called Section 235. It works like this:

The Department of Housing and Urban Development (HUD) pays the difference between the payment required on the mortgage at the market interest rate and the sum which the family can pay with one-fifth of their income, or as little as 4% of the interest rate.

In effect, the government-assistance funds for Section 235 housing are interest subsidies, allowing the families to obtain low-interest financing.

This interest assistance diminishes in amount as the family's income rises and the family is able to apply a greater dollar amount to payment of the mortgage, eventually to the point where the homeowner assumes full responsibility for his payments. Like any homeowners, the owners eventually can sell their homes, take the profit and trade up to another home. Of course, they no longer would get a subsidy.

Significantly, a sample HUD survey of the first new-home purchasers under the Section 235 program showed that after the first two years of occupancy the incomes of almost 10% of the purchasers had increased to such levels that they no longer needed the interest subsidy. This was due to increases in the incomes of the heads of the families and more income from additional members getting jobs because of their changed circumstances. The survey also showed a total reduction of 5% in the subsidies still being paid.

Section 235 housing, therefore, is serving a number of sectors of the population, generally in income ranges up to about $20,000 a year—the starting professionals, the operating worker, the factory hand, the unskilled, the displaced family, the ill-housed, and other people who have been behind financially in today's economy because of various circumstances.

Check the HUD-FHA office in your area or the local government housing agency to see if any will be available in your community.

Getting the Best House for Your Money; Stretch Yourself

Whether you are a first-time buyer, or looking to move up to a bigger and better house, there are things you can do to make the best possible investment.

What sounds like big money today may look like little money in two or three years. That is the reason we advise people to stretch their budget as much as they can.

What does that mean?

If you think you can afford a $40,000 house, chances are

that you could—if you really stretched it out—afford a $50,000 house.

The best example of this stretching is a young family with a gross pay of $1,400 a month, buying a $50,000 home with 20% down and an 11% mortgage rate. The payment for mortgage, principal, insurance and property taxes comes to about $470 per month. Meaning: $470 is 33.5% of their monthly income, and that is really stretching it. A typical family would pay between 20%–25% for shelter. Add to the $470 a utility cost of, say, $100 a month, and their total monthly expenses are a staggering 41% of their income.

But the $1,400 pay is going to be $1,600 in the next 12 months, since both husband and wife are going to get pay increases. That means that they will be down to 29% of their income spent for housing. And that is still a lot, but obviously much better. In five years, if they just get more due to inflation, they will be making around $2,300 a month. Then the $470 monthly payment will be down to 20%. Do you see what we mean by "stretching yourself"?

Lenders generally require that monthly payments for interest, property taxes and insurance not exceed 25% to 30% of a home buyer's gross monthly income. MGIC Investment Corp., the nation's largest private insurer of home mortgages, allows house payments up to 33% of gross income. But most will be flexible about the limit if a buyer's earning power seems likely to grow. The following table shows how you can stretch the buying power of your income by initially allotting a larger share of it for housing costs (Table 5-1)—assuming that you get a fixed rate mortgage.

For an idea of what kind of mortgage payments other people pay across the country, for new and used homes, take a look at the following summary of home purchases in 1980.

Check Those Mortgage Rates

Remember that high mortgage rates make a dramatic difference in your monthly house payments and what you can afford. For a 30-year, $40,000 mortgage at 9% interest, the principal and interest amount to $322 a month. But for the same loan at a 14% rate, the monthly payment is $150 higher, or $474.

Table 5-1

Your Down Payment and Income Needed

Sales Price	Down Payment 30 Years		Monthly Payments[1]	Income Needed[2]	
				25%	30%
$40,000	10%	$ 4,000	$413	$19,380	$16,350
	20	8,000	375	18,000	14,850
	25	10,000	356	17,100	14,100
$50,000	10%	$ 5,000	$518	$24,860	$20,500
	20	10,000	470	22,560	18,600
	25	12,500	446	21,400	17,670
$60,000	10%	$ 6,000	$610	$29,850	$24,160
	20	12,000	552	26,500	21,860
	25	15,000	524	25,150	20,750

[1] Including Principal, Interest, Property Tax and Insurance at an 11% rate
[2] Percent of Monthly Gross Income Allowed against Mortgage Payment

Share of $23,000 Income Needed For a $50,000 House at Various Levels of Down Payment

Down Payment	Share of Income
5%	28%
10	27
20	25
25	23
30	22

How Shifting Rates Affect Monthly Payments

House Price	8% Interest		10% Interest		12% Interest		14% Interest		16% Interest	
	Monthly Payment	Needed Annual Salary	Monthly Payment	Needed Annual Salary	Monthly Payment	Needed Annual Salary	Monthly Payment	Needed Annual Salary	Monthly Payment	Needed Annual Salary
$45,000	$297	$14,256	$356	$17,088	$417	$20,016	$480	$23,040	$545	$26,142
55,000	363	17,424	435	20,880	509	24,432	587	28,176	666	31,951
65,000	429	20,592	514	24,672	602	28,896	693	33,264	787	37,761
75,000	495	23,760	593	28,464	695	33,360	800	38,400	908	43,570
85,000	562	26,976	672	32,356	787	37,776	907	43,536	1029	49,379

Assumes 10% down payment, 30-year mortgage term, with 25% of gross monthly salary for mortgage payment (principal and interest only).
Source: MGIC Investment Corp.

Table 5-2

Comparative Home Purchase Data For Selected Metropolitan Areas, January, 1981

City	Purchase Price	Effective Rate	Loan-to-Value Ratio	Term To Maturity	Monthly Payment (P + I)
Atlanta	$ 89,400	13.62%	74%	29 yrs	$ 765.95
Baltimore	62,200	13.55	81	29	580.56
Boston	79,400	14.19	72	29	687.51
Chicago	68,100	13.53	72	28	565.92
Cleveland	64,600	13.88	74	26	550.32
Columbus	70,900	12.95	79	30	617.41
Dallas	108,400	14.00	74	29	952.68
Denver	89,600	12.55	77	29	741.39
Detroit	66,300	13.97	72	29	565.80
Greensboro*	53,100	13.83	78	26	491.10
Honolulu	94,900	12.75	77	30	794.08
Houston	83,500	12.55	81	30	724.46
Indianapolis	64,000	13.71	77	29	574.04
Kansas City	63,900	13.77	76	27	571.45
Los Angeles	107,600	14.37	76	30	992.94
Louisville	58,400	13.48	72	29	482.22
Miami	83,000	14.45	73	29	741.11
Milwaukee	74,300	14.17	84	26	756.39
Minneapolis	88,500	12.64	70	30	667.90
New York	89,300	14.00	64	27	682.70
Philadelphia	66,800	13.78	72	28	564.48
Phoenix	96,500	13.11	69	30	742.29
Pittsburgh	57,200	13.56	78	30	513.14
Portland	58,000	13.23	81	30	528.15
Rochester	48,900	12.98	82	28	445.73
St. Louis	60,900	13.88	72	26	521.60
Salt Lake City*	72,100	13.12	82	30	659.56
San Diego	124,900	13.99	71	30	1,050.03
San Francisco	123,900	14.61	76	30	1,114.98
Seattle	80,100	13.54	80	30	736.00
Tampa	70,500	14.49	77	29	665.71
Washington D.C.	119,300	13.86	75	30	1,050.26

Don't Think This is the Last House You Will Buy

Think positively. Don't get stuck with the idea that you are going to die in the house. We have not yet reached the point where, as people in Austria say, "The only time people leave their homes is feet first."

You must think that the house you are buying today is only a step toward a better house or a step toward something which your needs may dictate. If you are young, think in terms of staying 4 to 5 years and moving into a larger, more modern and comfortable house. If your children are gone, you may be thinking of buying a smaller house or a condominium.

Whatever the reason for buying today's house, always remember that this must not be the last one—there is always something else to look forward to.

Advantages of a Small Down Payment

To make a small down payment or a big one is an individual decision. But with certain exceptions that we will discuss later, we would advise putting down as little as you can while still having monthly payments you can afford. This is because:

- *You get "leverage," which in real-estate talk means using the least to get the most*. Here is an example of how it is used by real-estate investors:

Leverage Example

Item	Mr. King		Mr. Smith	
Purchase Price	$50,000		$100,000	
Down payment	10,000	(20%)	10,000	(10%)
Mortgage	$40,000		$ 90,000	
Annual Interest Payments	3,300*		7,900*	
If Rented:				
Annual Income	$ 5,000		$ 10,000	
Minus Interest	−3,300		−7,900	
Annual Equity Return	$ 1,700		$ 2,100	
% Equity Return (on original investment of $110,000)	17%		21%	

*Tax deductible

Leverage and Taxable Income

Item	Mr. King	Mr. Smith
Purchase Price	$50,000	$100,000
Less Land	− 10,000	− 20,000
Improvement	$40,000	$ 80,000
Annual Depreciation (4% straight line)	1,600	3,200
Less Annual Equity Return (from above table)	1,700	2,100
Taxable Income (Loss)	+$ 100	(−$ 1,100)

In the first example, Mr. King is getting a 17% return on his investment; not bad at all. But Mr. Smith is getting on the same $10,000 a return of 21%.

In the second example, Mr. King will have a net taxable income of $100, while Mr. Smith is going to have a tax-deductible loss of $1,100 with the same investment. (In both cases one assumes that the units purchased were rented out, and that the relation of price to rent was about the same in both cases.) But the general idea applies to ownership as well, simply because there is more interest to be paid, which is tax deductible.

A low down payment offers other advantages as well.

· *You can often get more house with a smaller down payment.* That sounds crazy. But let's say you earn a good income, but have only $5,000 available for a down payment. With 20% down, you could get only a $25,000 home, but with the same $5,000 and a 10% down payment, you could get a $50,000 home. You see? And generally, the better home you can buy, the better the investment. This is another way to stretch yourself if you expect your income to rise.

· *Lower down payment makes your tax and interest deductions higher.* Betty purchased a $60,000 new home because her old home was almost paid for, and she didn't have any tax deductions to speak of. She wanted as large a mortgage and monthly payment as she could get. She opted to put 10% down on the $60,000 house, even though the resale of her house brought her a net profit of close to $50,000. Since she was buying a new home that cost more than the sales price of her old one, her profit was tax-free, and with a minimum down payment, she had a big bundle left over to spend, save, or invest in something else.

· A low down payment may make your house easier to sell because a buyer may be able to assume your loan without having to pay a lot of cash.

It also is better to pay as little down as possible because:

· Even with nothing down, you will still need about 5% of the loan amount for all kinds of expenses such as settlement charges, fees, and taxes. For example, if you are buying a $50,000 existing house, you can count on spending about $2,500 for those things alone.

· You will probably need even more money than that. You have to move, and you'll probably buy bits and pieces of furniture. This is true even though you may have a house full of furniture now.

A small down payment obviously is best for people who can afford the monthly payments on a home, but who don't have much cash. But it also can be best for people who have stashed away a good chunk of money. If you don't have to, you don't want to tie up all your money in your house. Not when it could be growing in other investments, even if it is just a savings account.

If you have your bulk of money in passbook deposits paying 5½% and you borrow at 11%, your real rate is 5½%. That is not bad (actually, it is cheap money) but you may transfer some of this into Certificates of Deposit and get—say—10%. Then you will be making the 10% and paying 11% mortgage rate period.

Why should you pay on a bigger loan than you have to at 11%? Simply because 11% still is cheap money considering that the level of inflation is, say, 13% a year. The real rate at which you are borrowing money is the difference between 13% and 11%—a 2% REAL RATE. And that is cheap indeed.

Inflation, you see, is another reason why a big home loan can be a good investment. The lender loans you today's dollars, but you pay him back over as long as 30 years with dollars that are worth less every year.

One home mortgage that the Sumichrasts still are paying for carries only a 6% rate. With 13% inflation, they are actually ahead 7 percentage points. At the time of this purchase in 1967, they thought that 6% was an incredibly high rate to pay. But they did. And there still are many people paying 4½% to 5% rates!

Smaller Isn't Always Better; Advantages of a Large Down Payment

Of course, a low down payment isn't the best idea for everybody. If your situation is that you have some cash but not the income to carry large monthly payments, then you should opt for a larger down payment to keep your monthly payments down.

For instance, a divorced woman with four children was able to sell a house for $92,000 and netted $31,775. She then purchased a smaller home for $46,500. This is what she has to pay:

Sales Price	$46,500	
Settlement	2,625	
Total	49,125	100%
Cash Paid Down	21,930	44.6%
Loan	$27,195	55.4%

The woman was netting about $1,000 per month; at 10% down she would have to carry nearly $400 for principal and interest, or 40% of her income. With a 44.6% down payment her monthly payment was only $245—still high, but only 24.5% of her income. It was hard, but she could make it. One year later, the share of her income dropped below 20% as she made more money and two of her sons brought in additional income.

- *A bigger down payment may make the difference in enabling you to qualify for a loan.* Look back at the chart on down payments and income in this chapter and you will easily see how a few more bucks down can make a difference in your monthly payment. For example, with 10%, or $4,000 down, on a $40,000 home, your monthly payments would be about $413 and you

would need an annual income of between $16,300 and
$19,300 to qualify for a 30-year loan. But with 20%
down, or $8,000, your monthly payments would drop
to $375 and your income could be as low as $14,850 to
quality. Moreover, you usually can get a lower interest
rate with a bigger down payment.

· *Some people are just nervous about carrying a big
monthly mortgage payment.* If you are one of them,
you should put as much down as possible to keep the
payments lower and to keep your peace of mind.

In all the points about down payments, there is one thing
to remember:

· *"Low as possible" down payment is relative.* If you're
trading up to, say, an $80,000 house, and the only way
you can afford it is to put all of your old-house profit
down to keep the mortgage at, say $50,000, then that
for you is the "lowest possible down payment."

Should you ever pay cash or pay off your loan? Usually
not—you lose tax deductions and tie up your money which
could be invested more profitably elsewhere. The exception
may be older people, many of whom do pay cash for houses.

There are other ways you can use financing to help you get
the house you want.

Uncle Sam Can Help You

You can get a considerably lower down payment if you get
FHA (Federal Housing Administration) loans. Here the U.S.
Government insures the risk, so the lender is willing to take
as little as 3% of the first $25,000 of appraised value and 5%
of value over $25,000.

If you are a veteran, you can get a VA (Veterans Administration) home loan that is partly guaranteed by Uncle Sam.
With a VA loan, you can put as little as NOTHING down and
get up to a $100,000 mortgage or more. Lenders also like VA
loans because, unlike the FHA loans which have lots of red
tape, VA loans are easy to process.

Private Mortgage Insurance

If you can't get a low down payment through either FHA or VA, you can try private mortgage insurance. Then you could get a loan with, say, 10% down rather than the 20% to 25% that many lenders require; you still have to pay insurance fees, but you keep much of the money. We'll give you more details on both privately-insured loans and government-backed mortgages in the chapter on financing.

Second Mortgages

Many people buying their first house lack the down payment. The best thing to do is to borrow additional money and get a "second mortgage." This may be $3,000 on a $50,000 house, repayable, say, in 2 to 4 years. With an expected increase in income, this is repaid pretty much the same way as one would repay any other loan on things such as a car, furniture and so on.

True, mortgage rates are steep. Make sure you don't get into the hands of a loan shark. Most second mortgages are about 2 percentage points higher than regular mortgages. The best thing to do is to ask either the builder or the seller to take a second mortgage at the same interest rate as a permanent mortgage. The reason you can ask them to do that is that both are interested in selling the home. If they do, let them arrange to get you the second mortgage. In some cases people do go to third mortgage or even to fourth, but this is generally not recommended.

The Longest Possible Mortgage

You will make lower monthly payments on a 30-year loan than on a 20- to 25-year loan. This may be the deciding factor in getting the more expensive house you want. Sure, you pay more interest over 30 years, but chances are you won't have the mortgage that long—the average mortgage life is 10 years. Besides, the interest is deductible.

Assuming a Low-Interest Mortgage

In the early 1980s, mortgage rates climbed above 15%—and, Heaven help us, to 18% in some places. But many people still have mortgages with 5½% or 6% rates, or lower. So if a seller has a house with, say, a 6% loan and a remaining mortgage of, say, $30,000, you could buy the house and assume the 6% mortgage—that is, providing the mortgage contract specifically allows that and providing you get the approval of the lender.

The advantage is obvious. You, the buyer, can get a $30,000 loan at 6% rather than, say, 12%. The difference is $122.67 a month in mortgage payments, a 39% savings ($193.29 a month on the 6% loan vs. $315.97 monthly on the 12% loan on a 25-year mortgage).

There may be a catch, however. You may have to come up with a big down payment if the seller has a large equity in the house. You have to pay the seller the difference between the selling price of the house and the mortgage amount that you assume. Your best bet is to find a seller who made a low down payment on a mortgage he obtained in the past two or three years.

TRADING UP: THE NAME OF THE GAME

Most people aren't able to get their "dream" house—or anything close to it—the first time they buy a home. Home ownership is like climbing a ladder: you have to climb a step at a time. With the way prices are climbing these days, however, you often can skip some of those steps and scramble up that ladder a lot faster.

You don't have to be like the people in California who move each year. (Nationally, homeowners move about once every 7.5 years.) These buyers could be called housing gypsies. They hardly have enough time to unpack, hang curtains and settle down. But because many California buyers could sell their homes, and sell them fast, making huge profits each time, they did.

In most cases, trading up is done that way. Trading up is simply selling your own house and taking the equity—money you have in the house—and buying yourself another, more expensive house. Today, trading up has become the name of the home-investment game.

Here's how it works: Escalating resale prices mean that young homeowners like Stephen Bieri of Denver can rapidly trade up. He and his wife, Barbara, who both work for the

Denver Rockies professional hockey team, in 1977 bought a new, $72,500 house, their third house in two years.

The Bieris had to borrow from his parents to buy their first used home in 1975 in California. But a $5,000 profit from the sale of that house after six months gave them a down payment for a used house they bought in August, 1976, in Denver for $49,500. After seven more months, the Bieris sold that house at an $8,000 profit, and they had saved enough to make a $14,500 down payment on the new house. With a combined income of more than $30,000 a year, they could easily afford the $550 monthly payments.

Because the price of the house they bought in the spring of 1977 for $72,500 went up $3,100 in only a few months, Mr. Bieri figured, "We can't lose money on it, and if we'd waited any longer it would have been an $80,000 house, and we couldn't swing that"—yet.[10]

What you do in trading up is build up your profits from your previous houses so that you can afford to buy the next one—it's as simple as that.

Let's say that you bought a house in 1975 for $30,000 with $5,000 down, and you sell it for $55,000. After deducting expenses with the sale, let's say you end up with $25,000. Now you can take this $25,000 and buy yourself an $80,000 to $100,000 (either 20% or 25% down) home. If you did not have the "profit" of $25,000 plus the first $5,000 you could not purchase your new home. As a matter of fact, you could not have purchased your 1975 house, which by now has increased in price to $55,000. For your 1975 house you would now need $13,750 down payment (25%)— which you, of course, did not save.

And that is what's called "trading up."

Now you do it with your own house and your own figures: Put down how much you can get for it, deduct the mortgage and selling expenses, and see how much you end up with.

By making good housing investments, trading up and using your borrowing power, you don't have to be rich to move up to the home you really want.

Of course, you don't want to get so carried away with the process of pyramiding profits that you move up into a fancy home with bigger mortgage payments than you really can afford. One strategy is to trade up to a home that you want and then—if you can—stay put for a while so that your mortgage payments stay relatively stable while the value of your home grows.

GETTING A GOOD BUY

Whether you are buying your first home or your fifth, one way to start off in the right investment track is to get the home cheaper than the next guy. Here are some ways to consider.

Buy During a Recession or Tight-Money Times

It may sound crazy, but for many people the best time to buy a home is when the housing market is in a slump. Many sharp buyers do just that. They stay out of the market when everybody else is in it, then jump in when everybody is avoiding it.

When there are plenty of buyers and mortgage money is plentiful, housing sells quickly at top prices. Lots of people are bidding against each other, so the prices go up even more.

But when housing sales slow—because of a recession or because of high mortgage rates or the unavailability of mortgage money—then can be the BEST TIME TO BUY! Houses are sitting there and sellers are desperate for buyers. Prices are leveling off and sellers are willing to bargain.

If you are in a position to buy (and especially if you don't have a house you must sell first), here is what you can do:

- Make a ridiculously low offer on the home you want. You may not get your price, but you may get something close to it if yours is the only offer the seller gets. In any case, you probably will be able to buy a home at a good bit less than the asking price.
- Get the seller to pay some of your closing costs. Many will be willing to do so in order to sell a house during a time when buyers are scarce.
- Shop the new-home market. If sales are down and interest rates are high, builders may be willing to cut their selling price to avoid the high cost of the interest they must pay on an unsold house.

- If mortgage money is scarce or too costly, offer to rent a home with an option to buy later at a stated price (that can't be changed) when funds are available and rates have eased.
- Find ways to finance a home when other people can't. Check the section on "Tight-Money Tips" in Chapter 8 of this book for ways to find mortgage money. If you have to, go ahead and get a mortgage with a high interest rate, but make sure you can refinance the loan after a year or two without a penalty if rates go down.

Finally, follow our advice in earlier chapters to make sure you are really getting a good buy. Sometimes those price-cuts can be misleading. One New Orleans speculator confided that after spending $40,000 to buy and rehabilitate a home, he "ran it in the paper one week at $75,000. Then I waited a week before I ran it as 'drastically reduced to $58,800'—and sold it in one week."

Actually, the distress reduction was "just a come-on," the speculator said, "but sometimes they grab at the higher prices."

Remember, when you buy a home, you are actually making an investment that, the record shows, increases in value. If you wait until interest rates come down and for the housing market to pick up, any savings you realize from a lower rate probably will be more than offset by a higher price as home prices continue to rise. The moral: Get the cheapest interest rate you can, but it doesn't pay to wait.

Buy from the Owner Directly

The realtors will hate the seller, but you may get a house cheaper if you buy from the owner. You could save at least the amount of the broker's commission, or close to it. This is usually 6% of the sale price. So, if you buy a $50,000 home from the owner, your potential saving is $3,000.

Wait Until a New Housing Project Goes into Bankruptcy

Some of the best condominium buys were made in Ocean City, Maryland, and on the east coast of Florida after the condo bust of 1974. To get rid of the units, banks who took over made all kinds of deals—cheaper mortgage rates, sharply reduced prices (in some cases as much as 20-25%), and stretched loans.

Buy a Shell or a Run-Down House

For those who can work with their hands (you need a few brains, too), this is the best physical exercise. It is also the best way to learn a lot of tricks in the business. It's hard work, long evening hours and weekends, but it can pay.

How to get going? We are discussing this in Chapter 7, so wait for a while. Just remember that this is an option you have—and a very good one. You may even get the shell for $1. Yes, one green American dollar in central cities. We will tell you how.

From time to time the Federal Housing Administration may have foreclosed houses they put up for sale. Ask the local office for a schedule of these (in some cases they are available to brokers only). In most cases you need cash (or a large down payment) for these properties—but it may be worth trying.

Buy a Future

What the house looks like today is important. But equally or more important is what you could do with it. Can you finish the attic? Can you easily enclose the porch? Can you add another room? Are the bathrooms expandable?

The smart people develop an eye for such things and can easily interpret the potential value in what may look like a bad house. Be aware of the possibilities and dream a little.

Avoid Gimmicks; Buy to Fix Yourself— Not What Somebody Else Did

There are too many amateurs in the "fix-up" business. You don't want to buy their cover-up job. The cosmetic touches are not what you want to pay for.

There are several strategic places such "fixers" would attack.

- Front door—You see it and it looks great. It is the first invitation to disaster (after all, you are buying more than a door).

- Outside lights—They look pretty, especially in the evening, but they are just a good-looking light fixture you can pick up at Sears.

- Entry—A jazzed up entry is important, and especially when well-designed and executed. But remember—you have the whole house to look at.

- A loud, screeching wall paint could be very modern but may well cover the other things you should be looking for.

- A big fancy chandelier—oh, what a beauty! This you can also get at Sears for less than $200—remember that!

- The kitchen is usually a place where the "fixers" get to promote their handy work. Don't be misled by what you may see. Look at the quality. It is not hard to recognize a butcher job. Just use your common sense. (Do the corners fit? Are the backs of the cabinets painted or is it raw wood?)

- Bathrooms are another—look beyond the shower curtains; look at the caulking, stains, floors.

You may be so impressed by the colors, wallpaper, and light that you neglect to see the ailing furnace, water marks in the basement, flaking paint, sagging windows and flying termites.

Look at separations between front brick and the house, the sunken porch, stairs giving way, hole under the porch where all the critters now live, sagging downspouts, and deteriorating soffits (this is the stuff you see if you turn your head and look straight up toward the side of the house covering the roof overhead).

Look for a House That is Cheaper for a Reason

It may be a house that nobody wants because it was not finished as the builder went down the drain, or it may be a house that for some reason was abandoned. Find out who owns it and buy it. It may be worth every penny you put into it.

It may be a house which nobody wants because of a busy street. (Who would get the kind of a house where children cannot play?) That kind of house may be hard to sell now. But tastes are changing—there are fewer people who buy with a lot of kids. Also, that kind of house may never be worth as much as the same house nearby, but it will get you in the area at a cut-rate price and will still appreciate in value.

Sometimes the Best Buys Are Found in Houses You Would Run Away from after the First Visit

The fact that everything is piled up everywhere and the house itself is a holy mess may not mean much. Just beneath the junk may be a pile of gold. The house may well be a jewel: good structure, well-maintained and well-built.

Remember the old houses with enormous kitchens? They really don't build them like that any more. There is something you can do with all of that space, if you have the imagination, patience, and can work hard.

A worn-out carpet may be an eyesore, but underneath there may well be the most beautiful hardwood floor you could find. The mess will distract you from finding a massive trim, installed many years ago, of solid oak; baseboards 4 inches wide rather than the 2 inches now generally being used; heavy solid hardwood doors which would be impossible to get today.

So look at the structure and what it is built of, rather than the messy furniture and dirty dishes.

Get Your Company to Help You Buy or Sell a House

It is becoming more and more difficult to move people. The cost of housing is one major reason. What one can get in one area of the country, he cannot get in another—at least not for the same price.

"To move people from the Midwest to Washington is becoming hard, if not impossible," said a president of a large real-estate company who helps people move around. "They just don't believe the prices of homes."

Because employees are becoming more reluctant to transfer due to higher housing costs, many big companies that transfer vast numbers of people each year are beginning to revamp their relocation policies to factor in cost-of-living effects. Employee Relocation Council, a Washington, D.C., association that studies corporate transfers, said that about 35% of its 530 member companies now offer a key new benefit: They pay the difference if an executive's new mortgage interest rate is higher than his or her old one. That is double the number that did so in 1974. About 70% pay closing costs, up from 35% formerly, the trade group said.

Avco Financial Services, Inc., a subsidiary of Avco Corporation, for example, offers higher-level executives 8% home-mortgage financing, compared with conventional rates as high as 10%, and saves them closing costs and "points," or payments for the mortgage itself. "When you get involved with inflation and the tremendous appreciation in real estate, people get apprehensive" about moving, said William Matheson, a personnel vice-president.

State Farm Mutual Automobile Insurance Company, on the other hand, makes a salary adjustment for professionals and managers moving to 52 high-cost counties. (But employees lose the bonus when transferring back to low-cost counties or when crossing the line to executive status, generally the $45,000 salary range.) State Farm's program "helps tilt the balance for employees deciding whether to go to, say, New York or New Jersey," said Ernest Hoffman, Jr., assistant vice-president, employee relations.

Companies like Howard Johnson Company that transfer fewer executives tend to deal with transferred employees' cost-of-living concerns on a case-by-case basis. The Braintree, Massachusetts, restaurant and lodging concern said executives are more likely than in the past to bring up questions about the cost of living before moving and to come knocking on the door again if they get "hit hard" in the new area. The company is more likely "to recommend a (further) pay increase" for those doing a solid job and "to reach a little higher" for those doing exceptional work, said Quentin Laue, a senior group vice-president.

An additional consideration is that more and more companies now guarantee to purchase a house if they have to move people to another location. In many cases companies themselves buy homes and sell them.

And that may be one source of a home for you. If you are lucky and your company does own homes, see whether you can buy one.

Buy a Piece of Land and Build on It

This may be more than you bargain for, but it can be fun! There is nothing more exciting than having your own piece of land, planning what you will put on it, and actually seeing it go up. This you can do at any age—and it can save you money.

Look at the description by Lew Sichelman, real-estate editor for the Washington Star, of Dr. George Wesley Buchanan and his wife, Harlene, building their own retirement house in 1978:

> They began four years ago to plan a retirement home they won't need for nine more years. Today, although it is far from finished, they're already living in it.
>
> "We had to think of the future," says Buchanan, a professor of the New Testament at Wesley Theological Seminary near American University in Washington, D.C. "Since inflation would eat up the interest we could earn

Photo by Wm. Volz © Washington Star

*with a savings account and then some, we decided to go
for broke and put everything we had into real estate."*

The Buchanans admit that what they had wasn't
much. "We've been out of debt for only the last five
years," says the 56-year-old former preacher, explaining
that heavy medical expenses left him and Harlene, 48,
with a negative cash flow for a number of years.

That didn't stop them, however. They borrowed $16,000
on their life insurance policies for a down payment on a
$63,000 house and adjoining lot on Newport Mill Road
in Kensington. They rented out the house and began
working on plans to build on the lot.

When the Montgomery County sewer moratorium was
lifted, they were one of 10 families who were granted
permits to build. To get financing, they transferred the
mortgage on the Maryland house to their home of 17
years in the District and took out a new $58,000 mort-
gage on the rented house.

While they were waiting for approval of that loan,
they borrowed $17,000 in two chunks from the credit
union "to get started." The credit union loan, for which
the Buchanans needed co-signers, was paid back when
the new mortgage came through.

"As it turned out, $58,000 wasn't enough to build the
house we wanted," says Buchanan, "but it was enough
to get the basics done."

Acting as his own general contractor, Buchanan had
the foundation dug, the slab laid, the exterior walls
blocked in, the roof put on and the basic carpentry and
electrical and plumbing work done.

When the "basics" were completed, the Buchanans
rented their District house and moved into the new
house. Since February 10, 1978, they have lived in a
house in which the subflooring is covered only by several
area rugs, a few interior walls are finished with
gypsumboard, and the exterior walls remain naked
cinderblock.

According to Buchanan, he and his wife didn't need
an occupancy permit to move in. Once county building
inspectors determined that there were no safety hazards,
the kitchen and bath were functioning, and the floor and
joists, supporting walls and roof were installed properly,
they gave the Buchanans their blessing.

*"They wouldn't allow this if a contractor were build-
ing the house for us, but they know we're going to do the
rest of the work ourselves," he says.*

*The Buchanans are going about the task of finishing
their retirement home largely with used and discarded
materials.*

Building your own home obviously isn't for everyone.
But across the country, thousands of people are taking the
hardy and sometimes precarious step of becoming do-it-
yourself home builders. Dozens of companies now sell
either kits or partially-built houses to make it easier.

Although some of the do-it-yourselfers are brick masons,
carpenters, or other persons with a background in construction, authorities say most have had only a crash
course in building houses or no special training at all.
"People who have never built anything before are looking
for alternatives to buying a conventional house," says
Patricia Hennin, a partner in the Shelter Institute in
Maine, where over 600 people have each paid $250 for 60
hours of construction lessons.

The Census Bureau estimates that over 150,000 owner-
built houses are started each year. Do-it-yourself builders
can cut 10% to 50% from the cost of a house by saving part
or all of the wages usually paid to skilled tradesmen,
authorities say. For many builders, getting the corners
square and other details correct is a task vastly simplified
by the kit house: components that come with detailed
instructions for putting them together. Kit houses come in
dozens of models, and some makers will even make changes
in floor plans or make an entirely new kit to accommodate
a buyer. Kit prices range from $5,000 to $50,000, the
producers say.

Whether they're easy or difficult to put together, many
kit houses are certainly easy to buy. The makers themselves are often willing to finance the purchase after
collecting a small down payment, and some don't require
anything down. Once the house is built, the owner can
usually obtain a mortgage loan from a bank or savings and
loan company, enabling the initial financing to be repaid.
Thus, borrowers use "sweat equity" to gain a mortgage.[11]

Buy a Piece of Land and Put a Mobile Home on It—for the Time Being

One way to start is to buy a piece of undeveloped land and, if your county permits (better check it out first), buy yourself a mobile home. This will get you real estate and a temporary place to live while you are contemplating and building your own dream house. About 45% of new mobile-home sales each year are for individual lots.

Use your land as a starting point to get construction money (or mortgage money) to build.

Build a Log Cabin

Believe it or not, that's exactly what a lot of people are doing, particularly in the Northwest. Actually, these are log houses—not the log cabins of pioneer days—and the do-it-yourselfers can buy a kit with the logs already cut to size, peeled, and notched. The kits usually include only the logs for the walls, not materials for the roof, foundation, doors and windows. Those things, plus the land, cost extra. Kits range in price from $3,800 to $15,000 and in size from 1,000 to 4,000 square feet. For example, a log kit for a five-room house with three bedrooms costs $7,000 to $10,000, depending on the design.[12]

You can usually find home building kits—log or otherwise—advertised in popular housing magazines. A story about log cabins in The Wall Street Journal even prompted one writer to wax poetic:

> As construction know-how increases
> We may reach a new millennium:
> Economical luxury living
> In a log cabin condominium
>
> —Arnold J. Zarett

HOUSE-HUNTING HINTS

To wrap up the subject of investment strategies, here are some shopping tips to help you get the best housing buy.

Get There before the Crowd

If you find out what is coming on the market and are there at the very beginning, you may get it cheaper. Consider this: at the very beginning of the condo market craze in the early 1970s, a builder was about to open a new subdivision with 160 units. As always, he wasn't sure what the response of the market would be. He opened one Saturday morning with his knees trembling and his prices beginning at $28,500. By 10:30 a.m., he had a mob of people at his trailer (no model homes, just a trailer parked on a lot).

"Our prices are too low," he said. "But—we wanted to be sure to sell, so we started way down." At 1 p.m. he raised prices in the second section to $30,000, and by evening he was sold out.

There are two points here: One is that it is possible that you can get a better deal at the very beginning; second, it is very likely that prices of the last units in the subdivision—or the same units in the next section—will be higher than the first ones.

Learn to Spot Good Buys and Get There First

Find out what houses are priced at in the neighborhood where you want to buy. One way is to look up sales prices in Lusks or similar books at a library or at an office of your friendly real-estate agent. Some local newspapers also list sales. You can even go to the courthouse and look up home sales records. A friendly agent could tell you when a good buy is coming on the market, before it is advertised.

Sometimes the original owners will underprice their house because they can't believe prices have gone up so much since they bought 15 years ago. If you wait for the Sunday real-estate section to come out on Sunday morning, you may be too late. Pick up an early edition Saturday night, or Friday night since weekend ads may begin then, and try to get in ahead of the open house. Also, these sections are printed up and delivered to your paper boy or girl by Saturday morning. See if they will give you that section—the Sunday "shove" that is shoved inside the paper that comes out Sunday morning—on Saturday.

"Would you like to see something near the future park,
the future swimming pool, the future school . . . ?"

Negotiate a Price

You can learn from the speculators. There was a house for
sale in "as is" condition selling for $92,000. Two offers came at
$80,000 and $85,000, with one speculator offering $79,000
cash on the barrel. It was a ridiculous proposal. But the other
two offers did not go through, probably because the bidders
had difficulty securing financing, and the speculator got the
house.

The best advice we can give you is to make an offer, even
though it may sound very low. You can never tell what the
reaction of the seller may be. For one thing, yours may be
the only offer he will receive. For another, his house may be
overpriced. Third, if you come early and make a written offer
with few or no conditions, this may well be the determining
factor of the sale.

Buy Out—It's Usually Cheaper

Especially if you are buying your first house, get out of the
metropolitan area to where land is only one-half or one-third
as expensive and where builders can put up a $50,000 house
for which you may have to pay $65,000 in the metro area.

Workmanship may be better too. As well as the dream house, you may end up with a substantially larger land area.

A lot of things are cheaper outside most of the metro areas. The demand for land is usually much heavier within the metro areas; it seems that not as many people like to live in outlying areas. Therefore, land is cheaper, and builders can build less expensive homes. But consider the transportation and time that may be involved in traveling to work, shopping facilities, and the like.

On the average, new home buyer–heads of households travel 16 miles each day to work, or 26 minutes, according to the National Association of Home Builders survey, "Decisions for the 80's." But they are willing to travel 21 miles and be on the road for 33 minutes in the future when they are ready to buy another house.

Buy Off Season

The high price seasons are early in the year—March, April and May—and then again in September and October. Those are the times when demand is strongest. If you can buy in the middle of a slow period, in November-December or during a hot July-August when all the "normal" people are on vacations, you may get a better deal, since the demand is lower.

Or try after a period of heavy snow when nobody, but nobody, goes out, and when the sellers are spending weekends sitting in open houses, totally demoralized. Just about any offer would be one they couldn't refuse.

New-Home Buyers: Protect Yourselves in Fast-Escalating Price Periods

Traditionally, builders have been able to cost out a unit and quote the buyer a firm price for a house to be delivered several months later. Prices obtained from suppliers and subcontractors were firm for several months and left the builder with an adequate profit.

Now, with today's significantly higher rates of inflation, this process is no longer valid.

"We allow a 1.3% cost increase per month, or 15.6% annually, and I'm not sure that this is sufficient," said an Ohio builder. "Some of the contracts have an escalation clause in which we simply reserve the right to increase prices before settlement."

There's not a great deal a new-home buyer can do to combat escalating prices, but here are some ideas:

· Enter only into contracts with a firm sales price.

· If you must take a contract with an escalation clause, ask for a maximum price plus a period of time after the final price is known in which to cancel the contract.

· Look for finished and unsold new homes. Many builders have cancellations on already-built and previously-sold units. Chances are that such a unit is cheaper than one which is yet to be built.

· Major builders usually buy in large quantitites for forward deliveries and negotiate contracts with sub-contractors ahead of time. They are usually in a better position to offer firm prices. Quality, however, may well be very different from that of custom-built units.

· Check the cost per square foot of various houses being offered. You need to know two things: the price and the total living area in square feet. If, for example, the price is $50,000 and the living area 1,700 feet, $50,000 divided by 1,700 equals $29.41 per square foot.

· Get a firm mortgage commitment.

· Buy as soon as you can. The sooner you enter into a contract, the better your chances are of a lower final cost. Realistically, there is little hope that the price spiral will change.

Buy Defensively, Or: How to Protect Yourself from Salesmen

A great professional of selling real estate—Jim Mills—in the first chapter of his book called *Action Selling* describes an interesting process:

> "There's a technique in rugby known as 'Selling the Dummy,' which means to deceive the opponent by faking a pass. If you can sell (deceive) the dummy (the opponent), you're applauded for your great deception. Even

if you fail to sell (deceive) the dummy, you'll probably hear someone say 'Good show'; at least you tried to make a dummy out of your opponent.

"In games of all types, as you know, deception is not only permissible, it's highly regarded, considered clever, and in the case of a poker-type game, it's highly rewarded with local Gelt."

When you go out shopping for a home, you're sure to run into lots of people who want to help you make the best buy—for them. At new housing developments, these people are called salesmen, or saleswomen. At used homes, they are called real-estate agents. Their job is to *sell* you a home, and they can in fact be very helpful, as long as you remember this: Don't let yourself be sold a home; *you buy one!*

For example, using a real-estate agent to help you house hunt offers several advantages. Good agents know the market, they can save you shopping time and, best of all, their services are free. They get their commissions from the seller. That last point shouldn't be overlooked. Many real-estate people are sincerely interested in helping you find the house that you want. But you should remember they earn their biggest commissions if the house you want is their listing or at least with their agency; but if you buy a house that is listed with a competing agency, they have to share their commission with that agency and its agent.

Also, remember that you enter the real-estate wars with a distinct disadvantage. You are an amateur. Sales people are professionals, trained to convince buyers to buy.

So, to arm you with some defenses, we have taken a look at some of the training given sales people, especially real-estate sales people. By turning around the advice experts give sellers, you can become a sharp buyer.

Meet the Salesman

The good ones always smile, smile, smile. They don't rush to greet you. As Mills advises: "Don't swoop down on them."

The good ones are always way ahead of you. They know their product. You should ask a salesman questions, but you also should do your homework. Make sure the salesman does not intimidate you ("If you knew the market like I do, you'd know what a great buy this house is.").

The good ones are master psychologists. Remember: They can almost read your mind. Don't let them sell you the first time you walk in.

Good salesmen are trained not to object to what you may say. They know that if they argue, there is no way they can win—especially if this is in front of your spouse.

So what will they do?

They will use one of these statements: "I know just how you feel"; or, "I most certainly agree with what you say."

Now you must be on your guard, because your salesman is very far from agreeing with you. He just doesn't want to aggravate you.

You must be on your guard because what you will hear is what is called in the trade a "shelving." That means that after agreeing with you, chances are that the salesman will use one of these lead words: "However," "Although," or "We may possibly consider," or "Let's come back to that later."

An example: You say, "I think that the yard is terribly small."

The salesman replies with, "I know precisely how you feel. I have children myself and they generally prefer a larger yard. However, why don't we skip this item for now (shelving) and first look over the whole estate. I think in this particular house there is something quite unique, and I want to make sure you see it. A person like you will appreciate it."

You see how he got around you?

Next is to answer the objection with a question. If you think that the monthly payments are high, with a tone of surprise a good salesman will say, "Payments are high?" (This already makes you feel like a beggar. Of course they are high for you. But the salesman will now show you what a low-roller you are.) "Really, if you break it down the $450 a month is only $15 a day. The cheapest hotel room is $25 per day."

Some of the Words Used for Better Prospecting by Salesmen

These words are used to describe your personal values. They are motivating factors in your behavior.

In real estate, Glen Buyer of Cornell University suggested using these: family well-being, financial gain or loss, personal pleasure, freedom, self-gratification, equality, physical and mental health.

All of these words are thoughts which one way or another motivate you to buy a home. These and others are used by good salesmen to get you to sign a contract.

Just before Signing the Dotted Line

It would be hard to duplicate what a real "pro"—Tom Hopkins—in his Champion Unlimited series of lectures for real-estate sales people said about getting people to sign. He described this situation: you have the prospect in your office after a long session of driving around and getting the basic information about him on a piece of paper. Now, just before the final decision is made you will run into the "We just don't jump into things" objection.

This is what Tom Hopkins describes as what a good "champion" should do:

So, they're going ahead with you, now. You're excited, but suddenly they stop you. Suddenly, they say to you, "Well, Tom, we just don't jump into things. You know, we've always been the type that kind of like to sleep on it." Smile when they say that and say, "I can understand you wanting to possibly wait. I've been in this situation numerous times, and that's why I sit here, feeling the excitement that you both have for the home. I feel an obligation to try and help you get it. The other night I was reading about a man that we Americans have long considered one of our wisest men, Benjamin Franklin. Whenever ol' Ben found himself in a situation such as you're in today . . . Here's what ol' Ben used to do. He'd take a plain, white piece of paper. He'd draw a line down the middle and on this side (pointing to the left) he'd write 'yes' and he'd list all the reasons favoring his decision today. On the other side, all the reasons against it. Then, he simply counted up the columns and his answer was made for him. Why don't we give it a try, just to see what happens? If it's good enough for ol' Ben, it might be good enough for us, don't you think? Then I want you to take and turn that piece of paper around, hand him the pen and say, 'Help me, John, if you will.' Let's just put x's for the yeses. Mary, you mentioned the neighborhood, didn't you? Put an 'x', John. And of course the landscaping, John. Then, of course, the fire-

place. You were excited with the spacious living room, weren't you? Built-in kitchen . . . the home is on sewer. Something I think is important is the street lights out front for the kids at night. The carpeting and draperies are custom quality. Remember out in the covered patio? You'd better put that down. Of course, the fence-enclosed rear yard. You'd better make an 'x' there. Also, the location of the home itself. Can you think of any more? Well, then let's see how many reasons you can come up with against the decision." Now you shut up. You give them all the help you can on the yeses, and you let them take care of the noes. I have yet to have a person come up with more than two or three on the no side.

If you pour it on, you can go right through the home and tell them all the things that you tied them down on, then after they've pondered a while, put down a couple of things, then smile and say, "Well, let's see what we do have. Well, one, two, three, four, five, six, seven, eight, nine, ten, eleven, twelve, thirteen, fourteen, fifteen, sixteen, seventeen, eighteen. Well, that's eighteen on the 'yes' side. Let's see the 'no' side. That's three: don't you think the answer is really pretty obvious, John?" That's a major close.

Before *you* sign on the dotted line, make sure you are investing *your* money in the home *you* want. Benjamin Franklin's idea about writing down the pluses and the minuses is a good one; just remember "Ol' Ben" was a smart old bird ("A penny saved is a penny earned") who probably wouldn't be pressured into signing a contract, so don't you, either. If you do sign, sign because *you* have found the house that *you want.* Make sure the contract provides that the plumbing and electrical equipment will be in working order when you go to settlement, that the contract is contingent upon your getting financing (and upon selling your house, if you have to) and that the deal is subject to a satisfactory report by a professional inspector. Also include in the contract any items—such as carpeting and rugs, light fixtures and so forth—that are to be sold with the house. No matter how much you trust the sales person, get everything in writing. Oral promises aren't worth the paper they aren't written on. If you have any doubts, you might consider hiring a lawyer to check the contract.

Buy What Is Best for You

We are not telling you to shop defensively when dealing with real-estate sellers because we have anything against sales people. Some of our best friends are real-estate agents. And, as we said, good ones can be quite helpful to you.

The point is that only you can decide what home is best for you. Salesmen can't tell you. We can't tell you. Ignore our advice on what makes a good investment, if you want to. Buy the home you want to live in—something you really feel comfortable with and something that suits your lifestyle. Don't get a big yard if you hate outside work. Don't buy a fix-up house if you have two left hands.

Buy yourself a house you will feel at home in. After all, it is your home—or will be shortly.

SIX

A Home Isn't Always a House: Condominiums and Townhouses

"What's a condominium?"
"I know, it's a kind of fir tree."
"No, it's a new tonic."

Those are the kinds of comments people made in the early 1970s when condominiums started cropping up in real-estate ads. Condominiums are neither a fir tree nor a new tonic. They are simply another type of home ownership.

Not everybody's dream home is a detached, single-family house with a picket fence and a big, grassy yard. For many people the ideal home is an apartment with a mortgage instead of rent payments, a pool to swim in, and no yard to mow.

And, basically, that is what the condominium concept is. You buy an apartment that is all your own and you also buy part ownership of the development's "common elements," which include everything from the hallways to the swimming pool. You and the other owners hire somebody to cut the grass and maintain the development.

"A condominium has a lifestyle that suits me—no maintenance," explained one bachelor condo buyer.

150

Condos—The Rise, Decline, and Rebirth

The condo concept isn't a new idea. In fact, the first written documents for such housing date back to before the early Roman Empire. If you did as the ancient Romans did, you may well have lived in a condominium. Legend has it that even Julius Caesar went out one day and bought a condo unit; in the sales office, he ran into an old friend, who also was buying, and Caesar said: "Et tu, Brutus?"

All right, so we made up the last part. But the rest is true. The condo concept was around in Roman times, and condos have been widely used in Europe for centuries. But the real boom in Europe didn't begin until this century. The reason: high-density development forced by a shortage of land. We tend to forget that densities in the United States are among the lowest in the world—North America, for example, has 29 people per square mile compared with 250 per square mile in Europe. In all of the United States there are 60 people per square mile versus 250 in France, 647 in West Germany, and 935 in Belgium.

In America, condominiums came in with a big bang in the early 1970s. It started in California with duplexes, triplexes and fourplexes. Soon everybody was copying California, and the condo craze was on. Next came the high-rises in Florida, other ocean cities, and then metropolitan areas. In Washington, D.C., they called one strip of high-rises the Condo Canyon. Nationally condominium construction went from under 80,000 units, or 5.5% of the total housing market, in 1970 to over 300,000 units, or 15.6% of the market, by 1973 (Table 6-1). To cash in on the craze, landlords also rushed to convert their rental apartments to condominiums.

Between 1970 and April, 1975, the number of condominiums in the United States increased 15-fold to nearly 1.3 million units, according to a study by the U.S. Department of Housing and Urban Development. By 1981 there were more than 2 million units. Of these, about 25% were "second," or vacation, homes. About 400,000 rental units were converted to condominiums in the 1970s.

Of the total condo housing, the study said, nearly 50% were in Florida, California, and New York. Only 10 states accounted for 70% of all condominiums. But the condo concept was rapidly spreading. The report concluded that condominiums "will continue to constitute a significant portion of the annual addition to the nation's housing stock."

Table 6-1

Condominium Starts, As a Share of Total Starts, 1970-1981
(in thousands of units)

Year	Condo Starts	Total Starts	Condos as a % of Total Starts
1970	79	1,469	5.4%
1971	164	2,085	7.9%
1972	299	2,379	12.6%
1973	318	2,058	15.5%
1974	176	1,353	13.0%
1975	65	1,171	5.6%
1976	95	1,548	6.1%
1977	118	2,002	5.9%
1978	156	2,036	7.7%
1979	211	1,760	12.0%
1980	198	1,312	15.1%
1981*	204	1,070	19.1%
1987*	274	1,297	21.2%

*Estimates

Source: 1970-1976 figures, Department of Housing and Urban Development
1977-81 figures, National Association of Home Builders.

After the condo craze, however, came the condo crash. By 1974 it was clear that everyone had completely misread the market for condominiums. Many areas were vastly overbuilt. In Fort Lauderdale, Florida, between 1970 and 1975 there was a 1000% increase in condos to a total of 123,000 units. Due to this tremendous overbuilding, the area (Broward County) in 1975 had enough vacant units to supply the market for close to three years at the 1975 sales rate.

The same thing happened in other areas, including Atlanta, Washington, D.C., and Ocean City, Maryland. With the recession discouraging buyers, developers were stuck with thousands of unsold apartments. The banks, which owned the mortgages on the unsold units, suddenly found themselves the owners of thousands of foreclosed condominium buildings. Many areas were probably affected to some degree by the speculators who inflated the demand for the condos by making minimal down payments, only to drop out of sight when they were unable to find buyers for their options.

The result was huge distress sales, as lenders and builders cut prices and sales terms in an effort to sell their condo albatrosses. In Orlando, Florida, Atlanta, Georgia, and other places the unsold condos were literally put on the auction block.

In 1977, in Atlanta, with a nod of his head and a wink of his eye to the auctioneer, Jim Hinsdale, an Eastern Airlines pilot, bought for $59,000 a condominium originally advertised for $85,000.

"Ooohh, we did it, we did it," squealed Mrs. Hinsdale as her husband's offer ended the bidding on Unit 421—a three-story, three-bedroom, 2½-bath condominium with a spiral staircase, intercom and central vacuum system.

The Hinsdales were among a small but growing number of condo owners who bought their homes at good prices as developers and lenders, anxious to dispose of moribund projects, resorted to auctions. The buyers usually got a 30% to 40% discount on the original selling price. "I won't say it's a bargain," said Mrs. Hinsdale, a flight attendant for Eastern Airlines. "It's still expensive, but I think it's a fair price."

Such bargain buyers counted on the condo crash to be followed by a condo comeback. While there is still an over-supply of condos in some areas, in many areas condos have again begun to grow in popularity—though this time at a less heated pace.

The Condominium Market Today

In many ways, the condo shakeout was needed. Most of those who got burned financially were speculators, developers and lenders who were after a quick profit. Most buyers should come out ahead in the long run because, now that the condo craze is over, condo housing is settling into a growing, but normal, housing market that makes for a surer housing investment.

Today, the condominium concept is an accepted way of life. In 1980 six million people lived in 2.5 million units of condos and cooperatives. (We'll get to cooperatives shortly.) Condo production, after plummeting to under 70,000 units and back to only about 5½% of total housing starts in 1975, has climbed back to about 20% of annual construction activity.

Condominiums are here to stay. It is rather surprising that the idea did not gain larger acceptance much earlier in the United States. The production rate should continue to edge upward due to the cost advantages of building multi-family housing in relation to the cost pressure of land and expensive single-family homes. Thus, condo living is an affordable alternative for a growing number of buyers.

Who Buys Condos and Why?

Most condo buyers fall into one of two groups: young people—either singles or "young marrieds," childless couples between 25 and 34 years of age—and "empty nesters," couples over 45 years old whose children are no longer living at home. But all kinds of people buy condos, especially with today's trend towards smaller families.

What they are buying are the advantages of home ownership—tax deductions, a home of their own—without the upkeep of a house. They're also buying the "good life," with access to swimming pools, tennis courts and other amenities that come with their home. Many are buying more leisure time—as one housing official put it, "to condo buyers, the power boat has replaced the power mower as a status symbol."

A 26-year-old single woman who bought a $51,000 condominium in Madison, Wisconsin, summed it up this way:

"I wanted to own a house," she said, but she chose a condo rather than a single-family, detached house because "the maintenance is taken care of." She chose her particular condo because "the unit is well-constructed, the value of the condos continues to increase, and because of the security and the neighborhood." She visited six subdivisions before buying.

She is pleased with her investment, although not everything is perfect. "I can sometimes hear sounds from the unit next door," she said.

How Does a Condo Compare with a House?

First you should realize that not all condos are created equal. There are several kinds. The most common types are:

- High-rise condominiums—these are apartments in buildings of more than three stories. Some are 20 stories or more high.

- Low-rise, or garden, condominiums—these are apartments in buildings up to three stories high.

- Townhouses—these are row-housing type units connected by common walls. Townhouses are more like houses than apartments; many have an upstairs and a basement.

- Converted condominiums—this is a misnomer because they actually are converted rental apartments. These range from apartment buildings in which the rental units have been completely rehabilitated before being put up for sale, to buildings where the conversion basically involved taking down the "apartments for rent" sign and putting up a "condominiums for sale" sign.

- Cooperatives—Hold it. Cooperatives aren't condominiums at all, even though people often get the two confused because the names sound similar. In a coop, unlike a condo, residents don't own their apartments but instead own shares in the apartment building that entitles them to occupy a unit. An owner in a coop is liable for all debts of the coop. This is known as "joint liability." As a result, financial institutions apply more rigorous credit standards to buyers of a coop unit.

Because of such liabilities, the number of coops coming on the market has dwindled. The majority of the nation's half-million coop units were built before 1970. But advocates of coops argue that the coop concept has great potential for future housing.

They may be right. The coop market has boomed in New York City and is picking up elsewhere across the country. Savings and loan associations' lending rules for coops have been liberalized. Since many coops already have low-interest mortgages of up to 40 years, they can offer low down payments with low interest rates and lower monthly payments than are possible with new condominiums—plus no closing costs.

Condos Can Be Cheaper

A major advantage of condominiums is that you can still find many units selling for under $30,000.

That's hardly possible in most areas these days for single-family housing because of rising land costs. The reason, of course, is that many condo units, sharing common walls, can be built on a given amount of land. Nationally in 1980, the average size of a single lot was 11,565 square feet, while condo townhouses had only 2,940 square feet of land.

Costs, of course, vary widely, but the fact is that the condo conversion units are the cheapest way to buy these days. The second cheapest generally are low-rise condos. Next come townhouses. New, high-rise condos have the highest cost. But with all types of condos, prices cover the full gamut of the housing market, ranging up to $500,000 or more for some luxury penthouse units.

Naturally, condo units generally are smaller than houses, which, of course, also is the reason many people prefer condos. In 1980, the average living area of a newly built, single-family house was 1,658 square feet, compared with 1,237 square feet for a condominium unit. Houses also have more bedrooms—62% were built with three bedrooms and 23% had four or more in 1979. In condo units, 68% had two bedrooms, 18% had three and only 1% had four or more (see Table 6-2).

Your best condo buy could be a condominium that is converted from a rental apartment. The condo-conversion craze was spreading rapidly across the country in the early 1980s. And since the condos usually are in older, though presumably rehabilitated, buildings, prices often are lower than for newly built units.

To get the best buys, though, you need to keep your eye out for conversions and get there at the beginning. Many conversions offer lower pre-opening prices. And usually renters who already live in the buildings can buy at substantial discounts. Some people move into rental buildings before a conversion is announced in order to get a discount price. For that, of course, you need some inside information. In some localities, the potential conversions must be pre-registered in an office of housing, usually at the county level. So you may be able to find out ahead of time if an apartment project will be put on the market.

Increasingly, however, renters are fighting conversions, so you can't be sure a conversion will go through. And in any case, buying a converted condo-apartment in an older building can have its pitfalls, so you must check the unit and the building carefully before signing on the dotted line. But, in general, condo-conversions are about the cheapest way to enter home ownership.

What about Appreciation?

As we said earlier, condominiums and townhouses haven't increased in value as rapidly as single-family homes. One reason, of course, has been the glut of condos in some housing markets. But the glut is gone in many markets, and condos are making a comeback—and so are condo appreciations.

"Today, the rate of appreciation on condos is still slightly less than for single-family housing but the gap has closed noticeably," according to a survey by the National Association of Realtors. In fact, in 50 markets with significant condo resales, 20 reported "that appreciation was about the same as for single-family homes," while nine said that "the price advances were greater" for condos, according to the Realtors Association. By contrast, in 1975 condominiums were appreciating at half the rate of single-family homes, and declining values abounded.

"In cities where condominiums are a significant part of the housing stock, a strong resale market is emerging," the Realtors Association said. As with single-family homes, location is a prime factor—"some outstanding price jumps have been recorded for condominiums, townhouses and apartments which have a particularly good view or boast a prestige, intown address."

The survey noted that "although condominium activity is on the rise, this is a much saner market than the one that went from 'super boom' to 'super bust'" in 1975. "Builders and lenders are doing their homework before plunging into this market," the study said. "This cautious attitude is healthy and will perhaps prevent another spate of overbuilding."

The study also reported that condo living is more popular

in some parts of the country than others: "This type of ownership is particularly strong in and around major cities where high home prices and a scarcity of buildable land have made it an attractive alternative to single-family home ownership. Condominiums also thrive in resort and retirement areas where people wish to be free from the gardening and maintenance chores associated with single-family living."

In short, "We're convinced that the condominium market has gotten over its growing pains and that it's going to do very well," said Kenneth Kerin, director of the economics and research department of the National Association of Realtors. But before you plunge into condo living, consider this question:

Is Condo Living for You?

That is no idle question. The fact is that the condominium way of life isn't for everybody. In a condo project your neighbors are as close as the other side of your wall, and keeping the project running smoothly requires the cooperation of many residents. So think hard: What is your lifestyle? Do you prefer to be left alone or to mix with people? Do you prefer living near others your own age or with people of all ages?

As the HUD study noted: "Some of the most widespread problems in multi-family ownership structures are the problems of communal living. Both traditional renters, who have had the landlord as the arbitrator of disagreements, and traditional single-family home owners, who are often unprepared for high-density living, have significant adjustments to make in a multi-family ownership situation."

In a multi-family development, your condo may be your castle, but, unlike the owner of a house, you can't always do what you want with your home. Condo developments are run by rules set by the majority of the owners through their owners' association or elected board members. That means that if you want a blue door but the association says doors must be yellow, your door must be yellow. There also may be restrictions on such things as TV antennas and outside remodeling.

"Condominium living sometimes means bowing to the will of the majority as determined by the elected board of directors who run the project," said one Chicago property-

Table 6-2

Selected Characteristics of New Single-Family and Condominium Housing Units

	1980		1978	
	Single Family	Condo (for-sale)	Single Family	Condo (for-sale)
Average Lot Size				
(square feet)	11,736	2,377	12,155	2,772
Average Living Area				
(square feet)	1,658	1,237	1,694	1,321
No. of Bedrooms				
1 Bedroom	0%	13%	0%	7%
2 Bedrooms	14%	68%	9%	51%
3 Bedrooms	62%	18%	65%	40%
4 or more Bedrooms	23%	1%	26%	2%
No. of Bathrooms				
1 Bathroom	13%	18%	12%	14%
1.5 Bathrooms	11%	18%	12%	20%
2 Bathrooms	47%	49%	47%	47%
2.5 Bathrooms	21%	12%	19%	15%
3 or more Bathrooms	8%	3%	10%	4%
Parking Facility				
Garage-one car	17%	19%	14%	28%
Garage-two or more	64%	14%	76%	19%
Carport-one or more	3%	19%	3%	12%
None	15%	48%	7%	41%

Source: NAHB Economics Department, Home Owners Warranty Corporation

management company official. "But this can be trouble if the board decides, for example, to raise your assessment fee to pay for new tennis courts and you don't play tennis."

Such differences can lead to "internal strife," as the HUD study calls it. Problems often are greater in the biggest complexes—some Florida high-rise condos, for instance, have more than 5,000 units—than smaller ones, the study says.

One of the chief bones of contention isn't door colors or assessments, but whether pets should be banned or allowed. In the HUD study, "the third most-cited problem affecting condominium owners was the problem of pets—largely the conflict between the dog-lovers and the dog-haters of the world."

All this isn't meant to discourage you from going condo, but to make sure you know what you are getting into. Indeed, the HUD study cited above concluded that "overall, condo unit-owners appear basically satisfied with their unit and project." In a random sampling of 602 owners in six different areas, "an overwhelming number of unit owners—95%—replied that they were satisfied or very satisfied."

Condo Shopping; What to Look For

If you are ready to "go condo," here's what to watch out for.

When buying a condominium or townhouse, you should follow many of the same guidelines we have already discussed for single-family houses. Location is still a prime consideration. You will want to decide the pros and cons of a new unit vs. an older one. But there are some special condo considerations you'll also have to check.

• Construction. Poor construction quality was the most common complaint of condominium owners surveyed in the HUD study. Inadequate soundproofing was the deficiency most often cited. In other words, often the walls are too thin and there is too much noise from the unit next door. Make sure your walls won't have ears. Check out the soundproofing. When looking in an occupied development, even ask the next-door neighbor to a unit to turn up his stereo so you can hear how much sound comes through to your side.

Check the construction—some questions to ask yourself are: How is the quality of construction? Is the design satisfactory? What is under warranty? Are you satisfied with the overall structure and the finished workmanship? How does it look?

• *If you cannot check the construction quality yourself, find a home inspector who can*—just as you would hire one for a single-family house. But make sure he knows something about condos. In addition to your unit, you need to know about the quality of common areas, including the recreational facilities.

- If you are buying a condo that has been converted from a rental unit, *you should be able to get an engineering report on the condition of the entire project*. In fact, you should insist on one. The report should detail the condition and adequacy of the structure, the plumbing, the electrical and mechanical components, the heating plants, the roofs and other structural elements. There also should be an estimation of the remaining life of these various elements. Such reports are required with condominiums financed with federally-insured mortgages.

- Remember, checking the construction of all the facilities is important because *you share responsibility for all of them*. There are many scary examples when condo owners were stuck with large repair bills. Two years after one condominium project was built in Wisconsin, the owners complained that because of roof defects, the ceilings of some units had collapsed, but the builder refused to make repairs. As a result, all of the condo's project owners were left "holding the bag for approximately $100,000 of work to be done."

- *Make sure the owners' association at the project you buy into has replacement reserves sufficient to cover "one-time" expenses.* Experts say reserves should be equal to 10% to 20% of the total annual assessment.

- *Another word about recreational facilities.* Don't be dazzled by fancy swimming pools, tennis courts and other amenities. Check the basics—construction of the units, how the project is run and so forth. Look for amenities already in place; don't put too much trust in developer promises to build them later. "Not meeting promised completion dates appears to be a problem common in new condominium developments," the HUD study concluded. The problem relates most often to completion of recreational facilities.

- Maintenance Fees and "Low-Balling." As a condo buyer, you will be obligated to pay more than your mortgage payment and property taxes. You will also be charged a monthly fee to cover the upkeep of your project, including management of the development, the cost of operating recreational facilities, and other expenses.

- *Make sure you find out what the current maintenance charge is,* how recently it was increased and whether it is likely to go up again soon.
- *In new developments, one thing to watch out for is "low-balling,"* a procedure whereby the seller makes a low estimate of the monthly maintenance fee as a "sales tool" to attract buyers. "The buyer is not always fully aware that the developer is, in effect, subsidizing a portion of the monthly common expenses and that, once the developer leaves, the common expenses paid by each owner will rise substantially," the HUD study warned.

Such "low balling," whether calculated or not, "has been very common," said the president of the National Capital Condominium Federation, an owners group located in Kensington, Maryland. At one Washington, D.C., area complex, he said units were sold with a monthly maintenance fee of $10, but when the builder departed the owners discovered that operating expenses forced a boost in the monthly fee to a range of $40 to $60.

- *Fees that are unrealistically low can also be a problem in existing projects.* In a condo complex, a majority or more of the unit owners, or a board elected by them, must approve increases in the monthly assessments before such increases can go into effect. This approval often is difficult to obtain, even though a boost may be needed. The result can be a serious deficit. Moral: a low maintenance fee isn't always as good as it sounds. Go behind the numbers. Check with current owners or officers of the condo association, and check the project's operating budget to see if the fee looks realistic.

- Make Sure You Know Who Owns What. When you buy a condominium you should own not only your apartment but also a share of such common areas as the swimming pool and the clubhouse. But mainly in Florida, a widespread practice was for developers to retain ownership of recreational facilities and lease them back to the owners for steep fees on long-term contracts that ran as long as 99 years, even though the owners of most of the units had to pay all the maintenance expenses and taxes. The builders can foreclose on the units if the owners refuse to pay. What's more, many of these "recreational leases" contain escalator clauses that allow the builder to raise the lease payments periodically with the cost of living.

Because of the bad publicity generated by such practices, few builders use recreation leases now. But you should make sure that the unit owners also own the common elements in any project where you buy. For one thing, previous recreation leases with the built-in escalation clauses are still in force in some projects.

· Safeguard Your Purchase Deposit. When you buy a unit you probably will have to put down a deposit. Make sure your deposit is placed in a separate escrow account. This is especially important if construction of the unit you are buying hasn't been completed yet. Some builders have commingled deposits with other funds and then gone bankrupt, leaving the buyers without either their deposits or places to live.

If you are buying a new condo, also ask if there is a pre-sale agreement with a financial institution. Such an agreement often prohibits the builder from "closing" on your unit until a specific number of condominiums have been sold or reserved.

· Check Those Condo Documents. Here's where buying a condo becomes even more complex than buying a house. Since you also are becoming part-owner of an entire housing complex, you will be showered with documents that tell you your rights, responsibilities and what you are buying. The only trouble is that these documents can be from 50 to more than 200 pages long, and you may not be able to understand them without an interpreter.

Some states, however, have passed laws aimed at simplifying such documents. And some developers have taken steps to take the mystery out of such papers. Benny Kass, a Washington, D.C., lawyer who specializes in housing, noted that a Florida lawyer drafted the following "translation" to the legal requirements for a condo offering there: Where it read, "The developer will submit the fee-simple title to the condominium property to condominium ownership," the translation said: "This means that we're in the business of selling the stuff rather than renting it."

The basic documents you as a prospective buyer should receive and check are the Master Deed, also called the Declaration, the Condominium Unit Sales Contract, the By-Laws of the unit owner's association, the Management Contract and the Covenants and Restrictions.

THE MASTER DEED: This is the controlling condominium document. It should fully describe the size, location and mechanical equipment in each condominium home. For your protection, look for definitions and detailed descriptions of these additional items: the scope of the project itself, the owners' association, common elements, the purposes for which the building and each of the units may be used, provisions for assessments and charges and a management agency agreement.

THE CONDOMINIUM SALES CONTRACT: This is the first document you will be asked to sign. The agreement should completely describe your unit, the purchase price, and the method of payment. When you sign it, the seller usually will require an "earnest money" deposit. But don't sign it yet. Wait until you find out more about your prospective purchase.

THE BY-LAWS: These provide for administering and maintaining the condominium complex. These will greatly affect what you can and cannot do with your unit and could affect your ability to resell it in the future. Here are some of the most important points to check.

· What are the rules and regulations governing the owners' association? What are the duties and powers of the owners or their elected board of directors? If it is a new project, make sure that the developer does not have too much power. The point at which the developer will turn over control of the development to the owners should be clearly defined. If you are buying in an older project, check with other owners to see how well the owners' association manages the project.

The point to remember here is that you—and your fellow owners—are in charge of running your entire development once the developer leaves. And, "the period of transition from developer to unit-owner control appears to be one of the most difficult in the life of a condominium project," the HUD study said. "This period usually lasts for a year or so after the developer has turned over control of the unit-owners association to the owner."

This period is sometimes called the "Awakening Period," according to a report by a HUD regional office. That report concluded that unit associations go through three stages: "(1) The Honeymoon, (2) the Awakening, and (3) Coming of Age."

The "Awakening" is described as follows:

"At this point, owners come to realize that *they* are the HOA (Homeowners Association). Original buyers begin moving for various reasons. The owners of specific units become increasingly more difficult to keep current as the units are sold to new owners without HOA notifications. Dues collection begins to falter. Replacement reserves and methods for calculation and predicting costs are found to be inadequate. Latent construction defects surface, but the builder's one-year warranty has expired. Subcontractors can't be located . . . inadequately designed community facility equipment begins to fail, particularly swimming pools and irrigation system. Monthly fees are found to be inadequate to meet current expenses. HOA directors feel isolated, frustrated, and overworked. Having been left 'holding the bag' they either resign, drop out or refuse to run for additional terms. Residents begin to violate architectural, parking, and pet restrictions; HOA finds enforcement powers unspecified. . . ."

Most owner associations, however, overcome their growing pains. In the HUD survey of condo owners, the majority were "reasonably satisfied with their unit owners' association." With a little checking, you can find out if your prospective owners' association has "come of age" or is still in for a rude awakening.

- Budgets—The by-laws should detail the condo association's budget procedures. As a potential buyer, you should look at the association's operating budget. It should provide for landscaping, maintenance, utilities management, taxes and insurance. In many states, such records must be open for inspection by unit owners during business hours.

Two related points: Make sure the common elements are adequately insured to protect the co-owners from loss or damage by fire or other hazards. Regardless, you should carry your own insurance on your individual unit.

- Your assessment requirements also should be stated in the By-Laws. You should know what your annual expenses will be. Also, check the penalties should you fail to pay your monthly fee. Don't get stuck paying someone else's delinquent assessments if you buy a used condo or townhouse. If you buy a condo from someone who still owes assessments and he doesn't pay them, you can be legally liable for them. So when you agree to buy a used unit, get a statement in writing from the seller that his assessments are paid up to date.

THE MANAGEMENT CONTRACT: Most condos are run and maintained by professional management companies, hired by the owners. Initially, the developer often acts as the manager. In such cases, beware if the original management contract seems excessively long, includes big fees, and your future association has no direct control over the management company. That's called a "sweetheart contract," and likely doesn't favor you, the owner.

The owners' association should hire the managing agent, subject to approval by the owners. The agent's job is to maintain the common areas, including cutting the grass, operating the swimming pool and taking care of the buildings. The agent also may collect delinquent assessments.

Good management of a condo project can make the difference between a profitable home investment and a poor one. So ask plenty of questions. Who is the managing agent? What is the reputation of his company? Does he have a long-term contract? Can he be fired by the owners? Does he control a limited fund to be used without prior consent in emergencies? If so, what is the limit of this fund? What do the other owners say about him?

- Protect Your Resale Rights—Check those Covenants and Restrictions. The By-Laws should list restrictions that are placed on individual condo owners; in a new project, other restrictions may be added later by a majority or more of the owners, so choose your fellow-owners carefully.

- Resale Restrictions—What restrictions are their on your
  right to sell your unit? Can you sell it to anybody, or do
  you have to offer it first to the condominium association? This is called the "right of first refusal." Similarly,
  the association may have the right to clear prospective
  buyers before you can sell your unit to them.

The HUD study found that "a significant factor inhibiting
resales is the restrictions which many condominium documents place on reselling a unit." In HUD's nationwide survey
of condo buyers, 45% said they had reselling restrictions and
64% said their projects either require prior approval of the
resale by the unit owners' association or give the association a
right of first refusal.

Avoid any condo that comes with such restrictions. Condos
with such limitations can't be sold with loans insured by the
federal government, and the "right of first refusal" is prohibited
in some states.

- Advertising—Check to see if you will be prohibited
  from putting up a "for-sale" sign or any other advertising restrictions.
- Renting—Can individual units be rented, either by the
  builder or individual home owners? In a complex of
  permanent homes, widespread renting can detract from
  the value of the development for buyers. (Of course, in
  resort areas, you should make sure renting is allowed,
  since you may be counting on the rental income to help
  you pay for it.)
- Kids and Pets—Are they allowed to live in the condo
  development? Buyers with children are barred at some
  all-adult developments. Some complexes don't allow
  pets. You may want to live in a place without screaming
  kids and yapping dogs; or maybe you couldn't live
  without them—mainly because you have three kids, a
  cocker spaniel and two hamsters. It's up to you, but
  also think of your resale potential. One Washington,
  D.C., area condo owner had a sale all wrapped up until
  the buyer discovered that he wouldn't be able to move
  in with his dog because the project banned pets.

In summary, go ahead and buy that condo, but think of
yourself not as a buyer but as a future seller. It could pay off
in the long run.

Make sure to understand what you are getting into before you sign a condo purchase contract. Don't sign a Subscription and Purchase Agreement until you have received and read a copy of the Declaration, By-Laws, Operating Budget Agreement and Regulatory Agreement.

One problem here is that sometimes condo buyers aren't given such documents before signing a purchase agreement. Unless there is a "cooling off" period during which time a purchaser can cancel his purchase agreement and get back his deposit, it is too late for him to read the documents after he has signed a purchase agreement. Some states have a 10-day or 15-day "cooling off" period that provides such protection, and you should check the protections in your state. But even if there is a cooling-off period (called a rescission period), you ought to insist on seeing the documents before you sign a contract. And don't be put off with the claim that the papers can only be seen "at the local land office." Get a copy and take them home where you can study them in privacy. If you still have major questions, consider hiring a lawyer to help you. But make sure he, or she, knows something about condominiums. Not all real-estate lawyers do.

Don't hesitate to ask anything. One prospective buyer at Rossmoor Leisure World, an adult community located near Washington, D.C., gave Mrs. Sumichrast, who was Vice-President of Marketing at the community, a 12-page list of 77 questions. They ranged from "What units are owned by the developer?" to "Are there existing burial plots for unit owners?"

"I like people asking questions before they buy," Mrs. Sumichrast said. "It makes it so much easier later on."

If you want to learn more about condos, one of the best short versions of what to do and not to do is "Questions About Condominiums," published by the U.S. Department of Housing and Urban Development, available free from the Consumer Information Center, Department 597F, Pueblo, Colorado 81009. Another is the "Condominium Buyers Guide," prepared by the National Association of Home Builders, 15th and M Streets, N.W., Washington, D.C. 20005. You also can buy *The Condominium Book* by Lee Butcher, which, in spirit of full disclosure, is published by Dow Jones Books, Princeton, New Jersey 08540.

Despite the complexities, condo living offers a good life for a growing number of home buyers.

SEVEN

Born-Again Homes: Housing Rehabilitation

> "In the old days the winos would
> fall asleep in your yard.
> Now we have high-class drunks who
> come right up and look in your window."
>
> —**Homeowner in a restored
> Dayton, Ohio, neighborhood**

Back in 1971, Skinny Mulligan scraped together enough money to buy an old wreck of a house on Capitol Hill in Washington, D.C., for $19,000. The red-brick townhouse was boarded up and filthy as a house could be. Hobos slept there and rats rummaged around inside.

Most of Skinny's friends thought he had flipped out. "Who would pay so much for such a mess?" they asked. "You've got to be nuts to touch a shack like that," they said.

But Skinny worked hard and put about $10,000 in materials into the house. Some of it he purchased at stores, some he bought from the junkyards, and some he got from people on the street. The labor cost him nothing. He did the work himself.

In 1975 Skinny sold the house for $90,000 and a fat profit. In 1981, the same house would fetch $110,000.

The Return to the Cities

Today there are thousands of Skinny Mulligans in every part of the country. They are busy fixing up old houses in the cities for profit, for fun, or simply because they want to move back into the cities.

It is a movement that is revitalizing old neighborhoods in many cities.

In 1974, the 6900 block of South Crandon Avenue in Chicago looked like a candidate for the wrecker's ball. The middle-class families that used to live on the street had long since moved away, and the once-handsome three-story apartment buildings they had left behind were in an advanced state of disrepair. It was a pattern repeated countless times in Chicago and other big U.S. cities.

The property was taken over by a company called Chicago Area Renewal Effort Service Corporation, which is owned by about 55 local savings and loan associations. Instead of destroying the buildings, Rescorp, as it's known, spent $3.7 million to rehabilitate them, replacing roofs, windows and wiring, installing new kitchens and bathrooms, and redecorating throughout. Today, all the 148 apartments in the five buildings on the block are occupied by families who pay up to $360 a month for the three-bedroom units. The surrounding area is also showing signs of perking up.

"If the buildings had been demolished in the old urban-renewal way, we'd just have another vacant lot in a dying neighborhood," said Saul Klibanow, Rescorp's president. "By preserving the buildings, I think we helped to preserve the neighborhood."

Wave of the Future?

According to government officials, builders, lenders and others in the residential construction field, projects like the one on South Crandon Avenue may well be the wave of the future. They say the time is ripe for an unprecedented effort to make existing urban buildings an important part of the national housing scene.

In some cities, of course, the rehabilitation movement is well under way, led by affluent business and professional people with a preference for close-in urban living. Such neighborhoods as the Park Slope section of Brooklyn, Lincoln Park in Chicago, and Beacon Hill in Boston have been revived largely by individuals who buy and restore gracious older homes.

The Wall Street Journal

"Don't think 'overcrowded' — think 'the
richness of urban life.' "

Now, however, there are public and private rehabilitation
schemes afoot that promise to dwarf what has already
taken place. "For a long time, federal urban-renewal
policy was directed almost entirely toward knocking down
old buildings and erecting new ones, and its effects on city

172   THE COMPLETE BOOK OF HOME BUYING

neighborhoods were disastrous. We intend to change this, and housing rehabilitation will be our main tool," declared the Reverend Gino Baroni, an assistant secretary of the U.S. Department of Housing and Urban Development.

A major reason for the rehabilitation push is the soaring cost of new construction, which has helped increase the price of the average new home to around $90,000—a price many families can't afford—and slowed the pace of apartment construction. Rehabilitation costs have risen too, but the process still is generally cheaper than new work because it is less extensive, doesn't involve site preparation, and can be carried on in all weather.

The high and rising cost of commuting from suburbia is also a force behind the rehabilitation movement. So is the increase in the number of childless couples, who can enjoy the cultural offerings of city life without worrying about the quality of schools the way couples with children do.

Finally, those in the rehabilitation business assert that there is a growing appreciation for the solid construction and living amenities peculiar to older homes. "A lot of people are tired of living in small, square rooms with skimpy walls. They want the quality woodwork, masonry and floorings and generous room designs that the old buildings offer," said Gerald Schuster, president of Continental Wingate Company, a Boston firm that specializes in apartment rehabilitation.

One obstacle is that few builders have much experience doing rehabilitation work. But the National Association of Home Builders, which long has been concerned mostly with new construction, has established a committee on remodeling and rehabilitation that will seek to show members how to do this work economically. "If the money is going to start flowing in this area—and we've seen a lot of signs that it will—builders will find ways to do it," said Milton Smithman, vice-president for builders services of the home builders' association.[13]

Rising Values

The result of this back-to-the-city movement has been soaring values for homes in many areas where nobody would have wanted to live in the late 1960s and early 1970s. A shell of a house on Capitol Hill such as Skinny Mulligan bought for

$19,000 in 1971 would cost $50,000 to $60,000 today. Restored homes in that area now sell routinely for between $100,000 and $200,000. In Philadelphia's revitalized Spring Garden section, a shell that cost $1,500 in 1970 would cost more than $35,000 today.

Housing values have jumped sharply in other born-again neighborhoods in cities around the country. In many places, yesterday's slums have become enclaves of upper-income people amid pockets of poor people.

All of this doesn't mean that most cities still aren't losing population. They are. What it means is that the poorer families often are being forced out of inner-city neighborhoods while those moving in are younger people with few or no children. So the total number of households may remain the same, or increase, but the number of people in those houses may decline.

This raises concern among some urban experts that while the back-to-the-city movement may add to the vitality and the tax base of a city, it may do so to the detriment of the poor and working-class people who already live there. Most of the newcomers are affluent whites, while many of those who are forced out of homes they previously rented are poor minority-group members. As the restored neighborhoods become wealthier, they lose the diversity that attracted many back to the city in the first place.

In Washington, D.C., lower-income residents have fought back by invoking an old law that gives tenants first crack at buying their units in rented housing that is put up for sale. Some of these tenants, most of them blacks, have become homeowners for the first time in their lives. But for many the prices are out of reach.

Where to Look

If you are looking to buy and restore a house in the city, you may have to look hard. In many cities, the prices of homes in restored neighborhoods have climbed beyond the pocketbooks of countless people—most of the bargains are long gone. Finding new areas of potential restoration is risky. The trick is to determine which urban areas are likely to be revitalized and which are going to become—or remain—slums.

There aren't any magic answers. But from talking with

people whose business it is to spot and invest in urban growth areas, we can give you some guidelines for finding an area that may be ready to be born again.

The first guide is that, with certain exceptions, most restoration isn't taking place in the worst slum areas of cities. Instead, the rehabilitation usually is in working-class neighborhoods just beyond the central city. Often these are areas with architecturally distinctive houses such as brownstones or Victorian style homes.

Second, your best investment is to buy a home before restoration is too far along in a neighborhood. "I highly recommend an area where there is very little restoration," said Frank Calcara, president of Calcara Enterprises, Inc., a major housing-rehabilitation company in Washington, D.C. "There is where you get your best value."

By buying in such an area, you run the risk of losing money if you have to sell the home before the area improves, Mr. Calcara warns. Your goal, he said, should be to find an area that should start back uphill in about three years. In other words, the best time to buy is at the beginning.

How do you tell the beginning? Again, there isn't any sure-fire formula. Here is the strategy Mr. Calcara has followed successfully: "You go into an area that has been depressed, and in any depressed area there has always been a section that has been restored. Now if you'll go away from that area five blocks or 10 blocks, as you drive in a circle, you will see the potential growth areas."

Once the comeback begins, he said, "you will see the growth of that area and within a period of three years, you practically close that area." Initially, the cost of unrestored homes is cheaper as you move away from the first area of activity. The period of individual restoration often is followed by commercial rehabilitation and marketing by builders and speculators, which tends to push prices higher.

Ed Havlic, executive vice-president of COMCO, Inc., a Chicago rehabilitation company, said his company uses the following rule of thumb:

"As soon as 20% or so of the structures within a neighborhood area have begun regeneration, or are considered 'good' economic values, you have a potential for redevelopment. Below the 20% factor is obviously the best time to acquire property in the neighborhood. But unless you have the economic substance with which to make a concerted effort and a significant impact on the community in terms of getting the numbers up, in terms of increasing the value of property in a very tight area, then the chances of success are marginal. Twenty percent seems to be—based on the studies I've seen—the magic number. The regeneration of 20% of the inventory is the sweep that's necessary to bring the rest of the housing stock up."

In other words, the safest course is to buy early in a neighborhood that may rebound, but not too early. Look for signs that a rebirth actually is underway.

One of those signs sometimes is the commitment of a major investment in the downtown area of a city, said John O'Dannell, general partner of the State Street Development Company of Boston. Often, when revitalization occurs, "it starts with the private institutions or a governmental agency making a large investment in a downtown or commercial core area," Mr. O'Dannell said. "When this occurs, the city overnight stabilizes and confidence is re-established on the part of investors, developers and lending institutions to go back into the city and to undertake development in the area or neighborhood that just a short time back would have been considered too risky or undesirable," according to Mr. O'Dannell.

If you plan to buy and restore a house in an urban neighborhood, you should double check our advice in Chapter Four on investigating the future of a neighborhood. Another place to check is your city planner's office, to see what changes officials there expect in a neighborhood. A real-estate agent who is knowledgeable about the areas you are considering also can be a big help. And you might be able to get some private advice from officials at companies that rehabilitate inner-city homes for resale.

Choosing a House: What to Watch Out For

· Flippers—In the real-estate business, a flipper isn't a friendly dolphin. It's a term used to describe speculators who buy old houses at cheap prices with no intention of restoring them. These speculators almost immediately resell, or "flip," the houses at a profit to eager buyers anxious to move into the city.

Basically, such speculators are able to buy houses cheaply by offering cash to long-time owners who aren't aware that their neighborhood is on the verge of revitalization. Then they offer to finance the house for new buyers who fear they otherwise probably won't be able to get a loan for an inner-city house. A successful speculator can buy a house for $30,000 one day and "flip" it the next day for $40,000 or $50,000.

There isn't anything wrong with buying a house from a speculator if you are getting a good buy. The trouble is the house often is overpriced and you can get more for your money by buying elsewhere. And, as we'll discuss later, chances are good that you can get a mortgage from a reputable lender. What you should do is find out how much the seller paid for the house, and when, by checking home-sales reports at your library or at city hall. If the seller bought the house just a few weeks or months before, chances are all he has done to the house is boost the price.

Your safest course of action is to deal only with owners who live in a house and with people represented by reputable brokerage firms, or with reputable builders and housing-rehabilitation concerns.

· Cosmetic Repairs—Unlike flippers, some speculators buy old houses cheaply, make "cosmetic" repairs, and then jack up the price and peddle the houses as "restored." Cosmetic repairs mean things like painting the walls, patching a leaky roof, putting in reconditioned stoves and refrigerators, and adding electrical outlets (even though they may be more than the house's old wiring can handle).

Again, a reconditioned house can still be a good buy. Just be sure you don't mistake a cosmetic job for a complete overhaul and pay a fancy price for a "restored" house in which most of the basic work still needs to be done.

"As long as it is a good cosmetic job—and the price is right—there is nothing wrong with it," said Frank Calcara, the rehab expert. "But for Pete's sake, before you buy this house, please have someone look it over, someone who knows about a structure, because there are too many things that the average buyer doesn't know—things that even the average real-estate person that is selling you the house doesn't know."

Indeed, "I would recommend that anybody who buys a house—restored or unrestored, but especially unrestored—have someone inspect the building," Mr. Calcara said. "I suggest they check the roof—that is paramount. They should also check the furnace, the plumbing and the wiring to see what condition it is in."

The roofs of old houses also can be an especially serious problem. You should check, or have a roofer check, to see "if the roofing is good, especially the flashing," advised Mr. Calcara.

Flashing is the metal that fits underneath the roofing material. It can rust and become leaky on old houses, especially old houses with tin roofs. Often these roofs have been covered with slag, or hot tar, to cover up the leaks. But eventually, the tar disintegrates and the leaks start again. Repairing such roofs is costly. "People should not buy a house with an old roof," Mr. Calcara said.

Mr. Calcara, whose firm buys old homes, guts the inside entirely and then refurbishes the houses for resale, also offers the following advice when checking an old home, or a shell, to be restored:

"The basic items I'm concerned with are masonry structure, and if there is any bad deterioration, which could be a very costly thing," he said.

Basic items to be checked include the foundation, the floor structure and the roof structure—not just the roof, but the structure of the roof. The rest of a house can be redone, but the basic structure can't, except at a big cost.

The basic condition of an old house, of course, has a lot to do with how much it will cost you to restore it. Many old houses are basically sound structures with features that are irreplaceable and that need only partial restoring. Other old houses may be structurally sound, but most of the house isn't worth saving. In the next sections, we'll look at what you should watch out for when you are either partly restoring a house or gutting it and starting over, and how much it is likely to cost you.

The Costs of Restoring an Old House from Scratch

The initial cost of restoring an old house, of course, is the purchase price. That can vary widely depending on the area where you buy, the neighborhood, whether you buy a partially restored house or a shell. Then you must consider the additional investment you will have to put into the house to transform it into what you want.

At a minimum, the basic cost of the house plus remodeling shouldn't add up to more than you would pay for a newly-built house of comparable size in your metropolitan area. And from an investment standpoint, the restored house should cost less than a comparable new house, according to rehabber Frank Calcara.

"The rule of thumb, the way I look at it, is that you always ask yourself this question: When I do this house over, its cost shouldn't exceed two-thirds the cost of a basic new home that I could build."

For example, if you bought a shell for $15,000 and rehabilitating that house—figure $22 to $30 a square foot— cost about $30,000, the total cost would be about $45,000. To build a comparable house in your area should cost at least a third more, or about $60,000.

You can put your own figures into the formula. But "one-third is the safety factor," Mr. Calcara declared. "If the acquisition price is wrong (too high), the investment price is wrong."

Next we'll take a look at what repairs to look for in an old house and what it will cost to make them. Again, prices vary widely, and they usually go up, so the following are only estimates based on 1978 prices. But they will give you some indication of what to expect.

First, we will consider the costs for completely refurbishing a shell of a house in which basically only the flooring, outside walls and roof structure are retained. That may be more restoration than you plan, but it will cover much of what probably will have to be done in any old house. Later, we will look at what to watch out for in older houses that need less restoring, and how much those repairs generally cost.

The following estimates are for restoring a shell into a three-bedroom row house with two-and-a-half bathrooms. The house has about 1,600 square feet. Using an average fix-up cost of $22 per square foot, the remodeling costs add up to about $35,000.

According to Frank Calcara, the costs break down this way:

- Demolition—between $1,500 and $2,000.
- Replacement of all windows, window sashes and window frames—$1,600. Usually the frames must be replaced along with the windows because the wood is rotted. You can tell by poking the frames with a screwdriver. If they are rotted, they will disintegrate immediately. It's

easier to replace the frames now than later. A typical old house has 16 windows, and the replacement cost for windows, sashes, and frames averages about $100 a window.

· Replacement of exterior doors and doorjambs—$250. Metal doors are the best replacements. Cost: about $125 each.

· Replace flooring—$550. If your old house has hard-wood floors, naturally you'll want to keep them. But many old houses don't. In such cases, "If the floors are sound and there isn't any major problem, I recommend that you just put five-eighths-inch plywood over them," Mr. Calcara said. A plywood sheet four feet by eight feet—or 32 square feet—costs about $11. Divide 32 into 1,600 square feet and you get 50 sheets of ply-wood, or a cost of $550 to cover the flooring in the entire house.

· New interior walls—$2,500. While some walls some-times can be retained, this estimate is based on tearing out all interior walls and putting up drywall partitions. But drywall prices are going up fast.

· Rough lumber inside the house, plus labor—$3,200. This is the cost for basically rebuilding the inside of the house.

· Mill work—$1,500. This includes all sorts of carpentry work including doors, closets, hardware, woodwork and the like.

· Redoing the kitchen—$3,500. This is a basic cost, including the installation of a frost-free refrigerator (new), dishwasher, garbage disposal, stainless steel sink, and 30 square feet of cabinet space, flooring and so forth. This can run much higher depending on what you include.

· Redoing the bathrooms—$3,500. Includes plumbing, tub, a shower, three commodes, vanities and sinks for two-and-a-half bathrooms.

· Heating and air-conditioning—$2,800. Includes a 100,000 BTU furnace and a three-tone central air-conditioning system.

- New wiring—$1,500. A 1,600 square foot house would require between 160 to 200 AMP circuit breakers. Old wiring usually shouldn't be saved because of possible safety hazards.
- Insulation—$1,000. "This is a must," with today's energy costs, Mr. Calcara stressed. His firm uses ceiling insulation R-38, about 12 inches, and exterior wall insulation of about R-9 or R-13, about four inches thick.
- New roof—$2,250.
- Painting, inside and out—$1,500.
- Concrete work—$2,000. This includes repouring the basement, walks, and steps.
- Carpeting throughout the house—$1,000 to $2,000. (Depends on the price of carpeting and the number of rooms covered.)
- Exterior wall—$1,500. This involves putting on one or two coats of mortar—covering over the outside walls to keep the original.
- Exterior brick repairs—$500.
- Miscellaneous expenses, including contractor fees—$2,850 to $3,500.

A final word of advice from another major rehabber: "I have found in almost all cases that costs are higher than anticipated."

Summary of Costs

Demolition	$ 1,500—$ 2,000
Windows	$ 1,600—$ 2,000
Doors (interior and exterior)	$ 250—$ 350
Floor plywood	$ 550—$ 600
Interior walls	$ 2,500—$ 3,500
Rough lumber	$ 3,200—$ 4,000
Millwork	$ 1,500—$ 2,000
New kitchen	$ 3,500—$ 5,000
New bathrooms (2½)	$ 3,500—$ 4,000
Heating and A.C.	$ 2,800—$ 3,500
Wiring	$ 1,500—$ 2,200
Insulation	$ 1,000—$ 1,250
Roof	$ 2,250—$ 3,500

Painting		$ 1,500—$ 2,000
Concrete work		$ 2,000—$ 2,500
Carpeting		$ 1,000—$ 2,000
Exterior walls		$ 1,500—$ 2,000
Brick repairs		$ 500—$ 2,500
Miscellaneous		$ 2,850—$ 3,500
	Total	$35,000—$48,400

Common Costs for a Partially Restored Home

There is a good chance that you won't be starting from scratch with a shell of a house when you invest in an old house. But one that seemingly needs less renovation than a shell still can be costly. Again, the first step is to have the house inspected to make sure it is well built. Then you'll want to figure how much it will cost you to fix it up.

The following is a guide to the common problems and repair costs for a typical, wood-frame, two-story house with about 1,600 square feet of living space. The estimates were drawn up in 1978 by Gary Scheppke, executive director of the Wisconsin Builders Association, at the request of the Credit Union International Association, Inc., for an article in its magazine, *Everybody's Money*. Mr. Scheppke said the estimates are national averages, but that they may vary by as much as 30% in some areas.

Inspection—To determine the cost of remodeling, a thorough inspection is a must. Starting in the basement, check the foundation for settling. If there is uneven settling the entire frame of the house may be distorted. If the foundation is square and only hairline cracks are visible, it's probably adequate.

Now check beams for signs of dry rot and sagging. The cost for shoring up sagging beams is about $350, but if the foundation is so bad the structure needs to be raised, the bill will run from $4,000 to $5,000.

You'll also want to examine basement walls for water stains, a serious problem. If stains are the result of a high water table, you might do well to search for another house. If drain tiles can solve the problem, you'll probably need to spend $3 a foot, including tearing up and replacing the perimeter of the floor, and $350 for a sump pump. Also look for dripping water, a sign of plumbing leaks.

First floor—A check of the first floor reveals much about construction. Are the walls, ceilings and floor all plumb, square and level? Big cracks in the walls probably mean the foundation has shifted and will get worse in time.

Test the floor by jumping up and down several times. If the floor is springy it may require an underlayer of plywood or particle board at 75 cents a square foot. Too much sag may indicate that some or all of the joists supporting the floor are weak, rotten or insect infested; to repair them would be prohibitive in cost.

Second floor check—on the second floor inspect ceilings for large water patches, usually indicating a leaking roof. Replacing the roof with average weight shingles costs about $60 a "square" (100 square feet). If all new downspouts are needed, you can count on another $175.

You also should look for water stains around the windows. If moisture from rain has penetrated the window sashes and sills, you have to install new window units. An average double-size window costs $300.

Attic check—In the attic, inspect for sag or rot in the rafters; an excessive amount is a warning that the house has serious structural defects. Note, too, whether the attic is insulated, an omission that is likely in houses built before the energy crunch. Ceiling insulation costs about $350, but installing it is comparatively simple, you can save labor costs by doing it yourself. Insulating the rest of the house may require tearing out walls and may be too costly. Or you can blow in insulation, but the effectiveness of this type of insulation is currently being questioned.

Major systems check—older houses often have woefully inadequate or outdated electrical, heating and plumbing systems. To install 100 amp service (considered adequate for modern appliances) with circuit breakers will cost $400. Outlets and new wiring will cost about $30 per outlet or switch. Plan to spend $600 to $800 to install a forced-air furnace assuming the existing duct work is useable.

Plumbing costs depend on whether it's necessary to replace clogged lead or galvanized pipes. For a two *bathroom house new plumbing costs $2,500, but if the pipes are in good condition all that may be necessary is replacing badly stained or broken fixtures. Average prices for fixtures are $375 for tub; toilet—$210; vanity, $235; fiberglass tub and shower—$525; shower stall—$450.*

Reprinted with permission from the Summer '78 issue of *Everybody's Money*, the credit union magazine for consumers, published by Credit Union National Association, Inc., P.O. Box 431 B, Madison, WI.

Choosing a Contractor

The next question to ask yourself is whether you will hire somebody to refurbish your urban house or whether you will do most of the work yourself. If you are handy with tools and good at working with your hands, you may be able to cut costs by doing much of the labor yourself. Even so, experts say you should at least depend on professionals for electrical, plumbing and heating work. You can also count on taking about one year to complete what could be done professionally in about four months.

For many people, however, the best choice is to hire a professional contractor—a builder or housing rehab company—to redo your new old home. But choose carefully.

A good contractor can make the difference between your urban adventure having a happy ending or turning into the start of never-ending frustrations. "If you get a good one, you'll be amazed at how easily he can cut through red tape" and "anticipate problems and avoid them," said Mr. O'Dannell of Boston's State Street Development Company. "If you get a bad one, or a person that's inexperienced, you'll have a heck of a time and the delays can kill you."

Whether you do-it-yourself or have most of the work done, investigate the reputations of the people you hire. Ask your lender or people you know who have had rehab work done to recommend companies that you might hire. Check with local home-building associations, real-estate boards, consumer protection agencies and business watchdog bureaus to verify their track records. Get at least three bids for the work you want done. And remember, the lowest bid isn't necessarily the best bid (though it isn't necessarily the worst either). The best contractor "might seem like he is 5% or 10% higher, but in the long run he's cheaper because he turns out a good product," said Frank Calcara.

Before you complete your purchase, you will want to check local building codes and permit requirements. You probably will need a permit for your remodeling work, and your house probably will have to meet local building codes. There also may be zoning restrictions. Check your city's building inspection division. If you're planning to add on to your house, the city will probably send someone out to do a free inspection. The report will list deficiencies for code compliance but won't give price estimates.

Your major protection is your contract. The following are safeguards suggested by experts contacted by *Everybody's Money*.

· *Include a starting and completion date.*

· *Write a schedule of payments into the contract. Limit the down payment and schedule remaining payments as the work progresses. Insist on making the final payment 30 business days after completion; the contractor is more likely to correct defects if money is due him.*

· *Obtain a waiver or require the contractor to post a bond protecting you from liens filed by suppliers or laborers.*

· *Include a provision protecting you against liability suits and workmen's compensation.*

· *Include a "broom-clean" provision, which means the contractor is responsible for cleaning up after the job is done.*

   And remember, even if you hire someone to do most of the work, you will end up putting a lot of your own sweat into your home as well. "Remodeling an old house must be a labor of love," said Mr. Scheppke of the Wisconsin Builders Association. "You will commit yourself to a long period of dirt, dust and inconvenience."

Financing

Once you've checked out the house and the total cost, the next step is getting financing both for the home purchase and for the renovation. Until fairly recently, that wasn't easy.

Lenders often declined to make loans on older houses in inner-city areas, claiming such loans were too risky. This practice is called "redlining," because some lenders were thought to have drawn red lines on maps around neighborhoods where they wouldn't make home loans.

Today home loans in urban areas are easier to come by in most parts of the country. Under pressure from urban, consumer and minority groups, Congress passed an anti-redlining law requiring lenders to disclose general areas where they make their home loans. And in 1978, the Federal Home Loan Bank Board, which oversees federally-chartered savings and loan associations, approved regulations designed to keep such lenders from discriminating against older homes and older neighborhoods when granting mortgages.

The new rules prohibit savings and loans from "arbitrary refusals" in considering making a loan on property that is "old or located in an area which the institution may have assumed is declining." The rules don't forbid S&Ls to refuse to make loans in inner-city areas, but they must have a good reason.

The object is to help assure that mortgage funds are available in older inner-city areas where lenders have practiced redlining. "We firmly believe there are many loans to be made in urban areas, and they can be made on a prudent basis," said Robert McKinney, bank board chairman.

Increasingly, however, lenders don't have to be pressured into making home-loans in old urban neighborhoods. This is simply because such loans have become good business. "I think we'd be moving in that direction even without the outside pressures. All the trends indicate this is the era of rehabilitation," said Norman Strunk, executive vice-president of the U.S. League of Savings Associations, the primary trade group of savings and loan associations.

Mr. Strunk noted that only about 5% of the S&Ls' annual national loan volume of $80 billion went into rehabilitation projects in 1977, but he said that figure could be as high as 20% within five years "if things go right."

So don't have any qualms about marching into your friendly lender and asking for a home loan on an old house in the city. Basically, you have the same choice of financing as for any other house, as we'll discuss in a later chapter. The only difference may be that the lender will want a bigger down payment or shorter mortgage on an older house than he might on a newer one in the suburbs. And you'll be able to eliminate some of those differences if you have a good plan for modernizing your new purchase.

The other difference is that you probably will also need to borrow money for your renovation work. According to the experts, what you should do is to go to the lending institutions and tell them exactly what the house, or shell, you wish to buy will cost. Then you give them a complete set of plans and complete details about how you plan to renovate the house. These can be supplied by your builder if you have hired one to do the rehab work. If not, hire someone who knows rehabbing to give you a complete set of plans and a cost breakdown item by item.

The lender will review these plans and, if he approves them, give you a loan based on 75% or 80% of the total cost, *including purchase price and remodeling*. He will give you the remodeling money on a periodic disbursement so that you pay for the work as it is completed. For instance, the lender will give you 15% of the money when the house is gutted, he will hand over another 15% when the house is framed and the windows are put in, you'll get 20% when the house is ready to be closed in, and so forth. In other words, he will set up scheduled payments until all the work is completed. This protects both you and the lender from problems of uncompleted work.

Getting Help from the Government

- Homesteading—You may be able to get some financial help for your refurbishing effort. Both the federal government and many city governments have moved to encourage the back-to-the-city movement by offering enticements to would-be urban home buyers.

For example, you may be able to buy an inner-city house for as little as $1. That's right, one U.S. dollar—which, as you know, isn't worth too much these days. The only catch in such "homesteading" programs, as they are called, is that the buyer must agree to fix up the house within a specified period, usually one to two years, and to live in it for at least three years. The program began in Wilmington, Delaware, and has spread to numerous other cities. In Baltimore, demand was so strong that the city had to hold two lotteries to see who got the houses.

Such programs have been given a boost by the U.S. Department of Housing and Urban Development which in 1975 began a homesteading program in 23 areas. Under the program, which was expanded nationally in 1978, homesteaders pay $1 for homes Uncle Sam has repossessed for failure to keep up payments on government-backed mortgages.

Check your city housing office to see if your city has a local homesteading program.

  · Low-interest rehabilitation loans—An increasing number of cities are offering residents who buy or fix up homes in the city cut-rate loans to encourage such renovation.

One source of such funds is community development block grants parceled out to major cities annually by the U.S. Department of Housing and Urban Development. HUD is reviewing its various rehabilitation aid programs with an eye toward increasing them. The federal government has been funneling $300 million annually into such work, most of it coming from the application of block grants to cities; HUD officials say that could triple in the near future.

A growing number of cities have their own special housing program. A leader in this area is Baltimore, Maryland, which combines bonds and federal money to offer special low-interest mortgages and home-improvement loans to home buyers in older neighborhoods. In 1978 Chicago sold $100 million in tax-exempt municipal revenue bonds to create a mortgage pool for persons buying homes in the windy city. Under the program, buyers with combined incomes of less than $40,000 can get loans of up to $80,000 at a below-market interest rate of 7.99%.

More than 25 cities, from Minneapolis, Minn., to Pine Bluff, Ark., now offer such housing programs.

It might be worth your while to see if your city offers special incentives to people who buy or refurbish inner-city housing.

Restoring Historical Houses

One way to get financial help when restoring an old home is to buy and fix up one that is located in an area that has historical significance. The National Park Service, part of the U.S. Interior Department, is charged with preserving historically noteworthy American districts, and over the years the number of such districts has grown to almost 10,000, including large areas in Boston, Baltimore, Philadelphia, Washington, Dallas and New York. Owners of homes or apartments in such places can qualify for federal assistance for projects that help maintain the character of their neighborhoods, even if their buildings aren't historically significant.

Until recently, Park Service spending for residential preservation has been relatively small, averaging about $20 million annually. But Congress authorized $100 million for that purpose in fiscal years 1978 and 1979 (fiscal year 1978 began Oct. 1, 1977) and $150 million in fiscal years 1980 and 1981.

"We think our program to maintain historical districts can become an important part of the wider housing rehabilitation move," said Jerry Rogers, chief of the Park Service's Office of Architectural and Historic Preservation. For information, you can write the Park Service at the Interior Department in Washington, D.C., 20240.

Many cities also offer special low-interest loans for restoring homes in historical districts. Dayton, Ohio, for example, offers 20-year loans at a below-market interest rate for buyers of homes in that city's historical district.

Restoring historic houses can offer even more of a challenge than rehabilitating other old homes. For one reason, if you're like most buyers you will feel a moral obligation—and indeed, there may be a legal obligation under your city's building codes—to maintain the historical integrity of the home. That may mean paying more to save more rather than tearing down and starting from scratch.

But it is an obligation and a challenge that more and more people are taking up. One of them is Ben Kline, a reporter on the Dayton (Ohio) Daily News, who, along with his wife, Marybeth, in 1975 bought the old brick house at 28 Tecumseh Street in Dayton's downtown Oregon Historical District. The house was built around 1840 for the man who owned Dayton's leading hat store. It had long been vacant and unimproved, except for a new roof and new wood windows, when the Klines paid $29,000 for their "dream" house. But that was just the beginning, as Ben recounted in a series of articles for the Dayton Daily News.

One doesn't have to be a child to have wonderful fantasies about an old house.

I picture myself rising graciously from a parlor filled with guests, throwing open the enormous double doors to the dining room and saying, "Dinner is served!"

Trouble is the doors are missing and there's a sewer pipe coming down through the middle of the doorway.

Trying to match fantasy with reality, authenticity with pocketbook and practicality, is the continuing challenge of restoring a house like ours.

"Restore" is a nice word, somehow less commercial than "renovate" and less tarnished than "remodel." And it's the word people use in the Oregon District. Exactly what they mean may vary greatly. There are extremely modernistic interiors behind some of the district's old brick walls.

Martin Kelly, a local historian, told me the key thing is "try to retain the original structure as much as possible. Don't do anything that cannot be undone, that would destroy the value of the house."

Obviously, there are going to be some small compromises. The only way to insulate solid brick walls, for example, is to furr them out. That will give the windows a "sunken" look on the inside.

Our builder had told us the remodeling would take him four months, and we took him at his word. We sold our house with an October 15 moveout deadline. But as May turned to September, the work went very slowly and we eventually signed with a new builder. Faced with the necessity of moving someplace, we wanted a place that would be close to the house and cheap. What we found was four rooms for $85 a month, plus utilities, plus cockroaches and a few other interesting creatures.

Actually living in the Oregon neighborhood instead of driving there with carloads of boxes every night is a delight. Around every street corner is another intriguing old house, restored or otherwise.

Every day there are changes, particularly on houses where the exterior brick is being retored. The natural brick look is "in" but it doesn't come cheap. We talked to two companies about having the brickwork stripped on the outside of our house. One was very cautious and

Kline House "before"

wanted $2,100. The other was more confident, but bid $4,475. I also got a sandblast estimate of $3,000—before I learned how dangerous sandblasting is to the glazing of the old soft bricks.

We may have to settle for exterior painting and replacement of damaged bricks, and the stripping done later. The temptation is to have everything done now, but there are so many horror stories of budgets that went berserk.

The natural tendency in this type of project is to reach for decorator magazines or wallpaper catalogs. We did,

Kline House "after"

but we also reached for the crowbar, scraper knives, screwdriver, chisels, hammer, pipe wrench, shovels and chemical paint remover.

Knocking down bad ceilings in two rooms was my job. These consisted of plaster more than an inch thick, held together with horsehair, affixed to strips of wood called lath that are nailed to the rafters. The trick with the crowbar is to make the hunks of ceiling land next to you, not in your face. I wore an old riot helmet, which helped, and a hospital-type face mask, which fell apart from the perspiration.

Our discoveries behind mantelpieces or plaster have

been sparse. There's some interesting wallpaper, gas pipes, haphazard wiring. Only one dead bird "flew" past me from the attic to the bedroom floor.

Aside from sensory shocks, there are real dangers in stripping down old houses. Pigeon dropping can carry incurable histoplasmosis fungus afflicting one's eyes, lungs or spine. Old paint can produce lead poisoning. Cuts and scratches from rusty nails can bring on tetanus.

After seven months in the house and 19 gallons of paint remover, we are doing pretty well: four rooms are done, three almost done, three partly done and five undone.

Contrasts of elegance and filth, finished rooms and half-finished messes of elegance you live with if you live like most people in Oregon. Our kitchen may look like a page from "Better Homes and Gardens," but our front-hall still is of the "Late 40's Flophouse" decor with walls painted a color we all "Army Hospital Corridor Green."

There are still some great houses sitting empty, waiting for somebody to love them. People looking for "bargains" in financial terms are going to be disappointed. But a bargain is in the eye of the beholder, and houses like these simply are not being built anymore.

How much has Oregon really changed in a year? Well, when two winos passed out on the steps of Irv Bieser's house a couple of weeks ago, it was such an event that another neighbor went out and took snapshots of them.

By 1978, Ben had put $46,000 in improvements into the house, with more to be done. The house's market value is estimated at more than $100,000. He offers the following advice for would-be restorers:

> *You need imagination to see the potential of an old, rundown house you are thinking of buying. But there also are practical things to consider:*
>
> · *Don't let real-estate people romance you. If the place has "all the original woodwork," it may also have the original termites. Do your own research on the house's structural soundness, its history, current appraised value and the neighborhood where you find it.*

- Get a lawyer before you sign anything. If your house needs urgent repairs to prevent further deterioration, there may be a month or two time lapse before you take possession. A good lawyer can arrange for the seller to make necessary, interim repairs.

- Don't go crying to your banker if you get cold feet or the project begins to look like Lockheed's latest over-run. His job is to protect the bank's investment, not yours.

- Don't fight city hall; use it. The various city permits and inspections required for your project may seem ridiculous, especially if you are working on a house that obviously has not been "up to code" for years. But those city inspectors can protect you from a builder who might take shortcuts or do slipshod work.

- Get a written contract with the builder, with a firm price for the job. Many builders want only to do such jobs on a "time-materials" basis, which you accept only if you agree with the builder on a ceiling price.

- Be prepared to put your foot down to save some of what's left of your old house. We got the impression the whole world would be covered with drywall and plywood if builders had their way.

- Consider hiring an architect. We never doubted what we wanted our house to be, but the architect knew the right language to use in instructions to the builder.

- Don't confuse decorations with restoration. Those gorgeous wallpapers, paints, and carpets will have their place in your dreams, but your house may first need unglamorous things like complete rewiring or a new roof.

- We noticed on Oregon District house tours that the tourists always seemed to end up in the kitchens, admiring the new cabinets. The serious house restorer looks in the attic and cellar too.

- Don't be afraid to do some work yourself, to have fun, get dirty, lose weight, get your nose full of soot, scrape

The Wall Street Journal

"You might as well have told them my age after bragging
that we have a 5¼ percent mortgage on our house."

your hands on rusty nails, get paint on your clothes.
It's known as getting acquainted with your house.

· If you don't like the neighborhood or cannot see its
potential, think twice about buying. On the other hand,
don't let anybody scare you out of living in the city.
It's a darn good place to live. And getting better.

EIGHT

Financing Factors

> "Going ahead with the neutron
> bomb would be sheer waste. We
> already have something that
> destroys people and leaves
> buildings intact. It's called a
> 17% mortgage."
>
> —Bob Orben

If you are like most people, you will have to borrow money to pay for that home you want to buy. And if you are like most people—even if you have purchased a home before—you will probably feel a bit apprehensive about getting a mortgage loan.

For one reason, those folks who lend money have such foreboding images; you're sure they are just sitting at their desks waiting to turn you down for a loan. For another reason, the idea of taking on, say, a $50,000 mortgage debt can give you a queasy feeling in the pit of your stomach.

Both fears usually are greatly exaggerated. Yes, we've heard those stories about cold-hearted money lenders. Like the one about the man who needed a heart transplant and his doctor said he could choose a new heart from one of three donors—a terminally-ill star athlete, a Hollywood movie star, or a 60-year-old banker. The patient said he wanted the banker's heart because it had never been used.

Actually, those bad, bad money lenders usually are pretty friendly folks. And there is no reason to feel guilty about asking them for a mortgage loan. After all, most home buyers do get mortgages (only 3% pay cash). What's more, you should remember that the lender isn't doing you any favors. It's his business to loan money—with an interest charge, of course. And a home mortgage is about the safest loan he can make.

As for the mortgage itself, today's mortgages are designed to make it easier for more people to own homes. It's not like it was back in the 1920s when you usually had to make a 50% down payment on a house and then finance the rest of the cost over only five years. The five-year loan had a big "balloon" payment at the end, and if you couldn't pay off the loan then, or get a new one, you could lose your home. During the Great Depression in the 1930s, millions of people did lose their homes when they couldn't pay their mortgages or their property taxes.

The Wall Street Journal

"They're not as young as they look . . .
they have a 4½% mortgage!"

To avoid such problems, and to encourage home ownership in the United States, in the late 1930s Congress created the Federal Housing Administration, or FHA. Its job was to insure long-term loan mortgages that could be paid off in affordable monthly installments. With Uncle Sam's backing as an incentive, more lenders began offering such mortgages. Today, the amortized, or installment, mortgage is the backbone of home financing.

Today, you can get a mortgage for 25 or 30 years. Instead of a 50% down payment, you only have to put down as little as 5% or 10%, or, in some cases, nothing at all. You pay back the money in monthly installments. What's more, there are a lot of new ideas cropping up in home financing. All of them are designed to make it easier for you to buy a home.

So, as long as you keep a firm grip on your common sense, there isn't any reason to be apprehensive about applying for a mortgage. William Shakespeare may have said, "Neither a borrower nor a lender be," but he never had to buy a home in today's housing market.

Where to Get Mortgage Money

When you go shopping for a home loan, here are the kinds of places you can check:

- Savings and Loan Associations—These lending institutions are called Building and Loan Associations in some areas because their main business is lending money for home mortgages. S&Ls write about half of the nation's home mortgage loans. So your local S&Ls are a good place to start in your search for mortgage money. Most will lend up to 95% of a home's appraised value, including private mortgage insurance. It will help you to get a loan if you have a savings account at the S&L.

- Banks—The main function of commercial banks is to lend money to business. But they can be a good source of mortgage money as well. Banks generally are permitted to lend up to 75% of the value of the property, which translates into a 25% down payment. But they can make FHA and VA loans with lower down payments.

- Mutual Savings Banks—These "banks" are more similar

to S&Ls than commercial banks. They actually are the oldest type of savings institutions in the United States. They are run for the mutual benefit of their depositors, and most of their assets are invested in mortgages. They are good places to go for mortgages, but they are located only in 18 states and the Virgin Islands. The heaviest concentration is in New England.

· Credit Unions—These are the new boys on the housing-finance block, but they swing a lot of weight. Credit unions in the U.S. began in 1909 to provide cheap credit and encourage savings among individuals sharing a common bond, such as employment. Depositors own a credit union by holding shares in proportion to their savings. Most of the nation's more than 20,000 credit unions were formed by employees at the companies where they work, but lately credit unions have spread to groups ranging from feminists to former drug addicts. Nearly 34 million persons, or about one out of every six Americans, belong to a credit union.

If you belong to a credit union where you work, or can join one, it could be the cheapest source for a mortgage. Previously, such organizations couldn't make home loans. But in 1977, President Carter signed a bill extending to credit unions such banking functions as making long-term mortgages.

· Mortgage Bankers—Mortgage banking companies mainly are in the business of originating mortgages and selling them to institutional investors, such as life insurance companies or pension funds. They use the money they get from selling loans to make more loans. If you get a mortgage from a mortgage banker, he will probably sell your loan to somebody else but continue to collect the monthly payments from you.

Mortgage bankers aggressively seek loans and often work with real-estate agents. They specialize in FHA and VA loans, because such loans are easy to sell on the secondary, or resale, mortgage market.

· Home Builders—If you're buying a new home, a builder can help get you mortgage money. He doesn't lend money himself, of course, but he usually has a commitment with a local lender who promises to provide mortgage money at a pre-determined rate.

· Your Family—Unless you really do have a rich Uncle Bill, you're not likely to be able to borrow enough from your family to pay for a house. But your family might be able to help you get up the down payment that you need to get a house. Increasingly, in addition to everything else they do for their kids, mom and dad are being called on to help their offspring get started on the road to home ownership.

If your folks plan to help you buy a home, have them sign a notarized "gift letter" stating their intentions and how much they plan to give you. You can use the letter to convince a home seller that you can afford to buy this house, and it will be used by the lender in considering your loan.

· Individuals—Home sellers or other private individuals also loan money for mortgages. When mortgage money is scarce, you may want to consider borrowing from an individual. But we'll discuss that in more detail later in this chapter.

Common Types of Mortgages

Basically, home mortgages come in two varieties—those that are backed by the federal government and those that are not.

· Conventional Mortgages—A conventional mortgage is simply a home loan from a lender without any federal involvement. This is the kind of loan that more than 75% of all home buyers get. Generally, a conventional loan can be obtained quickly—usually within a week or so—and there is a minimum of red tape.

Typical terms are: 20% to 25% down payment; 25 years to 30 years to pay the mortgage; a fixed interest rate, which means the rate won't change over the life of the mortgage— some people who bought homes 25 years ago are paying interest rates of 5% or less.

- Privately-Insured Mortgages—If you want to get a conventional mortgage, but you want to make a smaller down payment than the 20-25% the lender requires, you can get a lower down payment by using private mortgage insurance. You'll still be getting a conventional loan, but a private mortgage insurance company will insure payment of a small part of the loan, typically 20% to 25%. With the added protection, the lender will require a smaller down payment from you. For example, if the lender wants a 25% down payment and private insurance will cover 20% of the loan, you'll only have to put 5% down.

Such mortgages sometimes are called "MAGIC Loans" because they were originated in the late 1950s by a Milwaukee-based company with the initials MGIC, more formally known as Mortgage Guaranteed Insurance Corporation. Until then, the mortgage insurance field pretty much had been limited to Uncle Sam, through the FHA. Today, there are dozens of companies that sell private mortgage insurance. Your lender likely will advise you whether you can use such services and will help you arrange them.

As we said, essentially what you will do is get insurance on a small part of your home loan. Basically, there are two types of plans. One is called an "annual plan," and each year you pay a premium equal to ½ of 1% of the declining balance of your mortgage. With the second plan, you pay a single premium to cover a 10-year term; the cost usually is about 2% of the mortgage. In addition, with either plan, when you buy the home you may have to pay a one-time fee. Lenders often will allow you to drop the private mortgage insurance after 7 to 10 years.

- FHA-Insured Mortgages—You can get up to a $90,000 mortgage insured by the Federal Housing Administration, which now is part of the U.S. Department of Housing and Urban Development. The FHA doesn't make loans itself; it just insures loans that meet its standards. In effect, this means that the government promises the lender that if a buyer doesn't make his payments, FHA will buy the mortgage. Since this cuts the risk for the lender, terms for FHA-insured loans are more lenient than for conventional loans. Income requirements also are lower than for conventional and private-insured mortgages.

FHA-insured loans offer a number of advantages which, unfortunately, are sometimes offset by disadvantages. The advantages include:

- A fixed mortgage rate that doesn't change over the life of the loan.

- Low Down Payments—With an FHA-insured loan, you can buy a house with a down payment equal to 3% of the first $25,000 of the purchase price and 5% of the balance. Thus, with a $50,000 house, for example, the down payment would be $750 on half the price and $1,250 on the rest, or a total of $2,000—a total down payment of only 4%.

- Long Mortgages—Most FHA-insured home loans are for 30 years or sometimes more.

- FHA Appraisal—The FHA will appraise the house you are buying to determine its fair market value. It also will inspect the house to make sure it meets basic structural requirements. If not, the seller will have to make and pay for repairs before you buy. FHA, however, doesn't guarantee the house, and its requirements don't amount to a home warranty program.

- Lower Interest Rates—The FHA sets a ceiling on how much interest lenders can charge on FHA-insured loans, and the maximum rate often is below the market rate. In addition, however, you also pay an insurance fee of ½ of 1% per year. And the lower interest rate, as we'll see next, can turn into a disadvantage.

The disadvantages of an FHA-insured mortgage include:

- Lower Interest Rates—How can a lower interest rate be a disadvantage? Simply because sometimes the government ceiling on the FHA rate is too low compared with the rates lenders are charging buyers who get conventional loans. To make up the difference, the lender will charge an extra fee, called "points," on your FHA-insured loan. A point is equal to 1% of the mortgage amount. Thus, 1% of a $50,000 mortgage would be

$500. When the FHA rate gets too far out of line with the market, the points can rise to five, six, 10 or sometimes more.

That may not seem to matter to you as a buyer, because buyers aren't allowed to pay more than a one-point loan origination fee with an FHA-insured loan. Thus, if the points rise, say, to five on a $50,000 mortgage, that means you would pay 1%, or $500, and the seller would be stuck with the other four points, or $2,000. Naturally, the seller isn't going to be anxious to pay that. The result: either he'll refuse to sell his house with an FHA-insured loan in the first place, or he'll make sure the price is high enough to compensate for the extra charges. In the latter case, you end up stuck with paying the added cost by paying a higher price than a non-FHA buyer would have to pay.

- Loan Limits—Unlike non-FHA loans, which can be about as big as lenders want to make them, FHA-insured loans can't be for more than $90,000. That's a big improvement, though, from the unrealistically low $45,000 limit that existed before Congress upped the ceiling to $62,500 in 1976. You also can get an FHA-insured loan of up to $15,000 on single-wide mobile homes and $20,000 for double-wide units—with up to 23 years terms.

- Red Tape—The major drawback to FHA-insured loans is that they require a lot of paperwork before they can be approved. Loan approvals that take days for a conventional loan can take weeks for an FHA-insured loan. For this reason, many sellers and lenders avoid FHA loans. As a result, you may have a hard time buying a home with an FHA-insured loan.

Because of the disadvantages and the competition from private-mortgage insurers, the appeal of FHA-insured mortgages has been steadily declining. FHA loans used to be a major factor in mortgage financing, accounting for as much as 25% of all mortgages written annually. By 1980, only about one of every eight home loans was FHA-insured.

VA Mortgages

If you are a veteran, you may be able to get a mortgage guaranteed by the Veterans Administration, another federal agency. These mortgages, which began after World War II, also are known as GI loans. Unlike FHA, the VA doesn't insure loans; instead, it guarantees up to 60% or $25,000, whichever is less, of a loan to buy a home. It also guarantees loans on mobile homes. Like the FHA, the VA doesn't directly loan money itself. To obtain a VA loan, you first need to get a Certificate of Eligibility.

The advantages of a VA-guaranteed loan include:

- A fixed mortgage rate.

- No Down Payment—A VA loan is about the only home mortgage you can get without putting a single dollar down. The VA guarantee usually takes the place of a down payment with the lender. Of course, you may wish to put a small down payment, or the lender may require one, to keep your monthly payments in line with your income. And a down payment is required if the selling price of the house is higher than its appraised value.

- No Loan Limits—Unlike FHA, there aren't any limits on the amount you can borrow. The amount of the loan is limited only by your ability to repay. The mortgages usually are for 25 to 30 years.

- VA Appraisal—The VA will appraise the fair market value of the home you buy and inspect it. As with FHA, this isn't a warranty program, but the VA will assist you in handling valid complaints to correct any defects in homes that were VA-inspected.

- Lower Interest Rates—The maximum rate is set by the Veterans Administration. Usually it is the same rate as for FHA-insured mortgages and slightly below market rates.

As with FHA loans, there are disadvantages to VA-backed mortgages. As mentioned before, the interest ceiling means that the lender may charge extra fees to make the loan. Though the VA prohibits the buyer from paying more than

1% of the mortgage amount, higher charges may be passed on to you in the form of a higher buying price for the home.

VA loans also involve more red tape than conventional loans. But the processing usually is much faster than for FHA-insured loans. As a result, lenders and sellers usually are happy to deal with buyers using VA-guaranteed loans.

Who Is Eligible for VA Loans?

About 27 million veterans or surviving spouses of veterans are eligible for VA-guaranteed home mortgages. This includes veterans who were on active duty for at least 90 days during specified periods of war. It also includes unmarried surviving spouses of military personnel who died in service or from a service-connected disability, as well as the spouses of serving members who have been captured or who are listed as missing in action.

More than 4 million veterans whose GI loans have been paid in full are potentially eligible for new loans guaranteed by the VA. New loans are also possible for the nearly 5 million vets who now have GI loans when those loans are paid off and the house is sold. Thus, even though you have used your VA home benefits, you can use them again if your loan obligation has been met. If your VA loan obligation hasn't been paid off, or if the home you purchased through VA hasn't been sold yet, you are still entitled to use the difference between the benefits you have used and the new limit of benefits.

For example, let's say you purchased a home through VA in 1965. You used your loan guarantee benefit to the then-maximum limit of $7,500. You now wish to purchase another home that you will occupy as your prime residence, but you don't want to sell your first home. You are now entitled to use up to a $17,500 VA loan guarantee on the new purchase (the difference between the $25,000 maximum and your original $7,500 guarantee).

Certain disabled veterans are entitled to guarantees of up to $35,000 toward their home purchase. For all veterans there is no time limit for using the benefits.

In 1978 Congress raised the limit on the VA guarantee to $25,000 from $17,500. It also expanded the eligibility of Vietnam War veterans by reducing the required active-duty service for veterans who served between August 5, 1964, and

May 7, 1975, from 181 days to 90 days, the same as for other war periods.

It is estimated that an additional 168,000 Vietnam era veterans are eligible for guaranteed loans. Check your local VA office for details on VA-guaranteed loans, or contact the Veterans Administration, Washington, D.C. 20420.

Farmers Home Administration Loans

You don't have to be a farmer to get a Farmers Home Administration, or FmHA loan. But you do have to live in a rural area or at least in a small community outside a metro-politan area. You also must be unable to obtain a conventional loan and have an annual income below $15,600. If you live in a rural area, an FmHA loan can get you started as a home-owner for as little as nothing down, up to 33 years financing, and below-market interest rates. There are special low-interest loans for people with low incomes. For details, contact the Farmers Home Administration in your county. It is part of the U.S. Agriculture Department and should be listed in the phone directory under "U.S. Government," or write the FmHA in Washington, D.C. 20250.

Innovative Mortgages

In addition to standard mortgages, there are a lot of new kinds of home financing that might make it easier for you to get a home loan. Some new mortgages, with payments that start low and then gradually rise as your income increases, are designed to help first-time buyers get into a house. Most new mortgages, though, are designed mainly to help lenders who are increasingly reluctant to offer long-term mortgages at fixed interest rates during times of super inflation.

The result is a confusing array of new types of mortgages, many of them with changeable interest rates that can go up and down over the life of the loan. They mean more uncer-tainty, and often higher costs, for home buyers. For most buyers, the best mortgage—if you can get one—will remain a fixed-rate mortgage.

These various new mortgages usually are described by their initials and served up as some sort of mortgage-market alphabet soup. Here is a simplified summary of the leading types:

The ABCs of Home Mortgages

FRM— Fixed Rate Mortgage
RRM— Renegotiable Rate Mortgage
VRM— Variable Rate Mortgage
AML— Adjustable Mortgage Loans
ARM— Adjustable Rate Mortgage
GPM— Graduated Payment Mortgage
GPAM—Graduated Payment Adjustable Mortgage
SAM— Shared Appreciation Mortgage
PLAM—Price Level Adjustable Mortgage
RAM— Reverse Annuity Mortgage
FLIP— Flexible Loan Insurance Mortgage
FLEX—Flexible Payment Mortgage
DIL— Deferred Interest Loan
HELP—Home Equity Loan Program

- Fixed Rate Mortgage (FRM)—This is the familiar mortgage with an interest rate that never changes over the life of the loan. Thus your mortgage payment stays the same as your income rises. The problem is that such loans will be harder to get as lenders try to switch to more inflation-proof (for them) loans. But, to paraphrase Mark Twain, the death of the fixed-rate mortgage has been greatly exaggerated.

- Renegotiable Rate Mortgage (RRM)—Also known as a "rollover" mortgage. These are long-term loans that are renegotiated every three to five years. Each time the loan is renewed, the mortgage rate is increased or lowered, depending on prevailing interest rates at the time.

  Rollover mortgages have long been used in Wisconsin, California, Washington State and Canada. But they came into wide use throughout the United States in 1980, when the Federal Home Loan Bank Board authorized their use by federally chartered savings and loan associations nationwide.

  Under the bank's initial rules, these loans must be automatically renewed every three to five years. At any renewable period, the interest rate can be increased or lowered a maximum of 0.5 percentage point for each year of the renewal period. The rate is tied to the bank board's monthly index of average interest rates on previously occupied homes. The maximum interest rate increase over the life of the mortgage is 5 percentage points.

Such renegotiated mortgages work like this: suppose you take out a $50,000, 30-year loan at an initial interest rate of 14% with rollover every three years. Your monthly payment for principal and interest would be $592 for the first three years.

If, at renewal time, the going rate of mortgages is the same as it was when the loan was negotiated, there isn't any change in the interest rate or monthly payments for the next three years. But if market rates rise or fall, so does your payment.

Since the maximum allowable adjustment is half a percentage point per year, or 1½ points for the three-year renewal, you could find yourself paying as much as 15½% or as little as 12½% when the loan is renewed. This translates into monthly payments as high as $651, or as low as $535.

By the 13th year of the loan, when it is renewed for the fourth time, it is theoretically possible for the interest rate to rise to 19%. It also could be as low as 9%. So after the 12th year, payments could range anywhere from $420 a month to $783.

Lenders like renegotiated rate mortgages because they can periodically boost the interest rate. And rollovers can be good for buyers who purchase homes when mortgage rates are high because their interest costs would be reduced if rates decline. They may also be able to get such loans at an initial lower rate than for a fixed-rate mortgage. Furthermore borrowers of these loans get 90 days before each renewal period to shop around for better terms from another lender.

The problem is that the buyer also could be faced with sharply higher monthly payments if interest rates go higher. That could be a heavy burden for buyers unless their incomes keep improving. The risk is increased by the fact that lenders are seeking to remove the limits on how much the rates on renegotiated rate mortgages can be increased.

· Variable Rate Mortgage (VRM)—As the name suggests, these mortgages rise and fall with changing money-market conditions. If interest rates generally go up, so does your mortgage rate. If rates drop, so does the interest cost of your mortgage.

Variable rate mortgages are widely used in California. And in 1979, the Federal Home Loan Bank Board authorized their used by federally chartered savings and loan associations across the United States.

The bank board rules allow rate increases of one-half of a percentage point a year, up to a maximum increase of 2½ percentage points over the life of the mortgage.

Of course, the rate also could be lowered, and there isn't any limit on how much it can be decreased. And while rate increases aren't mandatory, rates must be reduced if the S&L's cost-of-funds index falls.

The loans can be paid off without charge if prepayment is made within 90 days after notification of an increase in the mortgage rate. Because of such prepayment terms, lenders offering VRMs regard them as well-suited to homeowners who expect to own a home no more than five years.

· Adjustable Mortgage Loans (AML)—These are mortgages with interest rates that can be adjusted up and down in line with changing market conditions. Some experts believe that AMLs, which were approved for federally chartered savings and loan associations in 1981, will become the standard mortgage form.

Adjustable-rate mortgages are a dice roll for consumers. Generally, there aren't any limits on how much, or how often, the interest rate or monthly payment can be increased. Or, to keep monthly payments level, the lender can add the increased cost to the unpaid balance, a feature known as "negative amortization." On the other hand, while increases are optional, the mortgage must be adjusted downward if the index to which it is linked declines. So the best time to consider such mortgages is when interest rates are likely to go down.

Shop around for the best mortgage. Look for loans

for which the lender limits how much and how often
the interest rate and monthly payments can be increased. Also, make sure the mortgage is tied to a fair
index, such as the national average mortgage rate, and
not the lender's own cost of money. And you should be
able to get a lower initial rate than is being charged
for fixed-rate mortgages.

- Adjustable Rate Mortgage (ARM)—These are the
  bank's version of changeable-rate mortgages offered
  by savings and loan associations. As proposed in early
  1981, the rates on such loans could rise or fall by
  half a percentage point every six months—without any
  maximum for the life of the loan.

- Graduated Payment Mortgage (GPM)—These are
  mortgages with monthly payments that start lower
  than usual and then go up steadily for five to 10
  years. After that, the payment remains stable.

GPMs especially help younger buyers who might
not be able to afford the regular payments at first,
but whose incomes will increase over the years so
that they can afford higher payments later. The
Department of Housing and Urban Development
insures more than a half dozen FHA plans for
graduated payments. Such loans, of course, are
obtained through private lenders, many of whom
also now offer their own graduated payment loans.

Consider, for example, the Federal Home Loan
Bank Board's figures on a hypothetical $30,000,
30-year, 9% mortgage. Such a loan in standard form
would cost the borrower $241 a month for payment
of principal and interest over the entire 30 years.
But under the most popular graduated payment
plan, the initial amount would be sharply lower
—$182. The payment would increase 7.5% a year
for five years, reaching $262 a month. (Of course,
this example doesn't include payments for property
taxes and insurance, which also could go up.)

As the example shows, buyers using a graduated
mortgage plan end up paying higher monthly amounts
than they would on a conventional loan with a fixed
rate. And such buyers also build up little or no

equity in their homes during the early years of repayment.

One problem with GPMs is that they are ultimately more costly than standard mortgages, both in terms of higher payment later and in terms of total payout if the loan is carried to term. Also there is a degree of negative amortization, which means early payments don't cover all the interest due, so that future interest charges are made on unpaid interest as well as principal and the home buyer actually increases his debt.

· Graduated Payment Adjustable Mortgage (GPAM)— These are a combination of the graduated payment mortgage and the renegotiable rate mortgage. Under this plan, lenders would have the right to adjust the interest rate, up or down, every three to five years for 10 years in line with market conditions. The maximums would be 0.5 percentage points a year, but no more than 15% in any one year.

For example, consider a 30-year, $50,000 loan at an initial interest rate of 13%. A traditional, level-payment loan would carry a monthly payment of $553.10 in principal and interest, but the GPAM would cost only $428.09 a month in the first year.

However, the GPAM's payments would increase automatically to $460.20 in the second year and to $494.71 in the third year. And if interest rates rise to the maximum, in the fourth year the payment would jump to $568.92. By the sixth year, the payment would be $657.46 a month and the unpaid balance would be almost $5,000 more than was borrowed initially.

Of course, if interest rates declined, the graduated payments would go up as rapidly. The problem is that a combination of the built-in increase in payments plus a boost in the mortgage rate could put young home buyers in a financial squeeze if their incomes don't keep pace.

· Shared Appreciation Mortgage (SAM)—This is a share-the-wealth mortgage. You get the mortgage at a below-market rate when you buy the house—but when you sell the house, you share the profit (or appreciation) with the lender.

Terms vary, but under the most common arrangement, lenders provide mortgages at a rate about one-third lower than the prevailing rate—for example, a 10% mortgage in a 14.5% market. The lender then gets one-third of the profits after seven to 10 years, or when the house is sold, whichever comes first. If the home isn't sold within seven to 10 years, an appraiser would calculate its market price. And the borrower would pay to the lender a lump sum equal to the agreed share of the appreciation, less any improvements and the cost of the appraisal. The lender refinances the home, if the borrower wishes, to cover the unpaid balance and the amount that the homeowner had to repay in shared appreciation.

Here's how one shared appreciation plan works: The lender offered a mortgage at a bargain rate of 9.9% interest. But after seven years, the home buyer must pay the lender up to 40% of the home's increased value. At 8% annual appreciation, a $66,666 home will have increased in value by $47,588 after seven years. The home buyer would keep $28,553, but would owe the lender $19,035. In addition, despite having made a $522 payment every month— for a total of $43,848—the home buyer with a $60,000 mortgage would still owe $56,500 of that amount; and he would have to refinance the house.

There are problems with shared appreciation mortgages that could prevent them from being widely used. For lenders, there is a negative cash flow that may make such mortgages unattractive despite the large potential gain. For borrowers, there is the prospect that they will have to part with 30% or 40% of their potential profit. And they may wind up with a huge and costly new mortgage that they can't easily afford. Indeed, most buyers probably would be better off paying a higher mortgage rate from the beginning than giving up a large chunk of the increased value of their home.

Here are some theoretical examples of how home buyers might fare with a shared appreciation loan versus other loans:

Variations in Mortgage Plans

Type of Mortgage	Monthly Payments Average Interest Rate				Homeowners Equity[2] Including Unrealized Appreciation			
$66,000 house $60,000 mortgage	1-3 Years	4-5 Years	6-10 Years	11-30 Years	After 5 Years	After 10 Years	After 20 Years	After 30 Years
Fixed Rate	$711 14%	$711 14%	$711 14%	$711 14%	$47,235	$114,017	$125,400	$171,187
Variable Rate[1]	$735 14.5%	$794 15.75%	$783 15.5%	$718 14%	$47,051	$113,472	$124,963	$171,187
Renegotiable Rate[1]	$711 14%	$781 15.5%	$786 15.6%	$720 14.05%	$47,120	$113,498	$124,922	$171,187
Graduated Payment	$596 14%	$713 14%	$795 14%	$795 14%	$41,149	$108,178	$119,421	$171,187
Graduated Payment[1] (adjustable)	$596 14%	$764 15.5%	$885 15.6%	$818 14.05%	$40,495	$106,805	$118,259	$171,187
Shared Appreciation[3]	$505 9.5%	$505 9.5%	$505 9.5%	$1057 14%	$35,117	$ 82,000	$ 86,206	$103,126

[1] Assumes market rate of interest rises 0.5 percentage points a year for five years, then declines 0.5 points a year for next five years, and that rates remain level for ensuing 20 years.

[2] Assumes 10 percent annual increase in housing prices for ten years with no increase thereafter.

[3] Assumes owner refinances remaining balance of original loan plus the bank's share of appreciation after ten years.

Source: National Association of Home Builders, Economics Division

- Price Level Adjustable Mortgage (PLAM)—With this mortgage, the monthly payments are adjusted for inflation so that the payments remain constant in "real" terms—after inflation is taken into account. In this situation the adjustment isn't made by changing the interest rate, but by increasing the loan principal. The problem is that in times of roaring inflation, the mortgage payments could well climb beyond your ability to pay them. What's more, since the increase is tacked onto your principal, rather than your mortgage rate, you don't gain any added tax deductions and you add to the amount you owe on your loan.

One way to make these mortgages more feasible is to put a limit, or "cap," on how much the monthly payments can go up. That is what some lenders in California and North Carolina do.

Under this arrangement, the payments would remain level in the initial years of the loan. Then the payments would go up and down as money-market costs changed. There wouldn't be any limit on how much the payments could decline. But there would be a cap, say 5% to 8%, on how much the monthly payment could go up each year. "Negative amortization," or increases in the unpaid balance of the loan, still could be a problem, though.

- Reverse Annuity Mortgage (RAM)—This is a mortgage designed to help older homeowners borrow against the increased values of their homes. A typical plan works like this: The homeowner gets a loan for up to 70% to 80% of his home's market value. Part of the loan may be paid to the homeowners in a lump sum and the rest is paid in monthly installments over five, 10 or 15 years. The homeowner repays the loan with smaller payments. The loan becomes due on a specific date or when a specific event occurs, such as sale of the property or the death of the borrower.

Here is an example of a reverse equity loan offered by Broadview Savings and Loan Company of Cleveland, Ohio, which pioneered a plan providing a monthly check of between $200 and $1,500 for up to 10 years:

A widow with a debt-free, $60,000 house borrowed $48,000. Broadview agreed to pay the sum over five years, in installments rising to $900 a month from $600. At the same time, the woman began repaying the loan with smaller payments based on a 30-year amortization of the loan and due to rise month by month. These payments would be $137.61 in the 12th month and $413.24 by the 60th month (when the homeowner would be getting $900 monthly).

After five years, the woman can continue paying off the debt according to the schedule already set, or she may be able to refinance it, or she can sell the property and pay off the debt in one lump sum.

Reverse mortgages still are offered only by a handful of savings and loan associations. One drawback is that the loans drain the owner's equity in the house. Also, if the house should decline in value, refinancing might not be available. And some critics note that most reverse annuity mortgages aren't true "annuity" arrangements because the owner could outlive the loan payments and lose their homes.

But efforts are underway to improve such loans and to insure permanent payments through other arrangements. Under one plan, the older homeowner would sell their home to an investor who would agree to allow the seller to remain in the home as long as the seller wished. The buyer also would purchase an annuity for the seller, who would then pay rent out of income from the installment payments from the buyer and from the annuity.

· Flexible Payment Mortgage (FLEX)—This is similar to a graduated payment mortgage because the payments are low in the initial years. With flexible payment mortgages, instead of paying both the principal and interest, you pay only the interest for the first five years. After that, the payments are increased enough to pay off the loan by the time agreed upon. Such mortgages are aimed at upwardly mobile buyers. And, of course, you eventually end up making higher payments than on a fixed rate mortgage in the same amount.

· Flexible Loan Insurance Program mortgage (FLIP)—A FLIP mortgage is a combined savings and buying program that lets you put part of your down payment into a savings account and keep it there. Each month, the lender withdraws part of the savings to supplement your monthly payments, which are lower-than-usual for the first five years. Eventually, you end up making higher payments than you would with a regular mortgage, but FLIP mortgages help buyers qualify for loans who otherwise couldn't.

· Deferred Interest Loan (DIL)—A DIL is the reverse of the interest-only loans. In this case, you pay a lower-than-usual interest rate at first to hold down your monthly payments. But you repay all of the deferred interest later in the term of the mortgage or when the house is sold. Again, payments go up—along with your income, you hope—as the years go by.

At the end of the period the lender receives the accumulated deferred interest, plus a fee. The cost advantage of DILs is gained only if the house is sold within the initial period. Otherwise, refinancing is required.

· Home Equity Loan Program (HELP)—Designed by a Las Vegas builder and a developer from Hawaii, this proposed program would have builders sell 80% of the house and rent the other 20%.

For instance, on a $76,125 house, purchased with 10% down and 30-year loan at 14% interest, the monthly payment would be $811.79. Under HELP, the payment would be $649.43. The income needed to qualify for the loan would drop to $31,173 with HELP, from $38,966 for a regular loan. And the number of families who could qualify would increase to 14.1 million from 7.7 million.

Under HELP, the buyer purchases 80% of the house outright and leases the other 20% with an option to buy. The builder collects a nominal but increasing rent on his 20% investment. If the house increases in value, the buyer will have enough equity in a few years to buy the builder's share. With a 10% annual appreciation, most buyers would end up owning 100% of their house in two to seven years.

How to Get a Mortgage

Once you've decided to buy a house, it's time to go and buy a mortgage. And we mean *buy* a mortgage, because that is what you are doing. And just as with your house, you want to get the best buy for your money.

- Shop around. Get names of lenders and call the loan departments. Find out what terms they are offering for loans. If you are dealing with a real-estate agent, the agent may be able to provide you with a listing of lenders and their rates.

Remember, you need to know more than the mortgage-contract rate to make a comparison. Find out if there are any application fees, whether you'll have to pay any points (as we said, one point is 1% of the mortgage amount), and the costs of any other fees. The best way to make a comparison is to ask for the annual percentage rate on the loan. This includes service charges, discount points or private mortgage insurance premiums and any penalties you will be charged if you pay off your mortgage early. The Truth-in-Lending law requires the lender who gives you a loan to give you a statement disclosing the annual percentage rate you will pay, but this isn't required at the time that you apply. So you'll have to ask for it.

- Find out about what kinds of loans the lender will make and what size of down payments are required. Generally, the bigger the down payment, the lower the interest rate. Find out if you can get a 30-year loan, or whether the lender will insist on a shorter term. Ask if someone can assume, or take over, your mortgage when you sell your house.

You'll also want to check these items, which could save you money in the long run:

- Can you pay off your loan ahead of time without paying penalty costs? Sometimes lenders charge a "pre-payment" fee if you pay off your loan before three years or so. Usually, you won't pay off your mortgage that soon unless you move and sell the house. But that could happen, so you should try to get a loan without pre-payment penalties. Such fees aren't allowed on FHA-insured and VA-guaranteed loans.

· Can you pay your property taxes and insurance? Usually, the lender pays these bills after collecting the money as part of your monthly mortgage payment. But in some states, lenders are required to pay you interest on the money that is set aside for such payments. If the lender doesn't want to pay you interest for such funds, you should see if you can pay these bills yourself. That way, you can put the money in a savings account and collect interest until the bills come due. Just remember to pay your tax bill, or the tax man could take your house.

· Can you get an "open-end" mortgage? This is a regular mortgage with a clause that allows you, after you've paid a certain amount on your loan, to borrow up to a specified amount to finance home improvements. The best deal is an arrangement that allows you to pay the same rate on your home-improvement financing as on your regular mortgage. Usually, however, a new interest rate would be charged for the added part of the mortgage. Generally, your monthly payments wouldn't go up with the added loan; instead, the length of the mortgage would be extended.

How to Figure Your Mortgage Payments

Before you sign up for a loan, you should sit down and figure your home-ownership costs and what you would be paying on your loan. In most cases, your monthly payment will be made up of four different expenses. They are the amount that goes to pay off the principal or the loan-amount itself; the interest on the loan; an amount roughly equal to 1/12th of your annual property taxes; and 1/12th of your annual homeowner's insurance premium. These four items—principal, interest, taxes, and insurance—are generally referred to as your PITI.

With most mortgages, the monthly principal and interest cost will stay the same throughout the life of your mortgage, but the monthly charges for taxes and insurance can go up. Generally, lenders require that you don't pay more than

25% to 30% of your gross income on your mortgage payment. But if your income potential is good, they may stretch that requirement.

You can figure your own monthly payments for principal and interest by using this simple table. To get your total monthly payment, add 1/12th of your estimated property taxes and homeowner's insurance cost.

Monthly Payment Table Per $1,000

	Duration of Loan (In Years)		
Annual Interest Rate	20	25	30
8¼	$ 8.525	$ 7.892	$ 7.517
8½	8.683	8.058	7.692
8¾	8.842	8.225	7.875
9	9.000	8.400	8.050
9¼	9.167	8.567	8.233
9½	9.325	8.742	8.417
9¾	9.492	8.917	8.592
10	9.813	9.087	8.780
10½	9.990	9.450	9.150
10¾	10.160	9.630	9.340
11	10.322	9.801	9.523
11½	10.664	10.165	9.903
12	11.011	10.532	10.286
12½	11.361	10.904	10.673
13	11.716	11.278	11.062
13½	12.074	11.656	11.454
14	12.435	12.038	11.849
15	13.168	12.808	12.640
16	13.913	13.589	13.270
17	14.668	14.378	14.060
18	15,433	15,174	15,071
19	16,207	15,977	15,889

Example: Monthly payment of principal and interest on a $33,400 mortgage loan for 30 years at 9¼%.

8.233	×	33.4	= $275 monthly
(from table)		(the number of thousands in the mortgage loan)	

In the beginning, very little of your monthly payment goes to paying off the principal. Most of it goes for interest, and over the lifetime of your loan the amount you pay in interest may total as much or more than the mortgage. Eventually, you pay more and more on the principal until the mortgage is paid off.

Consider, for example, a house purchased for $50,000 with a $10,000 down payment and a $40,000 mortgage payable over 25 years at a 9% annual interest rate. The monthly payment for principal and interest is $335.68. Of this, in the first year $298.40 is for interest, or about 89% of the monthly total.

Over the years, this is the way the outstanding balance on the $40,000 loan would change.

Table 8-1

Match Your Income to Mortgage Payments
(Figures Based on a 30-year Mortgage at 10% Interest Rate)

	$40,000 House		$50,000 House		$60,000 House	
	10% Down	20% Down	10% Down	20% Down	10% Down	20% Down
Down payment	$ 4,000	$ 8,000	$ 5,000	$10,000	$ 6,000	$12,000
Mortgage Amount	$36,000	$32,000	$45,000	$40,000	$54,000	$48,000
Monthly mortgage payment (principal and interest)	$315.93	$280.83	$394.91	$351.03	$473.89	$421.24
Insurance	$ 10.50	$ 10.50	$ 13.00	$ 13.00	$ 16.00	$ 16.00
Estimated Taxes	$ 61.00	$ 61.00	$ 76.00	$ 76.00	$ 91.00	$ 91.00
Total	$387.43	$352.33	$483.91	$440.03	$580.89	$528.24
Qualifying annual income range*						
25 percent	$18,597	$16,912	$23,228	$21,121	$27,883	$25,356
30 percent	$15,497	$14,093	$19,356	$13,201	$23,236	$21,130

*Annual mortgage payment and taxes and insurance should not exceed 25 to 30 percent of your gross annual income.

Applying For a Loan

When you apply, you will need the following items:

· A copy of the sales contract.
· The house location survey.

· The multiple-listing card for the house you bought
    (if you bought through a real-estate agent).
· A blank check, because you have to pay for the apprais-
    al fee (about $75 for houses under $100,000 and $100
    for those over) and a credit report (about $15 to $20).

Year	Outstanding loan balance of	
12 months	$39,549.00	
15 months	39,430.08	
9 years	34,042.40	
13 years & 6 months	30,076.40	
16 years & 9 months	23,247.60	
18 years & 4 months	19,960.80	(Halfway point on paying for house!)
19 years & 3 months	17,834.00	
21 years & 3 months	12,526.40	
23 years	7,054.80	
24 years & 6 months	1,620.40	
25 years	ALL PAID!	

Once you have applied for a loan, the first thing the lender
will do is run a credit check on you. If the credit agency calls
you for more details, be forthright—give all of the pertinent
information.

In determining what kind of terms to give you, the lender
will consider your income, your credit record, the stability of
your employment, how much debt you have, the appraisal of
the value of the house you are buying and the age and
characteristics of the house. You'll get extra points if you have
an established record of repayment on a previous house loan.

Perhaps most important, the lender will consider your
potential earning ability. If you are married, he also must
consider the income of your spouse. Until a few years ago,
many couples weren't able to qualify for the houses they
wanted because lenders refused to count the income of the
wife. Today, lenders not only must count a wife's income, but
they are forbidden to ask questions about whether a woman
plans to continue to work or whether she is planning to have
children. Under the Equal Credit Opportunity Act, lenders

WORKSHEET FOR MORTGAGE LOAN QUALIFICATIONS

Name **Robert J. and Maria S. Hall**   ROCKVILLE BANK AND TRUST COMPANY

Cost of Property $ **90,000**

Down Payment **18,000**   Down payment is **20** % Loan/Value **80** %

Mortgage Loan **72,000**   Interest Rate **13¾** % for **360** Months

1. **Monthly Housing Expense to Income Ratio** (MAXIMUM is 25%)

Income	Per Month	Housing Expense	Per Month	RATIO
Gross Normal	$ **2,400**	Principal & Int	$ **838.89**	Housing Expense
Co-Borrower	**1,450**	PMI	**N/A**	÷ Income
Dividends		Real Estate Tax	**95.00**	
Interest		Hazard Insurance	**23.11**	**957.00** / **3,850.00**
Rental (net)		Association Fee	**N/A**	
Other				RATIO **24.9** %
TOTAL	$ **3,850**	TOTAL HSG EXP (Ratio purpose)	$ **957.00**	**QUAL.**

2. **Monthly Debt to Income Ratio** (MAXIMUM is 33%)

Installment Debts (6 months or longer)	Per Month	
Revolving accounts	$ **40.00**	Total HSG EXP + Total Mo. Debt Pmts
First Nat'l Bank	**150.00**	Total Mo. Gross Income
Acme Fed'l Credit Union	**35.00**	$\frac{957.00 + 225.00}{3,850.00}$ = **30.7** %
TOTAL	$ **225.00**	**QUAL.**

3. **Cash required for settlement**

LIQUID ASSETS		CASH NEEDS	
Sales contract present house	$ ___ .	Contract sales price	$ **90,000**
Less ___ % commission		Est. settlement charges	+ **2,300**
Less mortgage & liens	.	R.E. Tax Escrow & Adj'mt	+ **1,140**
Less payoff of debts		Partial Assoc. fee	+ **N/A**
Plus savings	**17,500**	Less deposit	- **5,000**
Plus other (**Gift from parents**)	**5,000**	Less this mortgage loan	- **72,000**
TOTAL LIQUID ASSETS	$ **22,500**	TOTAL CASH NEEDS	$ **16,440**
NET SURPLUS/~~DEFICIT~~	$ **6,060** **OK**		

Qualified.
Harry S. Keller
HARRY S. KELLER
MORTGAGE REPRESENTATIVE

also can't discriminate against applicants because of their race, color, religion, national origin or marital status.

All of the good things you can bring up about your finances can help get you a mortgage or better terms on a mortgage. If you're in line for a big raise or promotion, have your boss put that in writing and pass the letter on to your lender when you apply for a mortgage. If you have been getting steady raises over the years, document that for the lender.

Take a look, too, at your present debts, including such things as car loans and revolving charge accounts. Lenders will look at all debt obligations that will take 8 to 10 months or longer to pay off. Generally, lenders require that your total monthly installment debt—including your house, car and credit-card payments—not exceed 33% of your gross monthly income. Again, that's being stretched by many lenders these days. But if you are saddled with some major debts, it's a good idea to pay off some of them before you apply for a mortgage loan. The less you owe elsewhere, the more you will be able to borrow to buy a home.

The lender also will want some assurance that you have enough money on hand to cover the down payment as well as the closing costs.

The application is gone over by the lender's loan committee, which approves or rejects it. If it is approved, the loan manager draws up a loan commitment stating interest rates and other terms of the loan and mails it to you for your signature. The commitment is good for a specified period—usually 60 to 90 days, or longer—and even if rates go up during that period, your contract is for the committed rate. But if you don't use it within the specified time, you have to negotiate a new loan. Before you sign the loan, you also should receive a Truth-in-Lending statement showing the annual percentage rate of the loan, including all charges.

What If You Don't Get the Loan?

Don't panic. If your mortgage application is rejected because your income is too low, you still have plenty of options:

- Increase the size of the down payment.
- Pay off your other debts.
- Try to stretch the repayment period from, say, 25 years to 30.
- Negotiate with another lender.
- Check into graduated-payment type mortgages.
- Save harder and try again later. Don't give up!

Closing Costs

The last home-buying step is the closing or settlement. This is when you, the seller, and the lender's representative all sit down together to complete the purchase so that you legally become the owner of your new home.

Right off, you should be aware that there are a lot of costs involved and that they have to be paid in cash at the time of settlement. The costs vary widely; they can amount to thousands of dollars in high-cost areas such as Washington, D.C., and hundreds of dollars in some non-metropolitan areas. Generally, you can count on about 5% of the sales price for closing costs. Thus, a $60,000 house will very likely require that you come up with $3,000.

The closing usually is held at the office of an attorney or title company. You should remember that the attorney represents the lender and not you. You all sit around the table, and the lawyer collects all the money that both the buyer and the seller are paying in closing costs. When all the money is paid and the papers are signed, the lawyer gives you the deed and keys to your new home.

In between, it is very complicated because the list of closing costs is long, complex, and, some critics think, excessive. Basically, they fall into two categories: one includes fees and other costs for arranging the loan and transferring the title. The other category involves prepaid items. For instance, the lender may require that you pay six months' or one-year's property taxes and insurance premiums ahead of time. The money is put into escrow, or a separate account, until the bills come due. As we said, you should try to get interest on this amount.

These are the major closing costs for borrowers. The actual amount you'll pay varies widely around the country. In some areas, sellers may pay some of these costs:

- Loan origination fee—The lender sometimes charges one point, or 1% of the mortgage amount, to make the loan. On a $50,000 loan, that amounts to $500. The seller also may be charged one point.

- Prepaid property taxes—This could range anywhere from a few hundred dollars to well over $1,000.

- Prepaid homeowners insurance—The lender will require you to take out a property insurance policy. The lender often collects the cost from you now as part of your monthly payment and pays the premium for you when it comes due.

- State and local transfer taxes—These can be anywhere from a couple of hundred dollars to well over $1,000.

- Title search fee—This is the cost of having an attorney or title insurance company search the title to your new home to make sure that there isn't any legal question that the home belongs to the seller.

- Title insurance premium—Just in case there is a flaw in the new title that wasn't found in the search, the lender takes out insurance to protect himself from a potential title problem. You, however, pay for the policy. If you want a separate homeowners title policy (you aren't covered by the lender's), you pay for that too. The cost for the title search and two policies can run from $100 to $250, depending on the price of the home. This is a one-time charge.

- Survey fee—If the lender requires it, you pay for a survey of the lot on which your new home is located. The cost: about $25–$75.

- Attorney's fee—You didn't think the closing attorney was doing this for nothing, did you? Figure on $100 to $300.

- Private mortgage insurance premium (if you are getting mortgage insurance).

There are also several other assorted costs ranging from notary fees to fees for preparing the documents.

Is this all necessary? Probably not. The complexity and costs of settlement procedures have been widely labeled excessive by critics ranging from Supreme Court Chief Justice Warren Burger to consumer advocate Ralph Nader.

Chief Justice Burger has contended that home-purchase closings are more complex—and therefore more costly—than they should be. In one speech, he said:

"When I began to practice law, the newest associate in the firm was assigned the task of examining titles and closing real-estate purchases. I examined many hundreds of land titles and closed an almost equal number of purchases and financing transactions. The costs at that time ranged from $15 to $30 for the purchase of a typical home.

"There is a growing practice of using title insurance, either as a substitute for, or in addition to, the lawyer's title option . . . the basic system of real-estate titles and transfers and the related matters concerning financing and purchase of homes cries out for re-examination and simplification. In a country that transfers not only expensive automobiles but multi-million-dollar airplanes with a few relatively simple pieces of paper covering liens and all, I believe that if American lawyers will put their ingenuity and inventiveness to work on the subject, they will be able to devise simpler methods than we now have."

In addition to the complexity of title searches, the costs of title checks and title insurance have come under fire from Ralph Nader's Housing Research Group. In a 1977 report, the Nader group charged that "consumers pay more than they should for title insurance because effective price competition is lacking in the title industry."

The group cited a study by the U.S. Department of Justice, which concluded that title-insurance costs aren't competitive because most buyers simply buy the insurance from whomever the lender or closing attorney recommends. "Due to lack of knowledge, lack of time and lack of interest, the purchaser of title insurance frequently exerts little influence on the selection of sellers," the Justice Department said.

Title insurance companies defend their services. But by shopping hard for title and settlement services, just as you do for the best loan buy, you can save money on closing costs.

Under the Real Estate Settlement Procedures Law, or RESPA, the lender is supposed to give you a "good faith" estimate of closing costs within three days after you apply for your mortgage. He should give you a copy of "A HUD Guide to Home Buyers," a publication of the U.S. Department of Housing and Urban Development. The law also requires that you be able to obtain a list of actual closing costs one day before you go to settlement.

The trouble with RESPA is that it requires much of the information to be given to you too late to do comparison shopping. So you'll have to do that on your own.

Among other things, you can save money by:

- Shopping around for a settlement attorney. Call several title companies and settlement attorneys and find out what they charge. (They're listed in the phone book.) You may be able to save some money.

- Shopping around for the cheapest survey. If your lender requires a survey of the property lines at the house you are buying, you may be able to find a surveyor who will do it for less than the one the lender hires. The best bet is the surveyor who did the job when the house previously changed hands, because you may be able to get a cut rate. This isn't a big saving, but every penny may count when you're buying a home.

- Shopping around for title insurance. Find out what company issued the title insurance to the current owner and check the same company. You should be able to get a reissue rate and save 10% to 25% if the policy was purchased in the past 10 years. Should you buy a homeowners title insurance policy? That's up to you. But if you don't, be sure to get a "record policy" indicating that the title search was done.

- Shop around for the most economic homeowners insurance policy. If you pay for it yourself instead of having the premiums taken out of your mortgage payments, be sure and take evidence that you have purchased a policy when you go to settlement.

You can save on other closing costs as well by comparing such costs with lenders when you shop for a mortgage. To help you determine your own closing costs in advance, we are including at the end of this chapter a work sheet for calculating a borrower's settlement costs and comparing costs of different lenders. The work sheet is reprinted from a Department of Housing and Urban Development booklet, "Settlement Costs and You."

Tight-Money Tips

When mortgage money is scarce, you may have a hard time getting any kind of home loan. If you can get one, there may be a limit on the size of the loan, you may have to make a bigger down payment than otherwise, and you most certainly will have to pay a higher interest rate. The added restrictions may make it harder for you to qualify for the loan.

Money gets tight for mortgages as a result of an overheated economy, or when the Federal Reserve Board (the government's central bank) keeps the nation's money supply at low levels and pushes all interest rates up. The Board often does this when it wants to cool inflationary money demands. When interest rates on short-term investments go up, many people stop putting their money in savings accounts, because the interest payment is limited by law, and instead put their funds into other higher-paying investments. As a result, the lending institutions lose money and you either can't get a loan or have to pay more for it.

What can you do?

· You could try to get an FHA-insured loan or, if you are eligible, a VA-guaranteed mortgage. These loans usually are still available during tight-money times because the lender can easily sell them to third parties, such as the Federal National Mortgage Association in Washington, D.C. FNMA—better known as Fannie Mae—is a privately held, federally-supervised buyer and seller of home mortgages. To aid the flow of mortgage funds when money gets scarce, Fannie Mae steps up her buying. The Federal Home Loan Mortgage Corp., or Freddie Mac, is another quasi-government concern that buys home mortgages. Though both Fannie Mae and Freddie Mac also buy conventional loans, FHA-VA loans are more marketable because they are backed by Uncle Sam.

· You can try to get a loan from a mortgage banker. You may have to pay a higher interest rate, but a mortgage banking company may be able to find the money for your loan. They are the major sellers of mortgages to Fannie Mae.

· Consider buying a newly built home. Builders often have financing available because they made mortgage-money commitments in advance with lenders. For that reason, the interest rate usually is lower than the prevailing rate because the loan was arranged before money got tight and rates went up.

· Find a seller who is willing to use "creative financing" to help you buy their home. Creative financing plans are based on two main elements: preservation of any existing loans on the house and some form of seller-backed financing, with either or both at below-market rates.

Here is a basic primer of creative-financing tools:

Assumption: You may not have to get a new loan if you can take over the mortgage and the monthly payments of the person who is selling the house. This also will offer the likely bonus of a lower interest rate than the going rate. However, you may have to come up with a big down payment if there is a big difference between the remaining amount of the mortgage and the sales price of the house. Also, lenders aren't very happy about somebody taking over a low-yielding mortgage and many have begun involving "due on sale" clauses that require a mortgage to be paid off when the home is sold. Some states require lenders to allow mortgages to be assumed, others don't, and the issue is in the courts in more than two dozen states. One alternative: many lenders will allow you to assume an existing loan if you agree to pay an interest rate that is higher than the one on the assumed loan, but less than the going market rate. All FHA and VA mortgages are automatically assumable.

Take-Back Mortgage: You can have the seller finance your purchase rather than going through a lender. Some sellers who own their homes free and clear are willing to act as the lender, usually with a 20% or so down payment and a below-market interest rate. They'll give you a 25-to-30-year mortgage and you pay them the monthly principal and interest. You would be responsible for paying property taxes and insurance. The seller retains a security in the home in case you default on the loan. Why would a seller be willing to wait so long for his money? For one reason, it may be the only way to find a buyer when mortgage money is scarce and costly. Or he may prefer installment payments for other reasons. An older couple, for instance, may be looking for a steady stream of retirement income—which would be your monthly payment.

Purchase-Money Mortgage: This is another type of owner-financing if the seller doesn't want to wait too long for his money. In this case, the seller agrees to give you a mortgage of, say, two to 10 years—although the payments are the same as they would be for a 25-to-30-year mortgage. At the end of the loan term, you have to renegotiate the loan or find new financing. But with the equity you have built up, it should be easier to get a regular mortgage.

Second Mortgage: If you come up a few thousand dollars short because of tighter lending requirements or the need to make a big down payment, you may be able to cover the difference by getting a second mortgage. This could be used to cover the extra costs associated with your home purchase, to put up a bigger down payment or to make up the difference between the restricted mortgage amount the lender will allow and what you need to pay for the home.

A second mortgage often is combined with a loan assumption or a take-back mortgage. If you want to assume a loan, but the down payment is more than you have in cash, sometimes the seller will accept a second deed of trust and you would make the payments directly to him. You are in a good position to negotiate such a loan at a favorable rate because the seller is anxious to sell and, because of the mortgage-money drought, he has a harder time finding a buyer. For example, take a $100,000 house that carries a first mortgage with an unpaid balance of $40,000. The buyer might make a $20,000 down payment and assume the 9% first mortgage, payable at $350 a month. Then the seller carries back a second deed of trust for the $40,000 balance at 12%, payable at $400 a month. The buyer thus pays a total of $750 a month and an overall interest rate of about 10½%. Just be sure you can afford both payments.

Wraparound Mortgage: This is a seller-financing arrangement that "wraps" old and new financing together. For example, take that $100,000 house with a $40,000 first mortgage at 9%. The buyer pays $20,000 down and owes $80,000, for which he gives the seller an all-inclusive deed of trust at 12% interest with payments of $800 a month. The seller agrees to continue paying the $350 a month on the old mortgage and keeps the remaining $450 a month. Wraparounds are popular because the seller, in this example, manages to sell his house and get a 12% return on $40,000 plus an interest bonus—the three-percentage-point spread between his old mortgage and the wraparound rate. The buyer gets a 12% loan in a 17% market. Again, lenders sometimes object to such loans because they remain stuck with the old, low-yielding mortgage.

But some lenders are starting to help arrange wraparounds to at least get part of the action.

Exchanges: Not to be confused with tax-free exchanges of income property, this device may be adapted to residential properties simply as a marketing tool. The buyer and seller exchange properties and then trade notes for any differences in values. Exchanges may involve a trading of real property, such as a home swap, or personal property of value, such as a diamond ring, in lieu of a down payment.

Although most creative financing is based on standard elements, "unlimited creativity is possible," said Richard Rosenthal, a Venice, California, realtor. He also said, "There's nothing sacred about the terms and conditions of a note." Within the basic framework of seller-backed financing, there is room for extra wrinkles, such as graduated payments for people who expect their income to rise.

How to Take the Profit out of Your Home without Moving

If you aren't planning to move in the near future, you may wonder what all this concern about buying a home as an investment means to you. Well, you don't have to be in the market for a home to be concerned about housing values. The fact is that your current home already is a big investment and one that you want to make sure keeps on growing.

That's why—just like home buyers—it is important that you keep up with what's happening to housing values in your area; you want to make sure your home, or investment, is generally keeping pace with increases elsewhere and not starting to slip. You should be on the alert for zoning changes and road-building that could hurt the value of your investment. When making home improvements, as we'll discuss in detail in a later chapter, you should consider what kinds of changes would add the most to the value of your home.

If you want to get the most out of your current housing investment, you have to protect it. The profit you have built up in your home may only be on paper now, but it may make a very real difference should you have to go back into today's high-priced housing market.

Even if you don't move, you can take the profit out of your house and use it while your investment keeps on growing. As a homeowner, you may have an untapped well of cash stored away. It is the profit you have already built up in your home as its value has appreciated over the years. Increasingly, homeowners are cashing in the rapidly rising values of their homes and using their profits to buy real estate or make other investments, to help pay the high cost of sending their kids to college, to make home improvements, to travel, or just to pay off bills.

How can you cash in on your profit without selling your house? There are a couple of ways:

Refinancing

One way is simply to trade in your old mortgage for a new one. This is called refinancing. In its simplest form, it works like this: you bought a home some years ago for $30,000 and took a $25,000 mortgage. Today, the value of your home has doubled to $60,000 and your mortgage is down to around $20,000. That means your equity—the difference between what you owe on your mortgage and what you could sell your house for—is $40,000. You could refinance your home with a new $30,000 mortgage which, after you paid off your old $20,000 loan, would give you $10,000 cash to use as you wish.

Of course, in the above example, you would end up with higher mortgage payments, both because of the increased loan amount and because the interest rate probably will be higher than that on your original loan. Also, when you refinance you pay closing costs, although they are substantially less than for a new loan. On a $30,000 new loan, you will pay about $700 (depending on where you live) for closing costs. And you may have to pay pre-payment penalties for paying off your loan entirely.

Because of such costs, you probably wouldn't want to refinance to take out a small amount of, say, less than $4,000. And if interest rates are high—in the 12% range, for instance—and you have a 6% loan, it probably wouldn't make sense to trade your cheap mortgage for a much costlier one.

But for some people, refinancing can make both dollars and sense. The best deal, of course, is to get a new loan with payments not much higher than before. That can happen, but chances are you will end up with a higher monthly payment.

Say that a person purchased a home in 1960 on a 25-year loan at a 6% interest rate. The sales price was $25,000 and he made a $3,000 down payment, leaving him with a $22,000 loan. Principal and interest payments on the house, which is now worth $60,000, total $144.32 per month. The owner decides to refinance his mortgage—with a balance of $9,600—at 11% and makes a loan for $40,000. His new monthly payments are increased to $392 per month, but he keeps the difference—$30,400—*in cash*.

If your income is going up, and you can easily manage the higher payment it may be worth it even when interest rates are higher. Let's say, for example, that 10 years ago you bought a $40,000 house with a $35,000 mortgage, at 6%. Your annual mortgage (principal and interest) payments are $2,700—or 18% of your income. Today, your house is worth $80,000 (you owe $26,600) and your income is $35,000. You can refinance for $55,000 at 11%, take out $28,400 cash, and you will still pay the same share of your income, or less, that you paid 10 years ago. In this case, you would pay $6,468 annually for principal and interest—or 18% of your income. And since you are in a higher tax bracket, the higher tax deduction will offset part of the increased payment.

Sometimes, refinancing even when rates are high can make sense. Of course, you wouldn't want to trade in a cheap mortgage for a high-priced one if all you're going to do is stick your cash in the bank. But if you have a chance for an investment that would pay a bigger return than you would lose by refinancing, getting a new loan might be the way to get your hands on the cash you need to make the investment. Each situation is different, and you have to sit down and "do the numbers"—figure both your costs and gains, including increased tax deductions from refinancing. And remember, your equity likely will continue to grow as the value of your home rises.

If you decide that you want to trade in a relatively cheap mortgage for a costlier one, your current lender may be willing to give you a cut-rate of, say 1% below the going interest cost, just to get rid of your old one. Some lenders will refinance only a portion of the value of your home, say 70% or 80%. But some may go higher if you are using the money to make a substantial improvement on the home. Also remember that if you have a FHA or VA loan, you would have to refinance with a conventional loan.

If your problem is that you got a loan when interest rates were high, you can save money simply by getting a new loan when rates go down. Make sure first, though, that you have held the mortgage long enough to avoid pre-payment penalties.

Refinancing isn't for everyone. But if you are sitting on a big profit in your home and don't plan to move soon, it can be something to consider. Refinancing to get a higher mortgage used to be unthinkable, "but values change when you have capital gains like these (in homes)," said Alan Greenspan, a former chairman of the President's Council of Economic Advisers in the Ford Administration. "People no longer think a mortgage is just something to take out to buy a home. It can be a means of cashing in on your gain," he said.

Second Mortgages

An alternative to refinancing is to take a second mortgage. This is another way to provide for your financial needs. You retain your cheap (first) mortgage and get a "junior" or second mortgage. It is called "junior" because the first has preference in case of a foreclosure.

As inflation continues to push up the price of houses, homeowners are taking increasing advantage of their "windfall" gain in equity by using it as collateral for a loan. Most second mortgages are written in the $4,000 to $10,000 range for a period of five to ten years with annual interest rates ranging from 11% to 18% or higher, depending on the risk factor and diverse state laws. Because of the greater security, second mortgages appeal to lenders. And the borrower usually commands a lower interest rate than is available on some other types of consumer loans.

In times when rates are high, second mortgages are especially attractive in relation to refinancing.

Ideally, taking out a new first mortgage can raise extra cash with no increase or a small increase in monthly payments. But the ideal situation may occur only if there is no penalty for prepaying the existing mortgage and if the interest rate on the new loan is equal to or less than the interest rate on the existing loan.

Generally, homeowners who wish to refinance existing mortgages find that they will have to replace low-rate loans with considerably higher-rate loans, increasing their total payments and finance costs.

An alternative: taking out a second mortgage. Although the interest rates on second mortgages are steep—12% to 16% is typical—borrowing on a second mortgage still can be cheaper than refinancing a first mortgage.

Here's an analysis by the National Consumer Finance Association, an organization of loan companies. It assumes an outstanding balance of $31,934.83 on a 6.75% first mortgage maturing in 17 years. The homeowner needs to raise an additional $8,500. To raise this amount by refinancing the existing mortgage plus $8,500 at 9.25% over 17 years would increase his monthly payments to $389.06 from $259.44. Over the next 17 years he would pay $79,368.24 of which $39,433.41 would be interest charges.

Taking out a 16.51%, $8,500 loan for 59 months would raise the homeowner's monthly mortgage payments to $479.74 over the 59-month period. However, because in this case he retains his lower interest first-mortgage loan, his total payments over 17 years amount to only $65,392.46, or $13,975 less than his total payments in taking out a new first mortgage.

It should be stressed that if the homeowner can borrow by any other means, he probably should do so. Unsecured personal loans generally may be had for less than 16.51%, and loans with securities as collateral may still be had for 10% or less. But in some circumstances, taking out a second mortgage could be more desirable—or at least less undesirable—than refinancing a first mortgage.[14]

Shop carefully before using the equity in your home to get cash from a second mortgage. Deal only with reputable lenders. Stay away from individuals who advertise second trusts in the open market. Also, remember that the interest rates advertised by some finance companies are higher than they seem. They may advertise 8% interest on a 36-month loan, but what they don't tell you is that you will be stuck with paying 8% for the full amount and not on the outstanding balance, even though you are repaying part of the loan each month. In such a case, the true interest rate is 14.55%. Remember, find out the annual percentage rate, which must be disclosed under the Truth-in-Lending Law.

By hand shopping, you probably will be able to get a

LOANS

ELI
STEIN

The Wall Street Journal

"Getting back to those interest rates, could you be a little more
specific than it's going to cost a pretty penny?"

second mortgage from a reputable lender at a reasonable
interest rate in most states (a few states, such as New York,
prohibit second mortgages). Below is a table showing a typical
repayment schedule for second mortgages offered by one
lender.

Second Mortgage Repayments
Annual Percentage Rate 14%

	Amount Financed	Monthly Payments	Total of Payments	Finance Charge
60 Months	$ 7,500.00	$174.51	$10,470.71	$ 2,970.71
	15,000.00	349.02	20,941.43	5,941.43
	25,000.00	581.71	34,902.38	9,902.38
84 Months	$ 7,500.00	$140.55	$11,806.21	$ 4,306.21
	15,000.00	281.10	23,612.41	8,612.41
	25,000.00	468.50	39,354.02	14,354.02
120 Months	$ 7,500.00	$116.45	$13,973.98	$ 6,473.98
	15,000.00	232.90	27,947.96	12,947.96
	25,000.00	388.17	46,579.93	21,579.93

If you are getting along in years, you should think twice about getting a refinanced mortgage or a second mortgage. You may want to avoid higher payments if you will still be paying them as you move into your retirement years when your income likely will shrink.

SETTLEMENT COSTS WORK SHEET Use this worksheet to compare the charges of various lenders and providers of settlement services.		Provider 1	Provider 2	Provider 3
800.	**ITEMS PAYABLE IN CONNECTION WITH LOAN:**			
801.	Loan Origination Fee %			
802.	Loan Discount %			
803.	Appraisal Fee to			
804.	Credit Report to			
805.	Lender's Inspection Fee.			
806.	Mortgage Insurance Application Fee to			
807.	Assumption Fee			
808.				
809.				
810.				
811.				
900.	**ITEMS REQUIRED BY LENDER TO BE PAID IN ADVANCE:**			
901.	Interest from to @ $ per day			
902.	Mortgage Insurance Premium for months to			
903.	Hazard Insurance Premium for years to			
904.	years to			
905.				
1000.	**RESERVES DEPOSITED WITH LENDER:**			
1001.	Hazard insurance months @ $ per month			
1002.	Mortgage insurance months @ $ per month			
1003.	City property taxes months @ $ per month			
1004.	County property taxes months @ $ per month			
1005.	Annual assessments months @ $ per month			
1006.	months @ $ per month			
1007.	months @ $ per month			
1008.	months @ $ per month			
1100.	**TITLE CHARGES:**			
1101.	Settlement or closing fee to			
1102.	Abstract or title search to			
1103.	Title examination to			
1104.	Title insurance binder to			
1105.	Document preparation to			
1106.	Notary fees to			
1107.	Attorney's fees to			
	(includes above items numbers:)			
1108.	Title insurance to			
	(includes above items numbers:)			
1109.	Lender's coverage $			
1110.	Owner's coverage $			
1111.				
1112.				
1113.				
1200.	**GOVERNMENT RECORDING AND TRANSFER CHARGES:**			
1201.	Recording fees Deed $; Mortgage $; Releases $			
1202.	City/county tax/stamps. Deed $; Mortgage $			
1203.	State tax/stamps. Deed $; Mortgage $			
1204.				
1205.				
1300.	**ADDITIONAL SETTLEMENT CHARGES:**			
1301.	Survey to			
1302.	Pest inspection to			
1303.				
1304.				
1305.				
1400.	**TOTAL SETTLEMENT CHARGES**			

NINE

Gimme Shelter:
You and the Tax Man

"Some taxpayers figure the IRS
might as well use this simplified
form: 1. How much did you make
last year? 2. How much did you
spend? 3. What do you have left? 4.
Mail it in."

—*U.S. News & World Report*

For most people, taxes are no laughing matter. But home-owners are one group of taxpayers who often have the last laugh on the tax man.

The reason is that your home, in addition to giving you a roof over your head, also provides you with a sturdy shelter from taxes. Your home comes with a host of built-in tax deductions that help lower your federal, state and local income taxes. What's more, if you sell your home for a profit, the tax on that profit is deferred if you trade up to a costlier home; if you decide to take the money and run, the bite still isn't as deep as with other taxes.

In short, owning a home is one of America's biggest tax breaks. And that is no accident. On the assumption that the American dream of a home-of-your-own is the American Way, it is the policy of the federal government to encourage home ownership by making it easier for people to own their homes. Through the years, the major focus of this policy has been tax breaks that help reduce the costs of home ownership. Even more home-ownership tax breaks are provided by state and local governments.

It's true that the tax laws are complicated. But the simple fact is that taking advantage of the many tax breaks available to you as a homeowner can save you money. And don't feel there is anything un-American about using those advantages. After all, Uncle Sam must have wanted homeowners to benefit from tax deductions because there are so many of them.

The Basic Homeowner Tax Deductions

If you itemize your tax deductions—and most homeowners do—two income-tax deductions stand head and shoulders above all others.

- *Mortgage Interest:* The interest you pay on your mortgage as part of your monthly house payment is deductible from your income when figuring your federal, state and local income taxes. As noted earlier, the interest you pay is highest in the first years of your mortgage, so the deductions are biggest then, too. For example, interest payments on a 25-year, $40,000 mortgage at an 11½% interest rate total about $4,844 the first year after you buy the home. This $4,844 is tax deductible.

Your lender will send you a statement each year at tax time showing how much interest you paid the previous year.

- *Property Taxes:* It may hurt to pay those property tax bills on your home, especially if they are going up as home values in your area escalate. But the good news is that those taxes also are deductible. Again, if your lender pays your taxes for you out of money he collects as part of your monthly payment, he will send you a statement telling you how much you can deduct. If you pay the taxes yourself, you will know the total from the bill you paid to your local government.

Deductions for mortgage interest and property taxes are the biggest tax savers for homeowners. In 1978, 40 million Americans claimed nearly $11 billion for such deductions.

These deductions lower the real cost of owning your home. The tax benefits increase as your family's income rises, pushing you into higher tax brackets.

Consider, as an example, the tax savings for a family in which the father earns $23,000 a year, the wife doesn't have a job outside the home, and they have two children. Let's say that a year ago the family put 10% down on a $55,000 home and started paying on a $49,500 mortgage for 25 years at a 9% annual interest rate.

The family's monthly mortgage payments—including principal and interest, private mortgage insurance, property taxes and homeowners insurance—would be about $500. But the deductions for interest and taxes, which would total about $5,300 for the full year, make the tax savings for the year about $1,100 compared with the same family's taxes if they didn't have the homeowner deductions.

The tax savings amount to about $90 a month. Thus, a family's monthly mortgage payment, in effect, is reduced by about 18% from $500 to $410. The actual savings would be even higher, because the same deductions would lower the family's state income-tax bill as well. What's more, the house probably would have increased in value that year, and that, along with the small amount being paid to principal, adds to their equity in their home.

Individual situations vary, of course. But, except in the last years of a mortgage, interest and property-tax deductions mean lower tax bills for most homeowners. You can figure it out for yourself by determining your tax bill using your current deductions and then figuring what your bill would be with the deductions you estimate you would have if you bought a house, moved up to a house with a bigger mortgage, or refinanced your existing mortgage.

Other Homeowner Tax Deductions

Although mortgage-interest and property-tax deductions are the heavyweights of homeowner tax savings, there are a variety of other potential tax savings that you should keep an eye out for. They include:

- *Interest payments:* The interest you pay on most loans is tax deductible. That includes not only the interest you pay on your home mortgage, but also the interest on any home improvement loans or on a second mortgage.

· *Utility Taxes:* Check your gas and electric bills closely. If part of the bill is for a utility tax that is at the same general rate as your state or local sales tax, then the utility tax is deductible just as a sales tax is.

· *Energy saving and the 1978 Tax Bill:* Now you can save energy and lower your federal income taxes at the same time. Under the tax-cut bill passed by Congress in 1978, certain home improvements that conserve energy are eligible for federal tax credits. Unlike tax deductions, the tax credits are subtracted from your final tax bill.

You can get a credit equal to 15% of the first $2,000 you spend to install eligible energy-conserving items, or a maximum credit of $300.

The credit can be used for the following items:

· Insulation.

· Furnace replacement burner.

· Automatic flue opening modifier.

· Automatic furnace ignition system.

· Exterior storm or thermal doors and windows.

· Automatic setback thermostat.

· Electric energy usage display meter.

· Exterior caulking or weatherstripping.

The new tax credit covers energy-conserving items installed between April 20, 1977, and December 31, 1985. The credit can only be used for improvements on principal residences, not vacation homes or second homes. But it only covers existing homes that were substantially built before April 20, 1977—homes built after that date aren't eligible. Cooperative apartment owners and condominium owners can use the credit as well as owners of single-family homes.

To limit the paperwork, you can't claim tax credits of less than $10 in one year. But you can save up your credits and claim them in a subsequent year when the total exceeds $10.

Homeowners (and renters) who install solar, wind or geothermal energy devices get a tax break, too. You can take a credit of 40% on the first $10,000 of such outlays, plus 20% of the next $8,000, for a maximum credit of $4,000.

The rules generally are the same as for installing insulation or other energy-saving improvements. The major exception is that the credit for solar, wind and geothermal energy devices covers homes built after April 19, 1977, as well as those built before.

For 1978, the first year for which the tax credits could be taken, about 6 million taxpayers claimed energy credits totaling $600 million, or an average of $100 per return. The IRS, however, has taken a narrow view of what is covered by the law. Items that it has ruled aren't eligible for the credit include carpeting, drapes, wood paneling, heat pumps, enclosed fireplaces and siding, even siding with insulating qualities. For further information, get a copy of IRS Publication No. 903, "Energy Credits for Individuals."

More energy tax credits may be added. The IRS is reviewing some of the exempted items, such as siding, so watch for new rulings. And in early 1980 Congress was about to expand tax credits for energy-efficient improvements as part of the legislation to place a "windfall profits" tax on oil companies.

- *State tax breaks:* In addition to the federal tax credits, your state also may offer tax breaks for energy-conserving improvements. You can get a tax credit or other tax incentives for installing solar heating devices in more than 20 states. These include Alaska, Arizona, Arkansas, California, Colorado, Connecticut, Georgia, Hawaii, Idaho, Kansas, Maine, Massachusetts, Montana, New Jersey, New Mexico, North Carolina, North Dakota, Oklahoma, Oregon, Texas, Vermont and Wisconsin.

In California, for example, you can get an income-tax credit of 55% of the cost of installing a solar system in a home, up to a maximum of $3,000. In Texas, the purchase of solar devices are exempted from the state sales tax. In Arkansas, the cost of installing solar equipment can be deducted from gross income. Check the tax office in your state for details on what solar tax breaks are available in your area.

- *Tax breaks for the elderly:* Many states have passed special tax credits for elderly homeowners faced with declining incomes and rising property taxes. An upward reassessment of homes on a street of elderly homeowners on fixed incomes can be a terrible blow, and some retired people find they can't afford to keep their homes.

To aid such homeowners, at least 29 states and the District of Columbia have adopted what is called a "circuit breaker" law that reduces the taxes owed by elderly people, usually those in their 60s and older, who meet certain income requirements. In 1977, those 30 jurisdictions paid out almost $1 billion in tax relief to five million households.

The Wall Street Journal

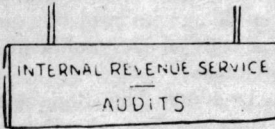

"First, the good news — you're in the running for our chutzpah-of-the-month award."

The states that offer such help are: Arizona, Alabama, California, Colorado, Connecticut, Hawaii, Idaho, Illinois, Indiana, Iowa, Kansas, Maine, Maryland, Michigan, Minnesota, Missouri, Nevada, New Mexico, New York, North Dakota, Ohio, Oklahoma, Oregon, Pennsylvania, Rhode Island, Utah, Vermont, West Virginia and Wisconsin, plus the District of Columbia.

Some states also offer other programs. In California, a 1977 law allows elderly homeowners to postpone payment of all or part of the tax on their homes. Actually, the state pays the tax for them and puts a lien on their property; interest of 7% is charged on the amount postponed. But the owners can put off payment indefinitely. The amount isn't payable until the home is sold, or the owners die, in which case their estate or heirs would pay off.

Major requirements are that all owners, except a spouse, live in the home and be at least 62 years old. Combined household income can't exceed $20,000 a year. About 400,000 applications were mailed to elderly homeowners the first year; officials didn't expect more than 10,000 to apply.

· *Damage to your home:* If a storm destroyed your garage door or tore off your roof, if part of your home or your furniture was damaged by fire, or if you suffered property damage because of a flood, part of the cost of losses may be tax deductible. Basically, casualty losses over $100 that aren't covered by insurance payments can be deducted. But your claims about the value of your property losses must be documented. It also helps to have pictures of your property before the damage and after the damage.

For example:	
Damage	$1,000
Less insurance payments	750
Damage	$ 250
Less $100 limit for each occurrence	$ 100
Tax deduction	$ 150

You also can deduct the cost of damage to your property caused by a contractor who, say, while adding a kitchen on the back of your home demolishes your patio and refuses to fix it. But you must make a serious effort to get him to repair the damage. If the amount is large enough, that means hiring a lawyer. Simply mailing complaint letters to the contractor may not be adequate proof of a "serious" effort.

You also may be able to deduct a bad debt connected with a home improvement. Say, for example, that the painter you hired (and paid in full) painted only half your house and refuses to do the rest—leaving you stuck with a house that is half green and half pink. But again, you must show that you made a serious effort to get the work completed or your money back.

- *Theft deductions:* If you don't catch the thief and get your jewelry or other stolen property back, you can deduct the loss of burglarized property. However, you will have to convince IRS that a criminal theft occurred. Again, you can deduct any loss over $100 that isn't covered by insurance reimbursements. Again, too, you'll need documentation regarding the value.

For more detailed discussion of casualty and theft losses, go to your local IRS office and get a free copy of publication 547, "Tax Information on Disasters, Casualty Losses and Thefts."

- *Home office deduction:* If you use a room, or part of a room, in your home as an office for business purposes, you may be able to claim the office as a tax deduction. But this isn't as easy as it used to be. The 1976 tax law substantially tightened the requirements for this claim, and the IRS also takes a narrow view of what qualifies as a home office.

Basically, you must meet two requirements:

One: You must be able to prove that the use of the room is needed for "the convenience of your employer." That means your boss must require you do work at home as part of your job. Moreover, a home office is deductible only if your employer doesn't provide you with local office space to do the work. Hence, a salesman or commissioned agent or other official who lives in, say, Detroit for a company headquartered in New York could have a room set up in his home as a tax-deductible office. An office also is generally acceptable for self-employed individuals such as writers, artists, consultants, doctors and lawyers who have no other office available to them. But if you could simply stay late at your own employer's office to do your work, then your home office may not pass the IRS's test. The best thing to do is to get a letter from your employer stating that a home office (or work-space) is required.

Two: Your home office must be used for business and not for personal enjoyment or convenience. If it is also used as a den or TV room, then you can deduct only a part of it for business use. The best way to prevent a hassle with the IRS is physically to separate the working space—such as by using a converted garage or a separate room.

If you claim a room as an office deduction, you can deduct a portion of the operating costs of your house. For example, if you own an eight-room house and use one room as an office, you can deduct one-eighth of your gas, electric and phone bills, homeowners insurance, maintenance costs, mortgage interest and property taxes (but be sure to subtract the interest and property-tax allocations from your total interest and property-tax deductions).

An even more accurate method of figuring deductions is to determine the square footage of your office as a percentage of the total footage of your home. Thus, if your office is 12 feet by 15 feet, or 180 square feet, and your home contains 1,800 square feet of floor space, then you would allocate 10% of your total costs as business expenses.

- *Home office improvements:* If you have a legitimate home office, you can deduct the cost of redecorating or improving it. Thus, if you put in new carpeting, a new desk or other equipment, the cost can be written off—not all in one year, but over a period of a few years.

- *Home office tax traps:* There are limits on what you can deduct for an office at home, so check with the IRS or a tax adviser. Also, be warned that should you sell your home, the IRS may try to tax your profit on that portion of the home you claimed for an office-at-home deduction, even if your claim wasn't allowed. Consider the following item from The Wall Street Journal's Tax Report:

AN OFFICE AT HOME wasn't deductible anymore, but it remained a tax trap.

A woman, referred to only as "Mrs. A" by the IRS, claimed 35% of her home was used for business, as an office needed for her school principal's job. She was allowed an office-at-home deduction for the years 1971–1975. But in 1976, Congress toughened the rules for the office-at-home deduction and she didn't qualify. That also was the year she sold her home and bought another.

Normally the gain from selling a home isn't taxed if another is bought within 24 months and the purchase price at least equals the sales price of the old house. This benefit applies only to a taxpayer's principal residence. Mrs. A's at-home office meant that 35% of her home was used for business and didn't qualify for the tax break on home sales, even though she couldn't deduct the office, the IRS said.

She should be taxed on 35% of the gain from selling her home, the IRS concluded.

- *Home improvements for medical reasons:* Some home improvements are tax deductible as medical expenses if they are done on a doctor's prescription. For instance, if you or a member of your family has asthma and your doctor prescribes central air-conditioning (perhaps with special filters) to help alleviate the asthma, you can write off the installation costs. Such deductible home improvements also could be projects like installing an elevator for people with heart trouble or a swimming pool for someone who needs physical therapy.

But you can deduct only the portion of the total cost that exceeds the added value of the item to your home. For example, if you pay $4,000 for the installation of a new air-conditioning system, and the new system adds a value of $2,500 to your home, you are allowed a $1,500 deduction as a medical expense. Remember, too, that all such home improvements made for medical reasons must be thoroughly documented.

- *Vacation Home:* If you buy a second home at the seashore, in the mountains or anywhere, you can deduct some of the costs of purchasing and maintaining it. But, as with home-office deductions, the tax writeoffs for vacation homes are restricted more than they used to be.

Before the 1976 tax laws changed the vacation-home rules, many people used their vacation homes whenever they wanted, rented them out when they could, and claimed the whole thing as a "rental" business for tax purposes. As a result, they were able to claim tax-deductible losses, since the expenses usually out-stripped the income from a few months' rental.

You can still use tax deductions to offset the cost of a vacation home, but if you want to write off business costs you have to meet certain requirements. The new rules are these:

1. If you use your vacation home mainly for personal use and rent it for less than 15 days a year, then you can't deduct any rental expenses. You also don't have to report any profit you make from rentals for less than 15 days. You can, of course, deduct the mortgage interest and property taxes, just as you can on your primary home.

2. You can claim certain rental deductions if you rent your second home for more than 15 days. But if you use the home yourself for more than 14 days in one year, or more than 10% of the total number of days that you rent to others, whichever is greater, then the amount of your deduction is limited to your gross rental income.

For example, let's say you use your beach condominum apartment yourself for four weeks in the summer and rent it out for eight weeks for a gross rental of $3,200. Your annual costs are $2,000 mortgage interest, $400 property taxes, $1,000 for maintenance and utilities, and $2,000 depreciation. That adds up to $5,400.

The most you can deduct is the $3,200, the same amount as your gross rental income. Since you used the home two-thirds of the time for rental, you first deduct two-thirds of the interest and tax payments—or $1,800—from the $3,200 rental. The remaining $1,400 is the limit that you can deduct for maintenance and utility costs plus depreciation.

In this case, two-thirds of the $3,000 in maintenance and utility costs plus depreciation is $2,000. But you may only deduct $1,400 of that for a total deduction of $3,200.

Of course, you also can deduct the rest of your mortgage interest and property taxes as well.

3. If you use your vacation home for less than 14 days, or 10% of the total rental time, you can claim full deductions as

a business expense. But you will have to show that it is a profit-motivated venture, and you may have to show a profit from rentals for at least two years during a five-year period.

If you can comply with the requirements, then you are entitled to claim full deductions for not only mortgage interest and property tax but also for all your maintenance, utility costs, depreciation and other costs connected with renting your unit. And you can claim a loss when expenses exceed rental income.

But you will need detailed records on when and to whom you rent your second home, plus records of your own use, to back up your claims. Indeed, you should keep records to back up your vacation-home deductions in any case.

Which Closing Costs Are Tax Deductible

When you pay closing costs while buying a home, some costs are deductible, but most aren't. You can deduct:

- *Points:* When a loan-origination fee is charged in the form of "points," you can deduct the cost from your income that year. Thus, if you paid one point, or one percent, on a $50,000 mortgage, that is $500 you can deduct. But the seller cannot deduct points paid on VA or FHA loans to his buyer, because such points are considered a reduction in the price of the home, not a loan fee.

- *Prepaid Interest:* When you buy a home, you will be charged for the interest on the mortgage between the time the loan is closed and the time you start making payments. This interest is part of your regular mortgage interest, and it is tax-deductible. Just be sure you don't deduct it twice when deducting the mortgage interest you pay for a whole year. Prepaid interest may be included on the year-end statement you receive from the lender.

- *Property-Tax Adjustments:* When you get to settlement, you may have to reimburse the seller for a share of the property taxes he already may have paid on the house you are buying. This tax, like all property taxes, is deductible.

Most other closing costs aren't tax deductible—including transfer taxes, attorney fees, title search fees and other charges. But keep all your records. Closing costs can be used when you sell your home to offset any profit—and tax obligation—you might have.

Deferred Taxes When You Sell

If you sell your home and make a big profit, that profit is taxable. But another bonus of home ownership is that chances are you won't have to pay any tax on your profit. If you reinvest in another principal residence that costs as much as, or more than, your older one within 24 months after you sold your old home, then the taxes on the profit are deferred indefinitely.

Let's say, for example, that you bought a home 10 years ago for $20,000 and you sell it for $35,000. That means you made a gross profit of $15,000. But if you buy another house and reinvest the entire $35,000—or more—then the profit on the sale of your old home won't be taxed for now.

And remember, you don't actually have to put all your cash-profit into the new home. You can make a low enough down payment, if you wish, so that you can keep some of the profit. You just have to buy a home costing as much as or more than the one you sold.

Moreover, your "profit" actually is smaller than the difference between what you paid for your old home and what you sold it for. The IRS lets you add certain costs to the price you paid for your old home and to subtract certain costs from the selling price. As a result, your "profit" is narrowed for tax-reporting purposes.

Although you don't pay taxes on your profit, you must report it when you sell a home and buy another one. This is done on a special IRS Form 2119, "Exchange or Sale of Personal Residence."

Here's what you do:

· First figure the selling price of your home. That's easy enough. That is how much the buyer paid for it.

· Next subtract your selling expenses. If you paid a real-estate commission to sell your house, subtract that.

Also subtract any "points" you paid at settlement time, including the points for a VA or FHA loan arranged for the buyer. You also can deduct any legal fees or closing costs.

The selling price minus selling costs equal the "amount realized," as the IRS puts it, from the sale of your home.

· Next you have to figure the "basis" of the home you sold. That's tax talk for how much it cost you, including buying costs.

Again, you start with the price you paid for the home. Then add those closing costs, including attorney's fees and transfer taxes that weren't tax deductible when you bought the place.

· Also add the costs of any home improvements that you made to the house, like remodeling the kitchen. Remember, these must be improvements and not normal repairs, like fixing the furnace. What's the difference between home improvements and routine repairs? The IRS explains it this way:

A home improvement materially adds to the value of your home, appreciably prolongs its useful life or adapts it to new uses. Putting in a recreation room in your unfinished basement, adding another bathroom or bedroom, putting up a fence, putting in new plumbing or wiring, installing a new roof or paving your driveway are improvements that are added to the basis of your home.

But, the IRS says,

A repair merely maintains your home in an ordinary efficient operating condition. It doesn't add value to your home, or appreciably prolong its life. Repainting your house inside or outside, fixing your gutters or floors, mending leaks and plastering and replacing broken window panes are examples of repairs.

But if the repairs are part of an extensive remodeling or restoration of a home, the entire job is considered an improvement and can be added to the cost-basis of a home, the IRS adds.

In any case, it is important that you keep detailed records of all home improvements, closing costs and selling costs. Otherwise, your cost claims probably won't stand if they are challenged by the IRS. Don't wait until the IRS comes calling. Start a record now. Put all your bills for home improvements and other costs in a file as you pay them.

For details on such costs, get IRS publication 530, "Tax Information for Homeowners."

· Now you take your selling price adjusted for selling expenses and subtract the "adjusted" cost of your old home after adding costs and improvements. The difference is your gain, or profit.

But wait; you can shrink that, too.

· You can subtract the cost of "fixing-up" repairs from the selling price of your home. These are things like having the house painted or the gutters repaired in order to get your home ready to sell. But to qualify, the repairs must be done during the 90-day period before the contract to sell your home is signed and the work must be paid for within 30 days after the date of the sale. Also the fixing-up expenses are considered only in determining the gain on which your tax is postponed. The costs aren't deductible in determining the actual profit on the sale of your old home.

· After subtracting fix-up costs, you have the "adjusted" sales price of your home. If the home you buy is more than that price, then the tax on your gain is postponed. But you subtract the deferred gain from the cost of your new home. That figure, then, becomes the base cost of your home the next time you sell.

Here is an example of how all this would work on a house you bought for $50,000 and sold for $70,000:

1. Selling price of old home	$50,000
Less selling expenses	3,000
Amount realized	$47,000
2. Basis of old home (with closing costs)	$32,000
Add: Improvements (family room)	4,000
Adjusted basis of old home	$36,000
3. Gain on old residence (1 minus 2)	$11,000
4. Amount realized on old home	$47,000
5. Less fix-up expenses (painting)	500
Adjusted sales price	$46,500
6. Cost of new home	$70,000
7. Gain to be taxes	-0-
8. Gain to be deferred	$11,000
9. Basis of new home (6 minus 8)	$59,000

If you sell your home and buy a cheaper one, you will owe taxes only on that part of your gain that isn't offset by your new home purchase. For example, says the IRS, if the adjusted sales price of your home is $29,000 and the cost of your new home is $28,600, you will owe taxes on a $400 gain ($29,000 − $28,600 = $400); the rest of your gain is deferred.

Until 1978, homeowners could defer taxes on the profit from a home sale only once within an 18-month period. As a result, many people who transferred job locations more than once during 18 months—and who bought and sold a home each time—got stuck with paying taxes on their home-sale profits even though they reinvested in another home. Under the 1978 tax-cut bill, you may be able to defer your profit more than once during an 18-month period if you move for employment purposes (Now 24 months).

Here is what Congress said would be required:

"Taxpayers generally will be allowed the benefits of this multiple rollover provision where there was a reasonable expectation at the time of the relocation that the taxpayer would be employed, or remain at the new location, for a substantial period of time. Thus, where the taxpayer is entitled to deduct moving expenses with respect to relocation falling within the 18-month period, the multiple rollover provision would be available so as to allow the nonrecognition of gain on the sale of a principal residence occupied by the taxpayer if, in fact, the taxpayer subsequently relocated within the 18-month period for employment purposes and acquired a new principal residence.

"However, in order to qualify for such treatment, a sale must be connected with the commencement of work by the taxpayer as an employe or as a self-employed individual at a new principal place of work, and that the taxpayer must satisfy both the geographic and length of employment requirements for deductibility of moving expenses."

For more details, you can get a copy of the IRS booklet, "Tax Information on Selling or Purchasing Your Home." But don't expect too much help from the helpful examples. Either the IRS booklet hasn't been updated in ages or IRS officials haven't purchased a home for a long time. About all of the detailed examples are about people who sell houses for under $30,000 and move down to a cheaper one—hardly a realistic prospect these days.

Taking Your Profit; Capital Gains and the 1978 Tax Bill

If you sell your home for a profit and don't buy another home—or if you buy a home that costs less than the one you sold—then you will owe federal taxes on your profit. But if you owned and occupied your home for at least one year the profit is considered a capital gain—a profit from the sale of real estate, stock and other capital assets. As a result, you will pay a capital-gains tax, which is lower than the tax you would pay if your profit were taxed at ordinary income-tax rates. The regular rates range from 14% to 70%, depending on your income.

The tax you pay on a capital gain was substantially lowered even more by Congress in the 1978 and 1981 tax-cut bills. The way it works is that you exclude 60% of your profit from your taxable income and then pay taxes on the remaining 40% at your regular tax rate. In effect, your entire profit is taxed at rates ranging from a low of 5.6% to a high of 20%, depending on your income bracket.

Under the old law, only 50% of your profit could be excluded from income. And, including certain other charges, the effective capital-gains rates ranged from a low of 7% to as high as 48%.

Here's an example of how to figure the capital gain and taxes on a home sale. Let's say you bought a home 15 years ago for $25,000 and sell it for $80,000. Then you buy a small condominium for $30,000. Your profit from the sale would be

254 THE COMPLETE BOOK OF HOME BUYING

Form 2119 (Rev. Oct. 1977)
Department of the Treasury
Internal Revenue Service

Sale or Exchange of Personal Residence

▶ Attach to Form 1040.

Taxable year: **1978**

Note: Do not include expenses which are deductible as moving expenses on Form 3903.

Name(s) as shown on Form 1040: **Herman and Henrietta Homeowner**

Your social security number: **123 : 45: 6789**

1(a) Date former residence sold: **July 4, 1978**

(b) Have you ever deferred any gain on the sale or exchange of a personal residence? — No: X

(c) Have you ever claimed a credit for purchase or construction of a new principal residence? (If "Yes," see Form 5405.) — No: X

2(a) Date new residence bought: **July 3, 1978**

(b) If new residence was constructed for or by you, date construction began

(c) Date you occupied new residence: **Sept. 1, 1978**

(d) Were both the old and new properties used as your principal residence? — Yes: X

(e) Were any rooms in either residence rented or used for business purposes at any time? (If "Yes," explain on separate sheet and attach.) — No: X

(f) If you were married, do you and your spouse have the same proportionate ownership interest in your new residence as you had in your old residence? (If "No," see the Consent on other side.) — Yes: X

3(a) Were you 65 or older on date of sale? (If "Yes," see Note below.) — No: X

(b) If you answered "Yes" to 3(a), did you use the property sold as your principal residence for a total of at least 5 years (except for short temporary absences) of the 8-year period preceding the sale?

(c) If you answered "Yes" to 3(b), do you want to elect to exclude gain on the sale from your gross income?

Computation of Gain and Adjusted Sales Price

4 Selling price of residence. (Do not include selling price of personal property items.)	4	$50,000
5 Less: Commissions and other expenses of sale (from Schedule I on other side)	5	3,000
6 Amount realized	6	47,000
7 Less: Basis of residence sold (from Schedule II on other side)	7	36,000
8 Gain on sale (subtract line 7 from line 6). If line 7 is more than line 6, there is no gain, so you should not make further entries on this form. A loss on the sale of a personal residence is nondeductible	8	11,000
9 Fixing-up expenses (from Schedule III on other side)	9	500
10 Adjusted sales price (subtract line 9 from line 6)	10	46,500

If you answered "No" to question 3(a) or 3(c), complete lines 11 through 14.
If you answered "Yes" to question 3(c), complete lines 15 through 17, or 15 through 20, whichever is applicable.

Computation of Gain to be Reported and Adjusted Basis of New Residence—General Rule

11 Cost of new residence	11	$70,000
12 Gain taxable this year (line 10 less line 11, but not more than line 8). If line 11 is more than line 10, enter zero. Enter here and on Schedule D (Form 1040), in column f, line 1, or line 6, whichever is applicable	12	0
13 Gain on which tax is to be deferred (subtract line 12 from line 8)	13	11,000
14 Adjusted basis of new residence (subtract line 13 from line 11)	14	59,000

Computation of Exclusion, Gain to be Reported, and Adjusted Basis of New Residence—Special Rule
(For use of taxpayers 65 years of age or over who checked "Yes," in 3(c) above.)

15 If line 10 above is $35,000 or less, the entire gain shown on line 8 is excludable from gross income. If line 10 is over $35,000, determine the excludable portion of the gain as follows:		
(a) Divide amount on line 10 into $35,000	15(a)	
(b) Excludable portion of gain (multiply amount on line 8 by figure on line 15(a) and enter result here)	15(b)	
16 Nonexcludable portion of gain (subtract line 15(b) from line 8)	16	
17 Cost of new residence. If a new principal residence was not purchased, enter "None," and do not complete the following lines. Then enter the amount shown on line 16 on Schedule D (Form 1040), in column f, line 6	17	
18 Gain taxable this year. (Subtract the sum of lines 15(b) and 17 from line 16.) But this amount may not exceed line 16.) If line 17 plus line 15(b) is more than line 10, enter zero. Enter here and on Schedule D (Form 1040), in column f, line 6	18	
19 Gain on which tax is to be deferred (subtract line 18 from line 16)	19	
20 Adjusted basis of new residence (subtract line 19 from line 17)	20	

Note: If you were 65 or older when you sold or exchanged your principal residence, and if that was your principal residence for 5 of the 8 years preceding the sale or exchange, you may elect to exclude part or all of the gain. If the property is held by you and your spouse as joint tenants, tenants by the entirety, or community property and you and your spouse file a joint return, only you or your spouse need meet the age requirement. You are only eligible for the exclusion once. This is true regardless of your marital status at the time you made the election.

Form 2119 (Rev. 10-77)

$55,000 ($80,000 minus $25,000). Deducting the $31,500 that you reinvest in another home would leave you a profit, or capital gain, of $23,500. You exclude 60% of that gain, or $14,000, and pay taxes on the remaining $9,400 at your regular tax rate.

Form 2119 (Rev. 10–77)   Page 2

Consent of You and Your Spouse to Apply Separate Gain on Sale of Old Residence to Basis of New Residence

Note: *The following Consent need not be completed if there was no gain on the sale of the old residence. If, however, there was a gain, and if the ownership interests of you and your spouse in the old and new residences were not in the same proportion, the separate gain on the sale of the old residence will be separately taxable to you and your spouse unless this Consent is filed.*

	Your portion	Spouse's portion
Adjusted sales price of old residence (from line 10)	$	$
Cost of new residence (from line 11 or 17)	$	$

The undersigned taxpayers, you and your spouse, consent to have the basis of the joint or separate interest in the new residence reduced by the amount of the joint or separate gain on the sale of the old residence which is not taxable solely by reason of the filing of this Consent.

Your signature	Date
Spouse's signature	Date

SCHEDULE I—Commissions and Other Expenses of Sale (Line 5)

This includes sales commissions, advertising expenses, attorney and legal fees, etc., incurred to effect the sale of the old residence. Enter the name and address of the payee and the date of payment for each item.

Item explanation	Amount
Real estate commission— Alice Agent	$ 3,000
77 Sales Street	
Anywhere, U.S.A.	
Aug. 30, 1978	

SCHEDULE II—Basis of Old Residence (Line 7)

This includes the original cost of the property to the taxpayer, commissions, and other expenses incurred in its purchase, the cost of improvements, etc., less the total of the depreciation allowed or allowable (if any), all casualty losses previously allowed (if any), and the nontaxable gain (if any) on the sale or exchange of a previous personal residence.

Item explanation	Amount
Original cost	$ 32,000
Home Improvements	4,000
Total	$36,000

SCHEDULE III—Fixing-up Expenses (Line 9)

These are decorating and repair expenses which were incurred solely to assist in the sale of the old property, and which are not ordinarily deductible in computing taxable income nor taken into account in computing the basis of the old residence or the amount realized from its sale. Fixing-up expenses must have been incurred for work performed within 90 days before the contract to sell was signed, and must have been paid for not later than 30 days after the sale.

Item explanation	Date work performed	Date paid	Amount
Interior Painting	6-10-78	6-14	$ 500

For more information obtain Publication 523, Tax Information on Selling or Purchasing Your Home, from your local IRS office.

☆ U.S. GOVERNMENT PRINTING OFFICE : 1977—O—218–309   33-0810708

Just as an example, if you are in the 30% tax bracket, you would pay a tax of $2,820 on your capital gain. That would, in effect, amount to a tax of only 12% on your total unreinvested gain of $23,500. Under the old law, with 50% of the gain excluded, your tax would have been $705 higher.

Of course, if you sell your home for a profit and don't buy another home, the entire profit is a capital gain. And, in any case, you would include various costs, such as improvements made to the home, in determining your profit, as discussed earlier in this chapter.

The 1978 tax-cut bill also saves homeowners money in other ways if they sell their homes for large capital gains. The legislation eliminated certain provisions that boosted the maximum tax on certain capital gains. And, under the bill, profits from a principal-home sale no longer are subject to a minimum tax that sometimes had to be paid in addition to the capital-gains tax.

Your Once-in-a-Lifetime Homeowners Tax Break

How would you like to make up to a $125,000 profit and not have to pay any taxes on your gain? If you are an older homeowner, you may be eligible for just such a tax break, thanks to the 1978 and 1981 tax-cut laws. The law gives homeowners who are 55 years old or older a one-time opportunity to take a tax-free profit of up to $125,500 on a home sale.

The new tax break is designed to enable older homeowners to sell their homes and move into smaller dwellings or rental units without having to pay a heavy tax penalty. The new provision replaced a previous once-in-a-lifetime tax break that allowed homeowners 65 years old or older to avoid taxes on the profit from a home sale if they sold their home for less than $35,000. As the sale price rose above $35,000, there was a diminishing amount of capital-gains relief.

The change adds up to a bonanza for many older homeowners. Let's say, for example, that you are in your late fifties, the kids have moved out, and you want to move out of your big, old house and into a rental apartment. The house you bought 30 years ago for about $20,000 sells for about $155,000. After adjusting for various selling and home-improvement costs, your profit amounts to $130,000. Of this total, $100,000 is excluded from your taxable income, and you won't have to pay federal taxes on it. The remaining $5,000 profit is a capital gain. Excluding 60% of the gain, or $3,000, you are left with a taxable gain of only $2,000.

Again, only as an example, if you are in the 30% tax

bracket, your tax on the $2,000 gain would be $600. In other words, of your $130,000 profit from your home sale, you would get $129,400 and the tax man would get only $600. Under the previous capital-gains law, you would have owed taxes of $19,500 on the same gain.

In addition, even if your profit exceeds $125,000, you may be able to avoid taxes on all or most of your gain if you buy another home instead of renting. Under the law, you are allowed to take your once-in-a-lifetime exclusion of $125,000 profit and also continue to defer that part of your gain that is reinvested in the purchase of another home. And, of course, if your gain is less than $125,000, you don't pay any taxes on the profit regardless of whether you buy another home or not.

So if you are approaching age 55, or your spouse is, you should consider waiting until you reach that age before selling your home in order to take advantage of this big, one-time tax break. If you qualify, it could give you a lot of extra dollars for retirement.

The rules are relatively simple. You or your spouse must be at least 55 years old when you sell your home. The home you sell must be your principal residence. It can't be a vacation home or second home. You must have owned and occupied the house for three of the past five years. (Under a special transition rule, you could qualify if you owned and occupied the home for five of the past eight years.) You must claim the tax break. It isn't automatic.

Remember that you can use this big tax break only once in your lifetime, so be sure you don't waste it on a relatively small gain. This rule covers married couples who are homeowners—a husband and a wife can't claim the $125,000 exclusions separately. However, if two people who took advantage of the tax break when independently selling their homes later marry each other, Congress said "there is to be no recapture of the taxes attributable to the gain excluded with respect to the sale of one of the residences." In other words, the IRS can't make one of them give the tax-savings back.

My Three Homes and Other Tax Rulings

Taxes, obviously, are complicated matters, or else we wouldn't have H & R Block offices on every corner to help us figure out what we owe Uncle Sam. Many of the tax rules depend on how the IRS and the courts interpret them. This includes tax rules that affect homeowners.

The special cases are something that you and the tax man will have to fight about. But as a guide, here are some tax rulings on housing as reported in The Wall Street Journal's Tax Report, which is edited by Sandy Jacobs.

MY THREE HOMES: How to tally tax if you sell two homes.

A tax break usually results if another residence is bought within 18 months of selling a principal residence: Profit on the first home is taxed only if it exceeds the new home's cost. A taxpayer who owned two residences sold one, moved into the other, making it his principal residence, then sold it and bought a third one—all within 24 months.

If he could lump the two sales together he would avoid tax on his profit by offsetting his gains against the third home's cost, which exceeded his profit on both sales. But he couldn't do that, the IRS ruled. He must offset the profit from the first home against the cost of buying the third one. His profit on the second sale is fully subject to tax, as he hadn't any home purchase to offset it.

* * *

THE WIFE GOT the house. Because she did, he owed the tax.

You can be in thrall to the tax collector when you make a divorce settlement that gives your half of the family home to your wife. That happened to a Jacksonville, Fla., pathologist when he divorced his wife after 35 years of marriage. The doctor didn't pay her alimony; he gave her his half-interest in their home, which she sold later for $303,000.

The IRS figured that the pathologist bought his wife's right to alimony and her other "marital rights" with his interest in the home. It was as if he had sold his half and given her the proceeds. So, the IRS said he owed tax on his "gain" on the deal based on his cost and the value of the home at the time of the divorce settlement. The Tax Court agreed with the IRS.

The doctor's half of the house cost him $44,200; the house was worth $250,000 at the time of the divorce pact, so he had a taxable gain of $80,800 ($125,000 minus $44,200).

* * *

IF YOU SELL YOUR HOME, expect strict enforcement of "rollover" deadlines.

Tax law permits you to avoid tax on your gain if you reinvest the proceeds in a more expensive home within a certain period. A Hyannis, Massachusetts, couple failed to qualify, however, because the Tax Court held them to the letter of the law. The couple had set out to build a seaside house, but their plans were stalled when the state issued a stop order halting work on a seawall they needed. It took almost a year to overturn the order.

That delay meant the couple weren't able to occupy their new home within 18 months of selling their old one, as tax law then required. (Currently, for a new house, construction must start within 18 months, and the home must be occupied within two years.) The couple argued in vain that they deserved more time because the state's ill-founded stop order had thwarted time. But the Tax Court ruled that the deadline applies precisely as written, even though the taxpayer makes a good-faith effort to meet it.

In the court's view, their problem with the state didn't really differ from, say, bad weather, illness, or similar factors that gum up people's plans.

* * *

OFF TO FLORIDA and a deduction, too, was their wish.

Basil and Barbara spent 11 days in the Sunshine State with their kids. They earlier signed to buy land there, and could cancel the contract only if they personally looked at the property. They did during the trip and cancelled. They also met with someone from International House of Pancakes about acquiring a franchise in Florida. They deducted nearly $1,000 for the trip.

The IRS barred the deduction. The trip wasn't for business, it was a vacation, the IRS said. Indeed, "pursuits which could conceivably qualify" as business-related took up only 2½ hours of their time in Florida, the Tax Court noted with disapproval.

However, if the pair had "substantiated" expenses connected directly to the land deal or the franchise discussion, they might be deductible, the court said. But they hadn't and could deduct nothing, the court concluded.

* * *

A SPECULATOR TROUNCES the IRS in a fight over a resort land sale.

Herman Slemers, a real-estate salesman in Hilton Head, South Carolina, bought a parcel of land from his employer for $18,000. He executed a promissory note for the purchase price and agreed to pay principal and interest on the note, as well as taxes and maintenance fees on the land. He paid nothing on these obligations until two years later, when he sold the land for $35,000. The day of the sale, he paid off the note, plus interest, taxes and fees that had accumulated from the date of purchase. Slemers treated his profit as a long-term capital gain.

Property must be held at least one year for the profit from a sale to qualify as a long-term gain. The IRS claimed that Slemers didn't really own the Hilton Head land until the day he sold it. For one thing, he didn't fulfill the tax and other obligations until then.

The Tax Court disagreed. It ruled that Slemers had borne the "burdens" of ownership, including liability for taxes and other expenses, from the time he bought the land, even though he didn't pay up until later.

* * *

A WIFE GAVE HER HUSBAND a share of the house he gave entirely to her.

Elena was the sole owner of the house she occupied with her husband in Bath, Maine. He paid for it but later put title in her name, and it stayed in her name for 20 years. But three months before her death, Elena put the house in both their names. Her estate excluded her half-interest from estate taxes, citing the exclusion for joint property a decedent acquired without paying for it. The IRS, though, wanted to include the house's entire value in Elena's estate.

The IRS argued that a transfer in contemplation of death is void, and ownership for estate-tax purposes is fixed as if the ownership change didn't take place. That meant only Elena owned the house when she died. But her estate contended that the joint ownership rule should apply. The house should be excluded, as she hadn't paid anything for the house when her husband put it in her name 20 years earlier.

The entire value of the house would have to be included, the Tax Court said recently. The transfer, so near her death, "was for no other purpose than to reduce" her estate's tax, the court asserted.

* * *

AN ESTRANGED COUPLE shared a house. But he claimed they were separated.

Husbands usually can deduct support payments to their wives during marital separation. Lugene S. filed to dissolve her marriage of 25 years with Richard. A temporary court order prior to their divorce directed the couple to "live separately but in the same house," and ordered Richard to go on paying their usual family bills. Richard deducted about $1,200 as support for Lugene for the period they occupied the house under the court order.

The Internal Revenue Service barred his deduction, contending it was available only if a separated couple lived apart. Richard argued that being separated was enough, and he and Lugene were apart despite being in the same house. They stayed in separate rooms, ate meals apart, did nothing together. But the Tax Court noted that Congress intended the deduction as a break for spouses who must support two households during separation. Sharing a house with Lugene barred Richard from the deduction, the court concluded, and added a prim assertion:

The court "shouldn't be required to delve into the

intimate question of whether husband and wife are in fact living apart while residing in the same house."

* * *

IS NAIVETE A CASUALTY? Not for tax purposes, the Tax Court declares.

A couple in California paid a deposit on a house they wanted to buy there. Then they decided to move to Ohio. The husband hired a lawyer to help him get his deposit back. The lawyer turned the matter over to a clerk, who eventually established an office of his own. The client knew the clerk wasn't a lawyer, but still permitted him to handle the case. The clerk led the couple to believe he had obtained a refund of their deposit. He said, however, that it had been necessary to use the money to pay the bill for moving their belongings to Ohio.

Meanwhile, the moving company was holding their furniture pending payment of the bill. The husband assured the company that the bill had been paid by his California representative. The company couldn't locate the man so, after a long wait, it sold the belongings to satisfy the moving and storage charges. The couple claimed a casualty deduction on their tax return, claiming the California man had lied to them and stolen the money. The Tax Court said no. The husband hadn't filed an insurance claim, reported the matter to the police, or even asked the representative to prove he had paid the moving bill.

"This loss cannot be considered unexpected, accidental or sudden as required by applying the term casualty," the court said. It ruled out a theft deduction, too.

* * *

HER $195,000 POOL was good medicine, but an appeals court won't swallow it.

Because Bonnie Bach Ferris had to swim daily to prevent paralysis from a back ailment, the Ferrises added an indoor pool to their home. It cost $195,000, largely because it matched the expensive cut-stone architecture of their Tudor-style home in Madison, Wis. The couple deducted as a medical expense $86,000, the balance after subtracting the cost of nonessential items in the addition and the value the pool added to their home.

The Internal Revenue Service argued that much of the outlay was caused by luxurious construction and shouldn't be deductible. But the Tax Court in 1977 said the law didn't require "barebone" spending for medical care. Still, the entire outlay for the pool can't be considered "for medical care," an appeals court asserted in 1978. "Only the minimum reasonable cost of a functionally adequate pool and housing structure" will count as spent "for medical care," the appeals court said.

The appeals court sent the Ferris-pool case back to Tax Court for determination of "minimum reasonable cost."

The Great Property Tax Revolt

Even with all the deductions, taxes can be a pain in the pocketbook for homeowners. The "most hated" tax of all, according to numerous polls, is the property tax that homeowners pay to local governments.

Property taxes vary widely around the nation. But in many places, such taxes are rising rapidly as home values escalate. Thus, you are affected by rising prices even if you don't plan to sell your home soon, because your property taxes go up right along with the soaring home-prices in your neighborhood.

If property taxes are skyrocketing in your area, what can you do about them?

· You can appeal excessive tax assessments. The fight against bloated taxes, literally, begins at home. Tax assessors are human, and they can make mistakes when determining the market value of your home. And if your home is over-valued, you are paying higher taxes than you should be.

Various studies indicate that the tax burden sometimes is unfairly apportioned because of either deliberate or unintentional assessment practices that discriminate against certain groups. Researchers from Georgia State University found that nonwhite neighborhoods in Atlanta tended to be over-assessed, as were low-value homes in higher-income neighborhoods. "Assessors may feel that the political power or knowledge of the appeal process is less for these groups," the researchers speculated. On the other hand, they found that very high-priced homes were under-assessed, as were those in areas where prices had risen above the citywide average.

If you think your home is over-valued, you can appeal to the tax assessor. You need evidence, though, to back up your protest. Ask your neighbors what values their homes are assessed at; if they won't tell you, you can find out the values by checking local tax records. If comparable homes in your neighborhood are assessed at lower values than yours, you have a solid case for seeking a tax rollback.

You also can appeal your assessment if the value of your property is reduced by some change in your neighborhood. Perhaps a road is constructed near you, the woods behind you are replaced by high-rise apartments, or your neighbor adds a monstrosity of a "home-improvement" to his house. If you feel any such change lowers the value of your property, take pictures of your home and the changes to use as evidence in your appeal.

In most areas, the process for appealing a tax assessment is relatively simple, so you can usually handle it yourself. But if you think there is a big error, you might want to consider seeking the advice of a lawyer and a real-estate appraiser. Remember, there usually is a time limit for appealing. If you miss it, you'll have to wait until next year to get any mistakes corrected.

· Another way to fight soaring property taxes is to join local citizens groups in the property-tax revolt. The rebellion came to a head in 1978 in California where, in the "vote heard 'round the nation," voters overwhelmingly approved Proposition 13 that slashed skyrocketing property-tax rates in that state to 1% of the 1975-76 level market value. The action sharply limits the ability of the state and local government to raise property taxes.

Critics contend Proposition 13 is a "meat axe" that mainly favors big landowners and hurts the poor by radically curtailing revenues for social programs. About two-thirds of the tax relief will go to large property owners, although some land-lords are expected to pass along the tax cuts in the form of lower rents. But the tax-rebels say radical action was the only

The Wall Street Journal

"As a firm believer in reincarnation,
I'm leaving everything to me."

way to get the government's attention. They say they support needed spending programs, but are opposed to run-away government spending and waste.

The tax revolt began in California in 1976 and 1977. As house prices in the state skyrocketed, hundreds of thousands of homeowners saw their property-tax bills rise as much as 200% in a single year.

In Los Angeles in 1977, Ralph Littrell, a manufacturers' representative in his 60s, posted a sign on the lawn of his comfortable, two-story brick and stucco home in the upper-middle-class Cheviot Hills section to voice his displeasures: "For Sale Soon, Our Beautiful Home for Life, Thanks to these . . . Big Red-Ink Writing Hoods."

The Littrells bought their house 15 years before for $50,000 and paid a property tax of $800. It was assessed in the mid-1960s at a market value of $65,560 and the taxes in 1976 were $2,238. The assessment rose in 1977 to $157,900 with an estimated tax of $5,180.

"We were hoping this would be our home for life, but you reach a point of diminishing return," Mr. Littrell said. "I don't argue with the assessment; it's the big spenders who caused this."

The tax revolt isn't limited to California. Proposition 13 "is a green Hulk emerging from the swamps in the West," said John Peterson, of the Municipal Finance Officers Association. Movements have sprung up elsewhere either to cut taxes or to hold down government spending.

Cook County, Illinois, homeowners, hit with a tax increase of as much as 300%, began talking about organizing a "tax strike" and withholding their payments. In Bucks County, Pennsylvania, an angry crowd of mostly middle-aged people and elderly residents threatened county commissioners with tarring and feathering after they proposed a property-tax increase of 126% in 1977. And in Hardenburgh, New York, homeowners were ordained en masse as ministers of a mail-order church so they could declare their homes as church property (like the nearby order of Tibetan monks) and thus evade the local property tax.

Few have gone that far, but the property tax seems to have been unpopular since the colony of Massachusetts began collecting it annually in 1646.

Property Taxes around the Nation

Of course, property taxes in most places aren't as high as in California. On the other hand, in some places they are higher. One place, for instance, is Massachusetts, which some residents refer to as "Taxachussetts," and where there was a Proposition 13-like tax revolt in 1980.

To give you an idea of the variations for a high-priced home, here are the property taxes that would be paid on a home with a market value of $100,000, according to *Time Magazine:*

Boston	$8,413
Los Angeles	3,100
New York	2,190
Atlanta	2,160
Chicago	1,989
Cleveland	1,966
Washington, D.C.	1,720
Seattle	1,711
Denver	1,486
New Orleans	422

As you can see, there is little uniformity in property taxes. In some areas, taxes are very high and in some quite low. Though it may seem hard for many homeowners to believe, property taxes actually aren't increasing as rapidly as a lot of other costs. The U.S. Bureau of the Census shows that between 1970-71 and 1975-76 property taxes in the largest 74 metropolitan areas increased at a lesser rate than overall inflation—property taxes rose 35.5% in the period, while inflation increased 39.5%.

This doesn't mean that cities and counties all of a sudden are spending money at lesser rates than before. In order to meet higher expenditures, just about all cities and counties are hitting the state and federal governments for more money.

Another way of measuring the impact of property taxes is to relate the taxes to the local population. This method, called per capita taxes, shows the amount of tax paid for each person living in the metropolitan area.

Here are the per capita property taxes for selected metropolitan areas in 1975-76:

Per Capita Property Taxes For 74 Major Metropolitan Areas, 1978/79 Versus 1974/75

SMSA	1978/79	1974/75	% CHANGE
Nassau-Suffolk	$715.25	$542.95	31.7%
Boston	597.75	461.83	29.4
Bridgeport-Stamford	557.69	416.41	33.9
Newark	554.20	440.84	25.7
New Brunswick	503.47	406.26	23.9
New York	493.38	384.61	28.3
Hartford	461.47	367.25	25.7
Jersey City	433.24	283.97	52.6
New Haven-West Haven	422.06	337.95	24.9
Springfield (Mass.)	419.77	307.79	36.4
Detroit	408.66	315.21	29.6
Houston	405.33	258.80	56.6
Milwaukee	401.88	331.85	21.1
Rochester	398.97	302.81	31.8
Worcester	397.93	374.58	6.2
Providence	390.69	255.42	53.0
Syracuse	386.77	267.38	44.7
Portland	384.16	288.18	33.3
Chicago	380.32	312.58	21.6
Minneapolis	376.71	276.62	36.2
Buffalo	367.86	292.00	26.0
Washington, D.C.	364.84	251.22	45.2
Albany	357.34	248.21	44.0
Denver-Boulder	357.20	226.56	57.7
Omaha	355.96	252.57	40.9
Flint	329.87	248.54	32.7
Miami	329.84	217.04	52.0
Cleveland	318.39	262.65	21.2
Atlanta	303.80	236.08	28.7
Phoenix	299.67	218.40	37.2
Philadelphia	298.95	214.57	39.3
Dallas-Ft. Worth	295.07	225.33	31.0
Gary-Hammond	293.91	289.99	1.4
Grand Rapids	293.09	230.07	27.4
Allentown	286.92	203.59	40.9
SF-Oakland	286.24	441.10	−35.1
Ft. Lauderdale-Hollywood	280.79	198.49	41.5
Toledo	278.35	199.21	39.7

SMSA	1978/79	1974/75	% CHANGE
Kansas City	275.65	222.36	24.0
Indianapolis	274.33	262.31	4.6
Akron	267.26	208.03	28.5
Pittsburgh	262.55	183.52	43.1
Richmond	260.88	183.50	42.2
San Jose	255.97	387.00	−33.9
Salt Lake City	254.45	164.63	54.6
Anaheim	254.02	332.81	−23.7
Los Angeles	250.98	382.80	−34.4
Columbus	247.27	176.79	39.9
Dayton	243.67	181.51	34.2
St. Louis	241.25	210.61	14.5
Orlando	240.18	180.74	32.9
Seattle	239.44	241.63	−0.9
Charlotte	238.20	182.74	30.3
Riverside-San Bernardino	226.22	324.02	−30.2
Cincinnati	226.12	174.06	29.9
Baltimore	222.67	180.04	23.7
Wilmington	217.66	163.64	33.0
Youngstown	214.52	197.71	8.5
Sacramento	211.36	291.84	−27.6
San Diego	210.86	303.86	−30.6
Memphis	209.68	159.64	31.3
Greensboro	202.71	138.88	46.0
Tampa-St. Pete	196.94	133.57	47.4
Tulsa	193.13	151.62	27.4
Jacksonville	188.61	125.28	50.6
Nashville	188.17	146.81	28.2
Honolulu	188.13	143.24	31.3
NE Penna	179.31	108.35	65.5
San Antonio	178.83	136.20	31.3
Oklahoma City	176.70	135.62	30.3
Norfolk	170.58	128.97	32.3
Louisville	153.27	113.33	35.2
New Orleans	105.87	90.01	17.6
Birmingham	102.33	69.81	46.6

Source: Bureau of the Census; Compilation by NAAB ECONOMICS DIVISION

Monitoring Your Property Taxes

Obviously, your fire for slashing property taxes likely depends on where you live. Most homeowners, however reluctantly, probably agree that reasonable taxes are necessary to maintain public services and needed programs. The trick, however, is to keep taxes and spending both reasonable and visible.

Theoretically, when rising home values boost property taxes, the added revenues should allow the local government to cut back the tax rate so that homeowners aren't faced with frighteningly sharp increases in their annual bills. If the local government needs more revenues, as most do, it should specifically seek a tax boost to raise them. But, in practice, most politicians find it easier merely to accept the windfall of rising property-tax revenues than seek publicly a new tax increase to pay for government needs. As a result, the tax assessor gets blamed for the problem instead of the politician.

One way to deal with this may be by seeking a "truth-in-tax" procedure. That, at least, is what Florida has adopted. State Representative Carl Ogden of Florida, who authored the legislation, described the procedure this way:

"Every year, the tax appraisers reassess homes in light of current market values, which generally are higher than the year before. The tax rate is then reduced, so as to generate no additional revenue from the reassessment. The only 'fudge factor' is new construction, which can be taxed outside the normal rolls for the first year.

"If last year's revenues plus the fudge factor aren't enough for this year's public expenditures, the taxing unit—for example, the city council—has to put the following quarter-page ad into the local newspaper of largest circulation: 'The City Council proposes to increase your property taxes. Hearings will be held on (such-and-such a date).' And lest you overlook the ad, it must be surrounded by a black border.

"If, after the public hearings, the council goes ahead and raises taxes, another black-bordered, quarter-page ad must be placed: 'The City Council has voted to raise your property taxes.' And after a second set of hearings, there's another vote. Only then can taxes actually be increased.

"Public officials call the ad 'the Death Notice,'" Mr. Ogden added. The idea is to force officials to be candid about who's raising taxes. "If the government can sell a tax increase to the people to cover inflation or specific city projects, fine," he said. "If it can't, that's tough luck."

Barring adoption of such a program, it's up to you and local citizens groups to keep an eye on property taxes. The experts say what you should look for are signs that the taxes are getting out of line in relation to market values of homes. "The best property tax is a moderate property tax," said John Shannon, assistant director of the Advisory Commission on Intergovernmental Relations, a Washington, D.C., agency that monitors local-government activities. "As with any other tax, the heavier it becomes the less obvious are its virtues and the more glaring are its defects."

Concluded Mr. Shannon: "In my view, a moderate property tax should fall in the 1.5% of market value range. Beyond 1.5% of market value, the amber warning light turns on—beyond 2% the red danger light flashes."

To see how the rate of property taxes to market value in your state compares with other states, check the following chart prepared by the Advisory Commission.

TABLE 9-1

Average Effective Property-Tax Rates
Existing Single-Family Homes
With FHA-Insured Mortgages

State and Region	1978	1971	1966	1962	1958
United States	1.56	1.98	1.70	1.53	1.34
New England					
Maine	1.58	2.43	2.17	1.81	1.58
New Hampshire	N.A.	3.14	2.38	2.03	1.81
Vermont	N.A.	2.53	2.27	2.10	1.63
Massachusetts	3.64	3.13	2.76	2.47	2.21
Rhode Island	N.A.	2.21	1.96	1.93	1.67
Connecticut	1.94	2.38	2.01	1.75	1.44
Mideast					
New York	3.02	2.72	2.40	2.23	2.09
New Jersey	3.30	3.01	2.57	2.22	1.77
Pennsylvania	1.91	2.16	1.88	1.75	1.50
Delaware	0.89	1.26	1.14	.91	.71
Maryland	1.72	2.24	2.05	1.74	1.47
Dist. of Columbia	1.76	1.80	1.37	1.18	1.08

State and Region	1978	1971	1966	1962	1958
Great Lakes					
Michigan	2.63	2.02	1.81	1.76	1.45
Ohio	1.20	1.47	1.44	1.24	1.07
Indiana	1.61	1.96	1.64	.96	.84
Illinois	1.81	2.15	1.96	1.79	1.35
Wisconsin	2.21	3.01	2.31	2.24	1.82
Plains					
Minnesota	1.33	2.05	2.14	1.79	1.57
Iowa	1.59	2.63	2.12	1.66	1.34
Missouri	1.45	1.79	1.64	1.36	1.12
North Dakota	1.18	2.08	1.81	1.70	1.54
South Dakota	1.69	2.71	2.64	2.31	2.01
Kansas	2.43	3.15	2.67	1.84	1.90
Southeast					
Virginia	1.20	1.32	1.13	1.03	.90
West Virginia	0.56	.69	.71	.79	.56
Kentucky	1.26	1.27	1.03	.94	.93
Tennessee	1.40	1.53	1.37	1.18	.97
North Carolina	1.35	1.58	1.31	1.17	.90
South Carolina	0.80	.94	.60	.53	.48
Georgia	1.28	1.44	1.30	.94	.84
Florida	1.14	1.41	1.09	.66	.76
Alabama	0.73	.85	.66	.52	.56
Mississippi	1.12	.96	.93	.76	.66
Louisiana	0.47	.56	.43	.49	.52
Arkansas	1.48	1.14	1.09	1.09	.84
Southwest					
Oklahoma	0.95	1.35	1.11	.86	.86
Texas	1.66	1.91	1.62	1.44	1.36
New Mexico	1.47	1.70	1.30	.98	.93
Arizona	1.69	1.65	2.41	2.27	2.14
Rocky Mountain					
Montana	1.23	2.19	1.70	1.58	1.32
Idaho	1.57	1.72	1.23	1.13	1.14
Wyoming	0.76	1.38	1.34	1.27	1.17
Colorado	1.74	2.45	2.20	1.85	1.72
Utah	0.99	1.49	1.52	1.31	1.05
Far West					
Washington	1.78	1.62	1.14	1.12	.92

State and Region	1978	1971	1966	1962	1958
Oregon	2.18	2.33	1.98	1.83	1.55
Nevada	1.72	1.48	1.47	1.31	1.06
California	2.26	2.48	2.03	1.71	1.50
Alaska	1.73	1.61	1.42	1.24	1.12
Hawaii	N.A.	.92	.81	.77	.62

N.A.—Data not available.

[1]Effective tax rate is the percentage that tax liability is of the market or true value of the house.

Source: Computed by ACIR staff from data contained in U.S. Department of Housing and Urban Development, Federal Housing Administration, Management Information Systems Division, *Data for States and Selected Areas on Characteristics of FHA Operations Under Section 203(b),* various years.

TEN

Home Improvements: Protecting Your Investment

"If your heart is set on an observatory in the attic or an aviary in the breakfast nook, understand that it will probably lower the value of your house."

—Business Week

The improvements you make to your house can make a big difference in the value of your home. In fact, the changes your neighbor makes to his home can make a difference to you. Sometimes the difference isn't for the better.

Consider, for example, the "improvements" added in 1976 in the retirement community of Sun City, Arizona, by a homeowner who celebrated American's Bicentennial year by going on a patriotic remodeling binge that included:

Painting a front-yard palm tree red, white and blue and stringing flags from it to the front of his home; erecting 13 red, white and blue poles up to 18 feet high and flying flags from some of them; putting a 10-foot red, white and blue tripod on the roof; painting an 8-by-16-foot American flag on the roof; erecting a 70-foot tower in the backyard from which to fly 18 more flags.

And, so help us Thomas Jefferson, that wasn't all. The homeowner also painted his rooftop air-conditioner red, white and blue and placed a large red, white and blue cattle-watering container in his front yard, equipping it with a fountain that splashed water 20 feet in the air. Moreover, he illuminated the entire display with lights and installed outdoor loudspeakers to blare musical accompaniment.

Many of the patriotic homeowner's neighbors were ready to start a new revolution. The man's next-door neighbor charged off to the local tax assessor, claiming that the bizarre changes had lowered the value of his own home. The tax assessors agreed. They reduced the assessed value of the complaining neighbor's $40,000 residence by almost $14,000.

The moral is that the wrong kind of home remodeling can detract from the value of a home. And, so can kooky remodeling by neighbors.

In most cases, however, the improvements you make to your home will add to its value—some more than others. Even if you are happy where you live now, and don't have any intention of moving in the near future, the right kind of home improvements can help your housing investment grow. You may decide you need to add some extra space or to modernize part of your house. Or you may decide to achieve your "dream house" by remodeling your present abode rather than buying a new one. In any case, if you are thinking about remodeling, you will be in good company. Millions of Americans are doing it all the time.

The Boom in Home Remodeling

Between 1970 and 1980, national expenditures for upkeep and improvement increased by 198%. In 1980 alone Americans spent a record $43 billion to fix up and add to what they owned. One-third of this was spent on maintenance and two-thirds on improving the structures.

And don't think for a minute that all of this money was put into old shacks; it was not. The improvement dollars were fairly well-distributed among the most recently built homes (since 1970) and those built between 1960 and 1970 and between 1950 and 1960.

The largest share of the dollar was spent by those people who just moved in. And about one-third of the jobs were done by the owners themselves, either entirely or partly using purchased materials.

The steady gains are due in part to sky-high home prices. One way to get a relative bargain-home buy is to purchase a house that needs fixing up after you move in. Another

The Wall Street Journal

"I'm sorry, sir, but we don't sell wallpaper
to gentlemen not accompanied by their wives."

influence is the "don't buy, remodel" syndrome that afflicts many people appalled by home prices these days.

One such couple is the Edward Vilds of Parma, Ohio. In anticipation of the birth of their third child, the gas company mechanic and his wife began to househunt because their $23,500 two-bedroom bungalow was cramped already. They soon found, however, that even the cheapest three-bedroom houses in Parma, a blue-collar suburb of Cleveland, cost at least $40,000, far beyond their means. So instead of moving, they decided to convert the attic of their present home into a master bedroom—at a relatively modest cost of $3,600.

The remodeling boom also is spurred by another major consideration. Higher fuel costs have triggered an upsurge in energy-saving outlays on items ranging from roofing to storm doors. One reason is that many homeowners figure that with today's rocketing energy costs, energy-saving improvements not only will add to their home's value when they sell but save them money in lower utility bills now.

Which Home Improvements Pay Off the Most

Installing a heart-shaped swimming pool in the backyard or remodeling that old-fashioned bathroom with the pink tiles— which is best? The home-improvements choice is up to you, and what you and your family want the most is certainly a prime consideration. But just remember, too, that all home improvements aren't valued equally when it comes to adding to the market value of your house. Don't expect to get your money back on every improvement you make. Many items will get you less than 50 cents on each dollar back in added value. But other improvements can get you most, or sometimes all, of each dollar back.

According to appraisers, tax assessors, remodelers, real-estate people and others, here are some of the blue-ribbon home improvement investments:

- *Kitchens*—Kitchen remodeling, experts agree, is the number one home improvement in terms of added value. Whatever you can do to bring an old kitchen up to date will make a difference: no-wax floors, a self-cleaning oven, bigger and easy-to-clean kitchen cabinets, no-nonsense work places, expansion of kitchen space, and similar items. Just about all these things will pay off in added value when you eventually sell your home.

This is one reason kitchen-remodeling is the biggest volume job in the home-improvement industry. Another reason is that kitchens seem to be the one room in the house with the most built-in obsolescence. The cost of remodeling a kitchen varies widely, depending on how fancy you want to get. Typical remodeling costs range between $4,000 and $6,000, but the price-tag can run up to $14,000 or even higher. A rule of thumb is that the total cost shouldn't be more than 10% of the estimated selling price of the home. Thus, in a $60,000 home, the kitchen-remodeling cost shouldn't be more than $6,000.

A word of caution: kitchens can over-improved. In 1977 the National Association of Realtors sent its members a publication stating that kitchens are one of the most "over-improved" rooms in today's houses. Today's energy-conscious buyers may look at fancy kitchen appliances as requiring too much energy. The association said that kitchen-renovation money should go into expanding work areas or creating compact work spaces and not into energy-eating frills.

- *Bathrooms*—Chances are you can get up to 100% of your investment dollar back in added sales value when remodeling or adding a bathroom. This is another room that frequently is out-of-date—but not out-of-sight when it comes time to sell your home. A bright, modern bathroom—with a vanity instead of sink with pipes showing underneath, for instance—is a big attraction. If nothing else, you may be getting rid of those ghastly pink and turquoise-blue bathrooms that were popular in houses built in the late 1950s and early 1960s. And adding a second bathroom to a one-bath home especially can add to the value of your house.

Again, don't get too fancy. Expensive and flashy faucets, for example, may impress some people, but they also may turn off many future buyers because of the extra upkeep.

- *Family rooms*—Adding a room may pay dividends, if it is located in the main living area and doesn't take away other valuable space, such as a garage. In newly-built

homes these days a family room is a "must," and people
are coming to expect one in about any house they buy.
This is a room where the family members can get away
to watch television, read, or just talk. Families with
family rooms hardly ever use their living rooms except
for entertaining. With such an addition, usually you can
recoup anywhere from 65% to 100% of your investment.

· Bedrooms—You probably can sleep easy when you add
a bedroom to your house. An extra bedroom in a
three-bedroom house (or a two-bedroom house) is almost certain to be a good investment because it adds to
the salability of a house. But don't overdo it. With
today's trend towards smaller families, adding a fifth or
sixth bedroom to your house may make it harder to
sell. Despite your extra investment, you might not be
able to get a better price than your neighbors would
get for their unimproved four-bedroom homes. Another
taboo: bedroom additions that can be entered only by
going through another bedroom.

· *Enclosed porches*—Like most room additions, enclos-
ing a porch or deck to create a new room can be a good
investment. Family rooms and dining rooms are two
possible choices. Because of the energy shortage,
screened-in porches also are again quite popular and
add more to the value of a house than only an open
deck or patio.

· *Central air-conditioning*—Once considered a luxury,
central air-conditioning has become a hot item, so to
speak. It is almost a necessity in the South and other
warm-climate areas. But even in northern regions,
air-conditioning is becoming almost standard equipment
in newly-built homes. So, adding central air-conditioning to your house probably will pay off, returning anywhere from 50% to 80% of its cost in added value. An
exception is when you also have to pay to have extra
ductwork installed.

· *Siding*—Adding aluminum siding is the second most
popular home improvement (next to kitchen remodeling),
according to the National Remodelers Association, so a
lot of homeowners think it is worth the average
$2,000–$4,000 expense. Because of the popularity of

siding, while you may not get all of your investment back, a quality siding job can be an asset when it comes time to sell your home.

Siding also is touted as an energy saver because it reduces heat loss in winter and heat gain in summer. But such claims sometimes are exaggerated. Siding with the maximum insulating value is made with a foam board that has an aluminum-foil skin. Adding siding with such an aluminum-foil skin could increase insulation value by 70%. A foam board without aluminum-foil skin provides somewhat less insulating value. And siding with a fiberboard backer offers half the insulating value of foam board.

One final warning: The siding industry historically has been plagued by a minority of fly-by-night operators who use deceptive means to sell inferior products at excessive prices. We'll tell you more about that later.

- *Garages*—A new two-car garage can be a good investment in colder climates. With the high prices of autos today, many people want a place to protect their four-wheeled investments as long as they can. In mild climates, adding a carport might be the best bet—except in coastal areas where auto rust caused by moisture can be a factor. Building a driveway, or resurfacing an existing one, also will usually be worth the cost in added value.

- *Carpeting and wallpaper*—Attractive, wall-to-wall carpeting can be largely recouped in added value if it is still attractive when it comes time to sell your house. But don't expect to pay top dollar and get top dollar back. Carpeting is carpeting to most buyers. Wallpaper can liven up a room at a relatively minimal cost and increase resale value. But, avoid exotic colors and patterns when choosing either carpeting or wallpaper. You may love that pink shag rug and the fuchsia-colored wallpaper, but you may have a hard time finding a buyer who feels the same way. Soft, neutral colors are best.

- *Fireplaces*—Fireplaces are making a strong comeback. If you have to build a new chimney, you won't get all of your money back in added value. Indeed, some experts say the best you can hope for is a 40% return. But that's changing. Fireplaces are "in" these days, even in warmer climates. More and more new houses are being built with fireplaces because of buyer demand. People think a roaring fire adds a touch of romance to a living room, and especially a bedroom, and coziness to a family room. Fireplaces recently have been exposed as energy wasters (too much cold air comes down the chimney), but many energy-conscious owners are turning to new glass-enclosed fireplaces that don't waste energy and have vents that can be used for heating. And a relatively inexpensive free-standing fireplace for $500 to $600 will pay for itself in added value.

· *Storm windows*—These items also are increasingly popular as energy savers. A house equipped with easy-to-use storm windows can be a big selling point with today's astronomical heating and cooling bills. The same goes for roof and attic fans that cut air-conditioning costs. All of these items are a good investment, but a costly storm door is a waste of money.

Insulation as an Investment

Increasing the insulation in your house can be one of the best home-improvement investments you can make. This is because it not only pays off when you sell but saves you money now by keeping down those distressingly high heating and cooling bills. But some homes would benefit more than others. Since this is a new and complex area, let's take a closer look at home-insulation as an investment:

According to industry estimates, the cost of heating and cooling an average home by utility-supplied natural gas has risen more than two-thirds since 1973. Natural gas heats more than half the nation's homes. The cost of heating oil, burned in more than 20% of the homes, has more than doubled. And the cost of electricity, used to heat about 12% of the homes, has increased by more than 50%.

To ease the burden, homeowners already have spent billions of dollars to insulate or to improve insulation in their homes. More than 14 million attics have been insulated since 1972, according to Owens-Corning Fiberglas

Corporation, a maker of insulation. Nevertheless, the Commerce Department estimates that about 25.5 million of the country's 42.5 million owner-occupied homes could use more insulation.

Government engineers documented the savings in one insulation project on a "tightly constructed" Gaithersburg, Maryland, house. They found that heat-energy use fell by 58.5%. Before the project the house had a minimal amount of attic insulation and weatherstripping around windows and doors, but no storm windows. Wall insulation cut heat-energy use by 19.7%, floor insulation by 7.5%, and additional attic insulation by 6.1%. Storm windows accounted for a 25.2% reduction.

A complete insulation job costs money, more than $1,000 for an average house and $3,000 or more for the kind of house that a typical professional or executive-level family might occupy. Peter Johnson, president of Comfort Control Corporation, Hackensack, New Jersey, analyzed costs and fuel savings in re-insulating a two-story, 11-room brick-front house built in 1965. Two inches of glass fiber in the attic already provided minimum insulation. To install wall insulation and properly insulate the attic would cost $3,000.

However, with caulking and weatherstripping, the new insulation would reduce the fuel-oil heating bill by as much as $780 a year from the $1,300 it was costing to heat the house, and the three-month summer air-conditioning bill of $300 would be cut in half. With total fuel savings of more than $900 a year, the owner could recover his investment in less than four years.

In smaller houses and houses better insulated to start with, such savings may be unattainable. Government engineers found that storm windows in the Gaithersburg house could pay for themselves in 5.4 years to 10.2 years, depending on the kind of heating plant. Additional insulation might take 9.5 years to 17.5 years. The size of a house, local climate and fuel costs, the house's location relative to the sun, the number and size of its windows, existing insulation, and the occupants' living habits all influence the economics of insulation.

As a result, there's no simple set of rules that will tell you whether your investment in insulation is wise. However, there are a number of guidelines and rules-of-thumb, and there's also a method of determining your home's insulation requirements with some precision.

The Department of Energy and the National Bureau of Standards say that glass-fiber batts 10 inches thick, or the equivalent in other materials, are generally desirable in attic insulation. In extra-cold places, as much as 16 inches of glass fiber in batts may be necessary. Such levels of insulation, the government says, offer the "greatest net savings" in fuel costs over periods of 20 and 30 years.

By contrast, guidelines developed by the National Association of Home Builders suggest six to ten inches of glass fiber in batts, or the equivalent, and twelve inches in very cold, high-cost situations—an electrically heated home in Minneapolis, for example. The guidelines assume yearly cost increases of 10% in energy, a yearly interest rate of 9%, and an investment payback period of seven years.

A useful workbook can help you to determine your best insulation strategy. It's a National Bureau of Standards publication called "Making the Most of Your Energy Dollars in Home Heating and Cooling." Priced at 70 cents, it is available from Consumer Information, Pueblo, Colorado 81009.

The National Bureau of Standards divides the 50 states into five winter heating zones and six summer cooling zones and provides tables of heating and cooling index figures that vary according to your location, the type of fuel you use and its cost per unit. The index figures permit you to determine, from other tables, insulation specifications for your attic floors and ducts, your other floors and your walls. The tables also show whether it will pay to fit your windows with storm windows.

Insulation packaging discloses the material's R-value ("R" is the measure of a material's ability to resist heat transfer) per inch of thickness. Dividing the price per square foot by the R-value permits you to compare the cost efficiency of different insulating materials.

For "Do-It-Your-Selfers," insulation in batts or rolls isn't unduly difficult to install. The key factors in proper installation are a snug fit and, to prevent moisture problems, the proper vapor barrier (kraft paper or foil facing on the insulation) and adequate ventilation. Loose fill can be hand-poured or machine-blown into hard-to-reach spaces like exterior walls. Manufacturers generally specify the number of bags of loose fill required to attain, over a certain area, a given R-value.

For walls, recommended R-values commonly range from R-11 to R-14. Lose fill or foam can be pumped into wall cavities through holes drilled in the wallboard or lath. For floors over unheated areas, R-19 is commonly recomended, but in moderate zones only R-11 may be needed, and in the coldest parts of the country R-22 may be required.

New windows are economical if they are double-glazed or even triple-glazed, without storm windows. But in most parts of the country, it will pay to put up storm windows in spaces of nine square feet or larger. Storm doors generally are considered optional. Unless your existing door has a large area of glass, the home builders figure, it may take more than seven years for a storm door to pay for itself.

In colder climates, basement walls and heating ducts may be insulated. One-inch or two-inch foil-backed wrapping typically is used.

Generally, costs of insulation materials have climbed more than 75 percent since 1973, according to Commerce Department figures. Costs vary by locality and installer. Complaints of price gouging have cropped up in some places. Generally, you can expect to pay 20 cents to 30 cents per square foot for R-19 insulation that you install yourself. Installed by a contractor, R-19 blowing rock-wool fiber should cost 30 cents to 40 cents a square foot. Plastic foam can cost 85 cents a square foot installed behind shingled walls, and more than $1 installed behind brick walls. Glass fiber accounts for about 60 percent of the market for insulation materials.

Even if your insulation job requires a contractor, you should consider installing the higher R-values. Labor costs, a large part of the total bill, change little by increasing the quantity or quality of insulation material. This means that for a relatively small premium in costs you may get a lot more insulation value.

One final note:

The home insulation business has attracted a number of dishonest or incompetent installers. Some have charged high prices for shoddy work that, years later, may cause serious damge to a house structure. People in the field say you should always get solid references, written estimates and signed contracts for insulation work. In addition, if the contractor's specifications appear unusually high or low in comparison with government or trade association guidelines, you should find out why.[15]

Home Improvements That Pay Off the Least

Most remodeling will add to the value of your home, but some projects will have only marginal value. By marginal, we mean improvements that return less than 40% to 50% of the cost in added value. That doesn't mean you shouldn't make them. After all, your home is your castle and if you want to dig a moat, that's up to you. Moreover, some maintenance items may not add value but are vital to keep up the value of your home investment. You should just be aware of the value you are getting for your home-improvement outlay.

The return on home improvements can vary from area to area, but the experts say you shouldn't expect more than a modest return on the following items:

• *Maintenance items*—You may consider that a new roof would be a big selling point, but don't expect some future buyer to be impressed. After all, every home buyer expects to get a roof over his head. The same goes for new furnaces, water heaters, as well as painting the exterior or interior of the house. People expect houses to have furnaces, water heaters and painted walls. That doesn't mean you should ignore such items, because they can detract from the value of your house if they aren't taken care of when needed. Moreover, a new roof (especially if it has special energy saving features) or furnace, or a fresh paint job, can add to the salability of your home, because the buyer knows he won't have to pay to take care of such items in the near future. Just don't expect to get back most of the money that you put into upkeep.

• *Basement recreation rooms*—Back in the happy days of the 1950s and 1960s, the basement "Rec" room was all the rage. In the approximately 30 million houses in the United States with basements, as many as half of the basements are finished in one way or another. But people have gotten tired of going down to the basement to relax; they prefer family rooms on the living level. As a result, basement recreation rooms are out. A finished basement, rather than a cement-block one, still is an asset if you already have one. But don't expect to get most of your money back in added value if you redo your basement now.

· *Coverting garages to family rooms*—We aren't saying that most Americans are more concerned about their cars than their families, but taking away a garage to add a family room usually turns out to be a poor investment. The main reason is that people want some place to put the cars, and they can't park in a family room. Besides, a family room created by a garage often looks strange from the outside; they are often poorly located in relation to the living space in the rest of the house. The moral: A family room is a good investment, but usually not at the expense of losing your garage.

· *Dens*—Dens and studies are nice, and they're often included in today's newly-built homes. But if you don't have one already, a den is hard to add on most houses, they can set you back as much as $12,000 or so, and it's doubtful that you'll be able to get 30% of that back in added value. So much for a den.

· *Finished attics*—That dark old attic that has been magically turned into a cheery bedroom for the children looks so picturesque in the housing magazine. And it may add the space you need. But a remodeled attic usually brings little back in added value. If you need the space, your best bet is to do it yourself and you may be able to recoup up to 50% of your cost—not counting your labor.

· *Landscaping*—Extensive landscaping looks terrific, but it rarely pays off in much added value. Don't expect the cost of 500 azaleas to bring you the price of 500 azaleas. To many people, a large amount of landscaping and planting means a large amount of extra yard work. A well-kept yard can add to the appeal of your house, however.

· *Appliances*—Special types of kitchen appliances may be of some attraction to future buyers, but don't count on getting back more than half of what you invested. As for washers and dryers, most sellers give them away as part of the house sale as an inducement to buy.

· *Baseboard heat*—Don't count on getting much return by installing baseboard radiant heat. If the baseboard heat is installed with separate controls for each room, so it can be turned off when not needed, it can offer some energy savings. The problem is that it is electric and, thus, costly to run.

· *Botched-up work*—Poor workmanship on a room addition or other remodeling job stands out like a sore thumb and detracts from the value of the project. This is often a problem—and a highly visible one—with do-it-yourself projects. Make sure the work is done properly if you want to get your money's worth. Also avoid flamboyant colors when painting your house as well as other extremes like the patriotic projects of the Arizona homeowner mentioned earlier.

· *Luxury items*—Generally, additions like tennis courts and greenhouses are valuable only in the eyes of other tennis players or plant lovers. Chances are, you won't get more than a portion of your investment back in added value. The same is true of elaborate patios and decks.

· *Swimming pools*—One of the riskiest luxury investments is a swimming pool. A backyard pool can add value in places like Hollywood, California, or other well-to-do neighborhoods in warm-weather areas. But in many places, buyers look on swimming pools as extra trouble, costly to maintain, and a potential hazard for their kids. At the same time, installing an in-ground pool is an expensive proposition, with prices ranging from about $10,000 for a small 18 foot by 32 foot pool to over $20,000 for a large pool of more than 20 feet by 40 feet. In many places, you will be fortunate to get half the cost back in added value.

Swimming Pool Swindles

If a swimming pool is what you have your heart set on, dive in. But look before you leap. Beware of swimming pool swindles.

These sellers rely on a time-tested procedure known as bait-and-switch. They lure customers with advertisements for a low-priced pool they usually haven't any intention of selling, then they talk buyers into switching to a high-priced—and often over-priced—model. The buyer soon discovers that the company's claims don't hold water, and, frequently, that their pools don't either.

The basic scheme works like this:

The seller runs big ads for a "bait pool" in the newspapers, often in the Sunday TV section. Typically, the ads "start off with 'save $500' and the pool's size is greatly exaggerated," said the Nassau County, New York, Commissioner of Consumer Affairs.

Indeed, he added, some pools pictured seem to contain "25 people, two rubber ducks and a partridge in a pear tree. The next ad probably will show a nuclear submarine."

When the consumer bites, a smooth-talking salesman visits him and quickly disparages the advertised pool and tries to sell him a costlier one. Or, in one variation, the salesman may actually sell the bait pool. As he starts out the door with the signed contract, he'll turn back and ask casually, "By the way, you *will* have the sand ready?"

"The sand?" you ask.

"Naturally—you realize at this low price that you have to prepare the pool yourself."

Naturally, you didn't realize this.

Before you can say Mark Spitz, the salesman whips out a model of another pool that "for only a few more dollars" comes completely installed. He generously offers to let you off the hook from your signed deal, when in fact he's starting to reel in his catch.

Such pool-peddling practices are deplored by the National Swimming Pool Institute, a trade group of 1,500 swimming-pool companies. The Institute has moved to expose bait ads in some local newspapers and to fight unethical sellers.

The best defense, the institute says, is to be wary when wading into a pool purchase. Check out not only the seller but also any subcontractor that does the actual installation; ask for names of other customers; if a salesman insists a bargain price is available "tonight only," show him the door; if you succumb to a sales pitch, remember the

Truth-in-Lending Law gives you three days to cancel most home-improvement credit contracts.[16]

The Risks of Over-Improving

Adding a new wing to your house may send the value of your home flying skyward. The only trouble is that it may send it flying way beyond the value of other homes in your neighborhood. That means your wing won't have a prayer of a chance of paying for itself when you sell your house.

"For example, if a $60,000 house is surrounded by $80,000 houses, then a $15,000 room addition will immediately be added in full to the market price" by tax assessors, said Russ Honza, Jr., president of the Northern California chapter of the Society of Governmental Appraisers. "But there will be little, if any, jump in the resale value if the surrounding houses are worth $50,000. Then we are talking about over-improvement for a neighborhood," Mr. Honza said.

What amounts to "over-improvement" depends on the housing market in your neighborhood. In an area of rapidly-rising prices, the value of a major overhaul may keep pace with the market. In an area of slower-growth, the same project may push you beyond the market. Home improvements are another reason you should keep abreast of values in your neighborhood even if you aren't planning to move anytime soon.

There aren't any hard-and-fast rules on how much you can expect to recover from a home-improvement project in added value. But barring over-improvement, Mr. Honza estimated for *Hudson Home Guide* that the remodeling of a home would have the following dollar-percentage return should the house be sold:

· 100% for adding space to the home.

· 75% for the modernization of existing rooms.

· 50% (or less) for "luxury type" items, such as a swimming pool, greenhouse, fireplace, patio, etc.

According to Mr. Honza, the following table in a sample of those used by governmental appraisers in establishing value increases related to home remodeling:

Adding New Space	Suggested Value Increase and % Investment Recovery
Bedroom additions	75-100%
New bath	70-100
New kitchen	60-100
Family or dining room additions	65-100
Two-car garage	60-100
MODERNIZING EXISTING ROOMS	
Basement to recreation room	30%
Garage to family rooms	30%
Attic to bedroom	30-50%
Bath modernization	45-55%
LUXURY OR SPECIAL ITEMS	
Greenhouse	20% or less
Fireplace addition	25-40%
Insulation	100%
Decking or patio	25%
Central air-conditioning	75-85%

Home-Improvement Costs

The costs of home improvements naturally vary widely depending on where you live and exactly what work you want done. Generally, for major additions you can count on a cost of $30 to $50 a square foot. The best way to check costs in your area is to contact several contractors or materials dealers. But to aid in your remodeling ruminations, we have obtained a long list of estimated costs for typical home-improvement or repair jobs. The following table on "Costs of Remodeling or Repair" was prepared by Home-Tech Systems of Bethesda, Maryland. The figures are based on what a contractor would charge a homeowner in the Washington, D.C./Baltimore, Maryland, metropolitan areas in 1981.

Home-Tech found that the costs include one-third for materials, one-third for labor, and one-third for profit. That means there is some leeway for bargaining with competing home improvers to get a lower price. And if you're handy with tools, you may be able to save up to two-thirds of the cost by doing the work yourself.

Choosing a Remodeler: What to Watch Out For

Remodeling is known as a business with a lot of rip-off artists. The Council of Better Business Bureaus says consumers ask for reports on home-remodeling contractors more often than on any other businesses, and that the settlement rate on complaints is well below the 76% average of all business.

Table 10-1

Costs of Remodeling or Repair (Washington-Baltimore Area) 1981

Remodel kitchen	$ 4000—$ 6000
Remodel bath	$ 2500—$ 4500
Add powder room	$ 1500—$ 2500
Add full bath	$ 2500—$ 4500
Increase electrical service to 200 amps	$ 400—$ 500
Run separate electrical line for dryer	$ 75—$ 100
Run separate electrical line for a/c	$ 75—$ 125
Install new warm air furnace	$ 800—$ 1200
Install central air-conditioning, electric	$ 1000—$ 1500
Install central air-conditioning, gas	$ 1500—$ 2000
Install humidifier	$ 180—$ 200
Install electrostatic air cleaner	$ 400—$ 550
Install new 40-gallon hot water heater	$ 200—$ 275
Install new 30-gallon hot water heater	$ 175—$ 225
Install attic ventilating fan	$ 150—$ 250
Install storm windows, each	$ 30—$ 40
Install replacement windows, each	$ 175—$ 250
Install new gutters and downspouts, $2.50 linear ft.	$ 300—$ 400
Install new asphalt shingle roof	$ 1000—$ 1800
Dig and install new well	$ 1500—$ 2500
Install new septic system	$ 1500—$ 2500
Build rear addition, approx. 300 sq. ft. $35 to $45/sq. ft.	$10000—$14000
Sand and finish floors, 50¢ to 70¢/sq. ft.	$ 600—$ 1200
Install new drywall ceiling over plaster, per room	$ 150—$ 250
Regrade around exterior	$ 250—$ 500
Install new sump pump	$ 250—$ 390
Install French drain and sump pump	$ 1500—$ 2500
Enclose porch	$ 2500—$ 4000
Install new hot-water boiler	$ 1000—$ 1800

Install new copper horizontal water pipes in basement	$ 500—$	900
Insulate attic, 50¢/square foot	$ 350—$	800
Remove interior non-loadbearing wall	$ 300—$	500
Remove exterior wall and install sliding doors	$ 800—$	1200
New single garage	$ 4000—$	5000
New double garage	$ 5000—$	8000
Masonry fireplace	$ 1500—$	2500
Pre-fab fireplace	$ 1100—$	1500
New kitchen floor-Solarian, $2.00/sq. ft.	$ 200—$	500
Basement apartment to meet code	$15000—$20000	
Gut and renovate two-story townhouse, $20.00 to $25.00/sq. ft.	$20000—$35000	
Replace disposal	$ 100—$	150
Install new disposal-drop waste	$ 200—$	300
Replace dishwasher	$ 300—$	500
Replace refrigerator	$ 350—$	700
Replace cooking equipment	$ 300—$	900
Install countertop with stainless steel sink	$ 250—$	350
Install bath vanity	$ 200—$	300
Drop concrete floor—townhouse	$ 2500—$	3500
Replace laundry tub—single fiberglas	$ 100—$	150
Install plumbing for laundry—within 5" of plumbing	$ 250—$	450
Vent dryer—easy access	$ 25—$	50
Pour concrete patio—$2.00–$3.00/sq. ft.	$ 300—$	800
Install overhead garage door—single	$ 175—$	250
Install overhead garage door—double	$ 350—$	500
Install garage door opener	$ 250—$	300
Replace flat roof—townhouse, selvage 4-ply built-up ($2/sq. ft.) galvanized	$ 1200—$	1800
Install storm door	$ 75—$	125
Reline fireplace with terra cotta	$ 1000—$	1400
Repoint brick exterior, $1 to $2/sq. ft.	$ 300—$	500
Install skylight	$ 500—$	800
Install bars on windows, $4 to $6/sq. ft. (ea.)	$ 60—$	75
Install wrought-iron door (ea.)	$ 150—$	200
Install ceramic tile in tub area—mastic	$ 250—$	350
mud	$ 350—$	500
Change sash cords in windows (per side)	$ 12	
Install aluminum siding, $1.50 to $2/sq. ft.	$ 2000—$	4000
Paint interior of house—small	$ 1000—$	1800
medium	$ 1500—$	2500
large	$ 2000—$	4000
Replace slate roof, $3 sq./ft.	$ 3000—$	7000
cedar shake roof, $2/sq. ft.	$ 2000—$	6000
Install disappearing stairway to attic	$ 125—$	150
Build redwoord or pressure-treated deck (sq. ft.)	$ 10—$	12
Basement conversion—component items	($ 1500—$	4000)

Kitchen	$3000—$5000		
Bath	$2000—$3500		
Electrical	$1200—$1800		
Heating and A/C—separate	$1500—$2500		
Heat-copper baseboard	$ 800—$1500		
Paint	$ 400—$ 700		
Drywall	$1500—$2500		
Carpentry	$1500—$2500		
Drop Floor	$2500—$3500		
Build 30′ shell dormer—finished exterior		$ 4000—$ 5000
Run new water line to street		$ 800—$ 1500
Install burglar alarm system if tied into central—monthly charge (per mo.)		$ 18—$ 25
Replace front door		$ 200—$ 500
Build closet		$ 300—$ 500

Actually, the rip-off artists are in the minority. But you should beware of the following possibilities:

· *Bait-and-switch tactics:* As we mentioned earlier with swimming pools, this is when the seller advertises an unrealistically low price for an item and then tries to switch you to a costlier product. These tactics show up often with such products as siding, carpeting and roofing. There also are sneaky variations, such as the following ploy:

You answer an advertisement for an aluminum siding bargain, and a salesman calls at your house. The salesman actually sells you the siding at the bargain price. On his way out the door, the salesman pauses and casually announces: "By the way, I forgot to tell you. We'll put your name and address on the back of the siding free of charge."

"Why," you ask, "would you want to do that?"

"Because," he replies, "if the wind gets above 30 miles an hour, this stuff will blow off. With your name on it, whoever finds it will be able to return it to you."

You begin to panic, since you have just signed a contract to buy the "stuff." No need to worry, the salesman says. "I have a better grade of siding that won't blow away. Of course, it costs a lot more." Anxious to get out of your deal, you sign up for the new siding which probably will clost you a lot more than if you had bought it from a reputable dealer.

- *The model-home scheme:* In this ploy, the sales person offers to sell you siding or some other improvement at a cut price if you will agree to allow your home to be used as a model of the company's work. What's more, the price will be reduced further for every customer who signs up for a similar job after seeing your house. Usually, there are no other customers, and the siding costs more than you would pay without such an arrangement.

- *Downgrading:* This is the practice of selling you a high-quality home-improvement item or materials at a premium price but then substituting lower quality— and cheaper—items when the work is actually performed. For example, the kitchen range may look like the one you're paying for as part of a modernization plan, but it could be the cheaper unit.

- *Construction liens:* If your contractor is in shaky financial condition and goes out of business or can't pay his bill, you could end up being liable for some of his debts. For example, if the bankrupt remodeler hasn't paid for the lumber he bought to use in your room addition, the supplier could come after you to pay the debt and legally, in many states, you would have to pay for it. There have been cases where consumers not only ended up paying a defunct contractor for work that never was done, but had to pay a second time for the materials that never were used on their house.

What can you do to protect yourself from such abuses? First, take the time to make sure you are dealing with a reputable dealer. Check his record with local consumer protection agencies and Better Business Bureaus. Get references from former customers and call them. Talk to your lender and ask him for a recommendation. Find out if the contractor is approved by a lender to do work under the Federal Housing Administration home-improvement program. You also might check to see if he is a member of either the National Remodelers Association or the National Home-Improvement Council, the leading remodelers' trade groups. Both groups screen members and can act as a go-between in case of disputes.

Be skeptical of unbelievably cheap prices because, in most

cases, they are just that—unbelievable. Be wary of bargain remodeling prices advertised in the TV sections of newspapers; such ads are poorly policed by the newspapers and many fall into the bait-and-switch category. A home-improvement booklet published by the U.S. Department of Housing and Urban Development offers its advice: "Avoid wild bargains. The best bargain is a good job."

HUD and other officials also give these suggestions:

- Get free, written estimates of the work you want done and make sure each bid is based on the same specifications and grade of material. Most reputable remodelers will use a cost book to calculate their estimates, so beware of people who offer quick estimates off the top of their heads. Ask for construction plans, and if you don't understand them, ask somebody who does. Show them to your lender. Don't be afraid to ask. It's your money you will be spending.

- Beware of the lowest bid if it seems too much lower than the others. Does it cover the same work, or is something missing?

- When you sign a contract, make sure the contract spells out the type and extent of improvements to be made. To make sure you get what you are paying for, the contract should cover the materials to be used, including brand names and model numbers. The contract should specify the cost of the job and the date or dates of payments. If the job involves a large expenditure, you might consider having a lawyer go over the contract before you sign it. Remember, the Truth-in-Lending Law gives you three days to cancel most home-improvement contracts.

- To curtail the chances of undue delay—one of the most common and aggravating remodeling problems—consider putting in the contract a date when the work is to begin and when it is to be completed. If you can, include penalties for non-completion after a specified time.

- Make sure the contract lists all interest and service charges. It also should include a payment schedule. A common schedule is to pay the remodeler a certain amount when he starts work, another payment when the job is half completed, and the rest when the job is finished to your satisfaction.

- Include a clause that says if the contractor goes bankrupt, you can't be held liable for debts he has for materials or labor. Have the contractor provide you with either a waiver of liens or verification that he is bonded against such costs.
- Never sign a completion certificate until all the work has been done to your satisfaction.

Do-It-Yourself Home Improvements

A do-it-yourself fever has gripped a growing number of homeowners and sent their remodeling expenditures soaring to an estimated $24.2 billion in 1980 from $8.9 billion in 1973, according to a survey by the Building Supply News, a Chicago-based trade publication.

Do-it-yourself has become chic. "It's an ego trip," one industry observer said. "Five years ago you'd throw a cocktail party, take people into the finished basement and say, 'Look what I just had done.' Now you throw a party, take them down and say, 'I just did this myself,'" he said.

But doing your own remodeling is much more than an ego trip. The do-it-yourself trend is spreading mainly because people are trying to stretch their budgets. Labor Department statistics show that between 1967 and 1978 the cost of home-maintenance repairs has jumped 92%, far outpacing the 65% increase in the overall cost-of-living index.

Experts estimate you can save one-half to two-thirds of the cost of a remodeling project by buying the materials and doing the labor yourself. So if you are handy with tools, go ahead. Just remember, though, that if you do a sloppy job, it can detract from the value of the improvement. And HUD warns that, "Unless you are skilled in wiring, plumbing, installing heat systems and cutting through walls, you should rely on professionals for such work."

Financing a Home Improvement

Once you have an estimate of how much your home improvement will cost, but before you sign a contract to have the work done, find out what kind of loan you can get to pay for it. You have a choice of a variety of government-backed loans or conventional loans that aren't backed by any government agency.

- FHA Home-Improvement Loans: What is called the FHA Title One Home-Improvement Loan is the work horse of home-improvement financing. You can get up to a $15,000, 15-year loan for most home-improvement jobs except for certain jobs that aren't part of the structure of the house, such as swimming pools.

FHA doesn't make the loan. You get the loan from your savings and loan association, bank, credit union or mutual savings bank. What FHA, a federal agency, does, is to insure 90% of the risk the lender is taking in granting you the loan.

The advantage of an FHA-insured loan is that the interest rate usually is the cheapest available, because the federal government sets a ceiling on how much lenders can charge. The disadvantage is that if the rate is too far below the private market level, lenders may stop making FHA loans for a while.

Another advantage is that for a contractor to do a job financed under the FHA program, he must be qualified for approval by an insured lender. That doesn't mean FHA is responsible for or guarantees the contractor's work. But you most certainly could complain to the FHA if you had a legitimate gripe.

- VA Loans: The U.S. Veterans Administration also guarantees home-improvement loans. But to get one, you must be a veteran and you must be buying your house under a VA mortgage. In addition, you may have to shop around to find a lender who makes VA home-improvement loans.

- Conventional Loans: This is an ordinary loan from your bank, savings and loan association, or credit union. You just apply for a personal loan and use it to pay for remodeling. If you need a relatively large amount, say, more than $7,500, the lender may require some kind of description of what you are going to be doing to your house, and he may insist on putting a lien on your house to protect himself.

Interst rates on such loans vary, so be sure to shop around for the best rate. To give you an idea of how much a loan is likely to cost you, reprinted below is a typical payment schedule for various loan amounts:

TABLE 10-2

Rate Payment Schedules
Annual Percentage Rate—11.5%

	THREE YEARS			FIVE YEARS		
Amount Financed	Monthly Payments	Finance Charge	Total of Payments	Monthly Payments	Finance Charge	Total of Payments
$ 3,000	$100.03	$ 601.08	$ 3,601.08	$ 66.71	$ 1,002.60	$ 4,002.60
4,000	133.32	799.52	4,799.52	88.91	1,334.60	5,334.60
5,000	166.61	997.96	5,997.96	111.11	1,666.60	6,666.60
6,000	199.90	1,196.40	7,196.40	133.31	1,998.60	7,998.60
7,000	233.18	1,394.48	8,394.31	155.52	2,331.20	9,331.20
8,000	266.47	1,592.92	9,592.92	177.72	2,663.20	10,663.20
9,000	299.76	1,791.36	10,791.36	199.92	2,995.20	11,995.20
10,000	332.89	1,984.04	11,984.04	222.01	3,320.60	13,320.60

	SEVEN YEARS			TEN YEARS		
Amount Financed	Monthly Payments	Finance Charge	Total of Payments	Monthly Payments	Finance Charge	Total of Payments
$ 5,000	$ 87.84	$2,378.56	$ 7,378.56			
6,000	105.39	2,852.76	8,852.76			
7,000	122.94	3,326.96	10,326.96	$ 99.42	$4,930.40	$11,930.40
8,000	140.49	3,801.16	11,801.16	113.61	5,633.20	13,633.20
9,000	158.05	4,276.20	13,276.20	127.80	6,336.00	15,336.00
10,000	175.51	4,742.84	14,742.84	141.93	7,031.60	17,031.60

Annual Percentage Rate—12%

	TEN YEARS			ELEVEN YEARS		
Amount Financed	Monthly Payments	Finance Charge	Total of Payments	Monthly Payments	Finance Charge	Total of Payments
$11,000	$159.38	$ 8,125.60	$19,125.60	$151.94	$ 9,056.08	$20,056.08
12,000	173.86	8,863.20	20,863.20	165.75	9,879.00	21,879.00
13,000	188.35	9,602.00	22,602.00	179.57	10,703.24	23,703.24
14,000	202.84	10,340.80	24,340.80	193.38	11,526.16	25,526.16
15,000	217.33	11,079.60	26,079.60	207.19	12,349.08	27,349.08

	TWELVE YEARS			FIFTEEN YEARS		
Amount Financed	Monthly Payments	Finance Charge	Total of Payments	Monthly Payments	Finance Charge	Total of Payments
$11,000	$145.90	$10,009.60	$21,009.60	$133.32	$12,997.60	$23,997.60
12,000	159.17	10,920.43	22,920.48	145.44	14,179.20	26,179.20
13,000	172.43	11,829.92	24,829.92	157.56	15,360.80	28,360.80
14,000	185.69	12,739.36	26,739.36	169.68	16,542.40	30,542.40
15,000	198.96	13,050.24	28,650.24	181.80	17,724.00	32,724.00

All quotations based on 60 days from contract date to first payment. Rates and terms for amounts up to $35,000 available on request.
As quoted by the Union First National Bank of Washington in summer 1978.

But if the financing is to be handled by a finance company, it will cost you more. Make sure you will be getting an FHA-insured or conventional loan from a bank or savings institution. Even then, be sure to find out if you can get a better rate by arranging your own loan. Some contractors now offer to finance projects themselves, but it may be better to keep a lender as a buffer between you and the contractor should problems arise.

ELEVEN

Be a FISBO,
and Other Ways to
Sell Your Home

"People either laugh or cry when
they see what home prices are
today. The laughers always buy.
The cryers usually do, too."

—Real-estate agent, Ridgewood, New Jersey

In the heydays of the California house rush in mid-1977, a
Berkeley stockbroker was advised by a local real-estate agent
that his late mother's house could be sold for a top price of
$68,500. The stockbroker decided to try to sell the house
himself. He put up a sign—it said, "For Sale By Owner"—
one day at noon. Five minutes later, a man came to the door
and asked, "How much?" The stockbroker decided to try for
$74,000, and the man bought the house on the spot.

Don't think for a moment that happens very often. You
would have to have the right house in the right market at the
right time to come close to matching it. And the fact of the
matter is that 9 out of 10 home sellers rely on real-estate
agents. But the point is that getting the most out of your
home when you sell depends on knowing how to market it.

You probably will have to put in more time and effort than
the Berkeley stockbroker, but—whether you sell your home
yourself or with help—you, too, can get top dollar. The key is
to know how to "sell" your house rather than just put it up for
sale. And when it comes time to sell, you have three basic
alternatives:

1. You can sell your home yourself. Real-estate people call such owner-sellers FISBOs, a name derived from the initials of For Sale By Owner, or FSBO. Real-estate people also call such do-it-yourselfers by other names that we can't repeat in a family book.

The major advantage of selling your own home, of course, is that you save the real-estate commission of 5% to 7% of the selling price (less your selling expenses, of course). For example, if the Berkeley stockbroker had hired an agent to sell his mother's home, a 6% commission on the $74,000 selling price would have cost him $4,440.

2. You can sell your home yourself, but with a little help from some hired friends. Sprouting up around the country are a growing number of real-estate concerns that specialize in for-sale-by-owner home sales. For a flat fee, usually between $500 and $800, these companies will provide certain marketing and legal services to help you sell your home yourself. And the cost still is less than you would pay a real-estate broker.

3. You can hire a real-estate company to sell your home. If you prefer not to sell your own home, or if you have a hard time peddling it, you can turn to a professional real-estate agent. As we said, an agent will charge a commission of 5% to 7% of the selling price, but you can negotiate a lower rate. And there are an increasing number of discount agencies that charge as low as 3% to 4% if you do some of the work yourself.

Which selling alternative is best for you depends on your circumstances. Selling a home can be hard work, and if you don't have the time or the inclination, a real-estate agent may be your best bet. The same is true if you will be moving to another town soon, especially if your employer will pick up the cost of the real-estate commission. But if you are determined to do it, you can sell your own home and put the money you save in your pocket—or into the home you are buying.

Selling Your Home Yourself

When there are spiraling home prices and booming housing demand in many areas, more and more home sellers are become their own real-estate agents. Nobody knows for sure how many of the 3½ million or so existing homes sold in the United States each year are sold by sell-it-yourselfers, but estimates run as high as 10%.

This FISBO phenomenon also is being fueled by consumer advocates and others in how-to-do-it articles and books. In Maine, for example, the fuel has been added by John Quinn, head of the state's Bureau of Consumer Protection. His office has put out a 20-page booklet—called "Down Easter III—For Sale by Owner"—that tells people how to sell their homes without a real-estate broker. ("Down Easter" is a term for a Maine fisherman.)

The Wall Street Journal

"Sure, I'll be happy to show you something in the $12,000 class. You're looking at it."

Maine real-estate agents are up in arms about the book, which has been in hot demand by consumers. Mr. Quinn said he is only doing his job, but that he can understand the flak "because already between 20% and 30% of Maine residents sell their own homes, and I guess the brokers don't want the habit to spread." The booklet is available free to Maine residents and for $1 to outsiders (to get a copy, write the Maine Bureau of Consumer Protection in Augusta, Maine 04333).

The sell-it-yourself approach especially "fits the person who absolutely has to have as much equity out as possible" from the home he is selling to move up to a better one, noted one real-estate seller who specializes in for-sale-by-owner sales.

If you are patient, you can sell your home yourself. But some circumstances are more favorable for do-it-yourself sales than others. If you are going to sell a house yourself instead of using a broker, these are the major market ingredients you should think about:

- Are you in a strong housing market? You don't have to live in a red-hot market like parts of California, but you need high demand and an upbeat market with lots of people looking and buying. This is known as a "seller's market." If demand is slow in the city or town where you live, and there are more homes than usual for sale, you are in a "buyer's market," and you may have a tough time selling your home yourself.

- Is your home in a good location? If your home is in an area that is sought after by large groups of potential buyers, then you are in a good position to sell your own home. But if you live in a part of town where house-hunters aren't likely to go looking on their own, you'll have to work harder to attract prospective buyers.

- Is mortgage money easily obtainable? If mortgage money is plentiful and buyers can get home-loans easily, your chances of selling your own home improve. But if money is tight, you may be at a disadvantage unless you are willing to finance the sale yourself. This is because your potential buyer may have trouble coming up with a mortgage. And, unlike a real-estate broker, who probably has built up connections with local lenders, you may be hard put to supply your customer with a lead on where to find mortgage money. You can find out what shape the local mortgage-money market is in by reading the financial pages of your newspaper; if lenders are advertising for home-loans and mortgage rates are relatively low, then money is generally available.

Selling-your-own-home isn't for everyone. But if market conditions are good, it's worth a try. You may find a buyer and save the real-estate commission. If you decide after a couple of weeks that do-it-yourself selling isn't for you, you can always hire a professional.

Whether you sell your own or hire an agent, there are two other factors to consider: Is your home in good, salable condition? And is it realistically priced?

Setting the Price

If there is a single key to selling your home—without or with a broker—it is in proper pricing. It may be even more important with do-it-yourselfers, because many buyers expect you to have a reasonable price since you are saving on the real-estate commission. Due to that savings, you may indeed have more bargaining room than otherwise, but there isn't any reason why you should sell your home at a cut-price. If you have a salable home in a good location, you should be able to get full market value—or even more. A Maryland man put his home, in a popular Washington, D.C., area, on the market for $100,000. The first day, the homeowner, who was selling the house himself, had four couples bidding in his living room. He sold the house that day for $104,000.

Proper pricing isn't an exact science. But it is more than guesswork. Here is what you can do:

· Don't rely on a "windshield" appraisal. This means you shouldn't drive around your neighborhood and guess what homes in your area would sell for. Rather, find out what other homes in your area are selling for.

· Start with the real-estate sections of your local newspaper. Look up classified ads for homes being sold in your neighborhood and see what the prices are. This will give you an idea what you will be competing with. But remember, these are the prices people hope to get, not what the houses actually sell for. To price your home correctly, you need to know actual sales prices.

· Check your newspapers again. In some areas, the local papers carry reports on home sales and list the actual selling prices of the homes.

· Check home-sales reports published by companies like Rufas S. Lusk & Son in Washington, D.C., and Real Estate Directory, Inc., in Philadelphia. There are similar services in most cities, and their reports usually are available at local libraries. With these reports you can see what houses in your neighborhood actually sold for.

· Go to the county courthouse and check home-sales records. Each sale must be registered, and the sales price is part of the public record.

· Have the value of your home appraised by the Veterans Administration. For $80, the VA will inspect your home and give you a written statement estimating its value. This is a good idea anyway, because with the VA appraisal you can advertise that your home can be purchased by a qualified veteran with a VA loan—a valuable selling aid. And you can use the appraisal as a guide for setting a price, whether you sell to a veteran or not.

· You can arrange for an appraisal by the Federal Housing Administration. But we advise against this unless you have a "live" buyer who is getting an FHA loan. An FHA appraisal, which costs $75, isn't acceptable to VA. But FHA will accept an appraisal by VA.

· Hire a private appraiser. Your lender may be able to recommend the one he uses. Or look up one in the Yellow Pages of your phone book (look under real-estate appraisers). Real-estate appraisers are professionals who will give you an appraisal based on three approaches to value—(1) comparable sales, (2) replacement value, (3) and market value. They generally charge $100 to $150. Many are members of the Real-Estate Appraisers or the Society of Real-Estate Appraisers, professional groups that set certain standards for members.

- Don't be too greedy. Set a realistic price. It doesn't do your pocket or your ego any good to let the house sit there week after week because you are asking too much. The general rule of thumb, real-estate people say, is that your house should be priced not more than 10% above, nor 10% below, comparable homes for sale in your neighborhood.

- Leave yourself some bargaining room. Real-estate experts suggest a leeway of 5% to 10% between your asking price and the minimum price you would accept. Thus, if you want to sell your home for $50,000, you could ask 5%, or $52,500 (or "the low $50's"). If you are in a strong market you can be firmer on your price.

Getting Your Home Ready to Sell

If you put some effort into making your house salable, you may be able to get just about every penny that you are asking.

Remember, first impressions are the most lasting. So start with the outside. Make sure your home invites people in rather than causes them to drive right by. Spend a few bucks to spruce up the place; it can pay off in a better price.

Outside the House

- Make sure the front door looks impressive. Fix it, paint it. Do whatever needs to be done to turn it into a welcoming mat.

- Scrape off the chipping paint on the gutters and have the gutters painted if you have to. Touch up the rough spots on the house with some paint. But don't paint the whole house unless it's really in bad shape.

- Trim the shaggy shrubbery, clean up the yard, and keep the grass cut. If you have time, spread some fertilizer on the grass to green it up some.

- Replace the broken steps leading to the door. Fix up the driveway. Put a fresh coat of sealer on the blacktop driveway.

- Wash the windows. Make them sparkle in the sunlight.

- Get rid of all the trash that's sitting around outside the house.

- If you have a garage, keep the garage door closed. Houses generally look better that way, If your garage is filled with so much junk that you couldn't squeeze a Volkswagen Beetle inside it, get rid of the junk. You need to show a roomy garage.

Inside the House

- Concentrate on the kitchen and the bathrooms. Those are the rooms that sell homes, so make them shine. Get everything off the kitchen countertop that doesn't make the kitchen more attractive. Get rid of excess tables or stools that take up space. Before prospects arrive, take the garbage out—your customer may stick his or her nose under your sink and/or wherever else your garbage bag may be.

In the bathroom, check the caulking around the tubs and clean and scrub the tiles. Buy a bright new shower curtain and toilet-seat cover. A few extra bucks here could pay big dividends. Neatly hang up some colorful towels and tell everyone in the family to use paper towels until after the lookers leave.

- Spruce up the bedrooms. These are big sellers, too. Make them cheery and bright. If you have a huge dresser in the smallest bedroom, move it somewhere else. People like spacious looking bedrooms.

- Make all the rooms look as roomy as possible. Push chairs and sofas against the walls to get a feeling of roominess. Get rid of all surplus dishes, pots and pans, and other things you don't use that make the house look cluttered.

- Clean up those faded walls. You don't have to redo the whole inside of the house, but a fresh coat of paint in a neutral color like white on the inside walls could brighten your whole house as well as your chances of getting a better price.

- Show big closets. You can't really make them bigger, of course. But you can make them look big by reorganizing or removing some clothing you have hung inside. Rent storage space if you have to, but make sure your closets aren't jammed with stuff.

- Stop the drips. Get the leaky faucets fixed. The leaks may be minor, but they are hard to explain and may make buyers think the plumbing is faulty.

- Clean up the basement. Get rid of all the accumulated junk you've been meaning to throw out for years. If the basement is too dark, put a light in. A coat of white water-proof paint might do wonders. Clean out the attic, too, if you have one. Remember, you are selling space, so don't hide it.

- Tighten all the door knobs. That may not seem important, but have you ever seen a prospective buyer who opened a door and ended up with a doorknob in his hand? It's not very funny if you are the seller.

Naturally, you'll want to make sure that basic parts of the house such as the heating and cooling system, the wiring, and the plumbing are in adequate working condition. But beyond that, the goal is to spruce up your home from top to bottom so that you can put its features to their best advantage.

Getting the Papers Ready

Before you start showing your house to potential buyers, you should get together all the papers you'll need for your sale. They include:

- The title, or deed, to your property.
- Your mortgage. (You'll want to check how much you owe on the mortgage and whether it can be assumed by another buyer.)
- A property plat. This is the map that you should have received when you bought your home. It shows the property lines of your land and how your home is situated on the land.
- A description of room sizes. If you don't have an old house plan, make a new one yourself. Figure the total space of the living area. Find out the size of your lot.
- An appraisal statement, if you had an appraisal done.

- A list of all appliances that will be sold with the home, and a list of items that will be removed. These also should be written into the sales contract.

- A list showing annual property taxes, monthly gas and electric bills, water bills, and any special assessments for your home.

- A list of, and receipts for, any home improvements which have added value to the home.

- A list of local schools and churches, swim clubs, tennis clubs, and recreational facilities. You may be able to get a booklet from your local Chamber of Commerce or local government that describes services in your area. This could be especially valuable to out-of-town buyers.

- If you are selling a condominium, you will need some extra papers. They include your declaration of covenants, or the master deed; the bylaws of your owners' association, and a list of rules governing the use of the property. You also may need copies of any ground leases or recreational leases, financial statements of your owners' association, and a statement showing you have paid your owners' assessment. If you are selling a converted condo, you may have to provide an engineering report. Remember to check any restrictions on selling your unit before putting it up for sale.

- In any case, you will need a sales contract. You can buy standard home-sales contracts at most office supply stores. Or you can have one drawn up by a lawyer, which we would suggest you do if you are selling your home yourself.

Hiring a Lawyer

As a do-it-yourself home seller, it's a good idea to hire a lawyer before you set out on your sales project. A lawyer can help you draw up a sales contract that suits your needs and protects your interests. You probably would need to hire an attorney at least before you go to settlement on a final sale; there are lots of legal papers that must be processed in the final stages of a home sale, and you probably will need someone to take care of them. And hiring a lawyer will be far cheaper than paying a real-estate commission.

Among other things, you also will need a third party to handle the money that a prospective buyer puts down as a deposit when he agrees to buy your home. He isn't likely to want to leave the money with you. Normally, the money is put in a special escrow account, held by a third party, until settlement. A lawyer can handle this arrangement for you. How do you find a lawyer? It's not easy. Look for a specialist in real estate. Your friends may be able to suggest one. So may your lender or—to make sure you get one who is consumer-protection oriented—you might ask public-interest groups in your town if they can suggest anyone.

Don't be afraid to ask a prospective lawyer how much he charges. You should pay a lawyer a pre-arranged fee, or one based on the time he works for you. Avoid lawyers who charge a percentage of the selling price of your home.

Lining Up Financing

Since you are the seller, you may wonder why you have to be concerned about the buyer's financing. And, in fact, your buyer may want to do his own shopping for a mortgage. But it just could be the clincher you need if a prospective buyer asks, "Where can I get financing?" and you can answer: "I have contacted the First National Savings and Loan, and they said they would make a 20%-down loan at 12% for 30 years to a qualified buyer."

You don't have to arrange a loan in advance, but you should get as much information as you can about the availability of financing.

- Check first with the lender holding the mortgage on your home. He put his money on your house once and may be willing to do so again if you come up with a qualified buyer.

- Call several lenders. Don't be afraid to ask them about their loan terms. Ask for the mortgage loan officers and find out if home loans are available, the down payments they require, their mortgage rates, and other fees. Find out about FHA, VA and special loans.

- Prepare a list of lenders you have talked with and the terms they offer. You can show this to your prospective

SHANNON & LUCHS
2600 University Blvd. W., Wheaton, Md. 20902

CONFIDENTIAL HOME REQUIREMENTS AND SURVEY

Name_____ Add _____ Home Phone _____
Bus._____ Add _____ Bus. Phone _____
No. in Family ____ Children's Ages _____

Other Family Members _____

Possession   Renting or   How Long
Needed When _____   Sell First _____   Looking (No.) _____
                                          Down   Monthly
Price $____ To $____ Max $_____ Pmt.$_____ Pmts. $_____
Necessary Anyone
Else See Home _____ Other _____

CHOICE FACTORS	REQUIREMENTS	HOME "A"	HOME "B"	HOME "C"
Type - 1st.				
- 2nd.				
Construction - 1st.				
- 2nd.				
Area Pref. - 1st.				
- 2nd.				
Bedrooms - No. & Sizes				
Den				
Baths				
Living Room - Style & Size Prefs.				
Dining Room - Size				
Kitchen - (T.S.)				
Recreation Room				
Basement ½ Full				
Workshop - Other Sp.				
Fireplace				
Storage - Extra				
Heat & Fuel				
Air Conditioning				
Garage, Carport, or Off-st. Parking				
Lot Size & Type Trees, Garden, Etc.				
Price				
Down Payment				
Possession				

SUMMARY..

School Requirements _____
Shopping _____
Transportation _____
Any other Special
Requirements

SHANNON & LUCHS
2600 University Blvd. W., Wheaton, Md. 20902

<u>ANALYSIS OF HOME OWNERSHIP COSTS</u>

(For Taxpayer Using Itemized Deductions)

PREPARED FOR: _____

By: _____

1. Sale Price of Home: $_____

2. Cash Required: $_____

3. Loan: $_____. ___ years at ___% interest.

4. Monthly Payments, principal and interest $_____

5. Monthly Deposit for taxes, approximately $_____

6. Monthly Deposit for insurance, approximately $_____

7. TOTAL MONTHLY PAYMENT: $_____

8. EXPENSE ITEMS FOR INCOME TAX PURPOSES:

9. First month interest: $_____

10. Monthly tax deposit: $_____

11. TOTAL DEDUCTIONS $_____

(12. In 50% tax bracket, deduct cash saving per month $_____
(13. In 40% tax bracket, deduct cash saving per month $_____
(14. In 30% tax bracket, deduct cash saving per month $_____
(15. In 20% tax bracket, deduct cash saving per month $_____

16. Total Monthly Payment: (Line #7) $_____

17. Subtract Applicable Deduction: (Line 12-13-14 or 15) $_____

18. ACTUAL MONTHLY PAYMENT: $_____

19. Subtract EQUITY which is being gained monthly: $_____

20. ACTUAL MONTHLY COST: $_____

Interest decreases by small amount each month, but equity increases
by the same amount.

buyer. Get loan applications that you can give to a buyer.

- Also prepare a cost sheet showing figures for down payment requirements of your home and what the monthly payment would be. You should also find out from the lenders the income requirements for a buyer to qualify for a loan on your home. We have included a cost-analysis sheet used by Shannon & Luchs, a major realtor in the Washington, D.C., area which you can use to figure the payments, and tax benefits, of a prospective home buyer. You can use the tables in the financing chapter of this book to calculate the figures. You also should be able to tell your buyer about what closing costs he can expect to pay.

- Use "creative financing," which means that you would be the lender for your buyer. During times when mortgage loans are hard to get and rates are out of sight, it might be the only way to sell your home.

For example, you can offer the buyer a low-interest loan—yours. This can be a big incentive if you have a fairly recent mortgage that can be assumed with an affordable down payment, or if you have an older mortgage with a low interest rate. Let's say, for example, that the current market rate is 11% and you have $30,000 left to pay on a mortgage with an interest rate of 6%. You could offer to let the buyer assume your 6% mortage, if the lender permits this.

The advantage to the buyer is obvious: He can get a $30,000 loan for 6% annual interest instead of 11%. The difference: $101.74 a month in mortgage payments, or a 23% savings ($193.30 versus $294.04 a month on a 25-year mortgage).

There are some catches, though. For one, if you made a big down payment or if the value of your home has increased greatly since you bought it, a $30,000 mortage won't cover most of the purchase price. That means the buyer must come up with a big down payment or you will have to take back a second mortgage and let the buyer make payments on that loan to you. If so, be sure he has a strong income and can afford to make the payments on both your old mortgage and the second mortgage.

Another potential catch for you as the seller is that you can still be held responsible if the buyer defaults on the assumed mortgage. On the other hand, the lender will still have the house as a security and probably would only move against you if he couldn't get his money from the new mortgage-holder or from selling the house.

The other problem is that lenders are invoking "due on sale" clauses to keep sellers from passing on their low-interest loans to buyers. And the Federal National Mortgage Association (Fannie Mae), the nation's biggest buyer of mortgages in the resale mortgage market, has refused to allow assumptions on loans it holds.

The issue is still being fought in the courts. The safest course is to find out who owns your mortgage and if the loan can be assumed, even at a slightly higher interest rate, if necessary. Send a letter and a self-addressed envelope to your lender, and he will mail you the information.

Check the "Tight Money Tips" section in Chapter Six of this book for other types of owner-financing that you can use. And if you decide to finance a buyer's mortgage yourself on an installment basis, Fannie Mae—this same company that is making assumptions more difficult —may be able to help you get cash for the loan. It has begun buying mortgages that homeowners accept as payment from buyers. The loans must be made on Fannie Mae's standard documents, must meet standard credit and appraisal standards and must be serviced (the payments collected) by an approved lender. Sellers who hold such mortgages would receive monthly and interest payments, minus whatever fee is charged by the servicing lender. The mortgages could be converted to cash by selling them to Fannie Mae.

Creative financing is a "must" if you have to sell your home when potential buyers can't get affordable mortgage loans, the experts say. It also can add to your profits. "We tell sellers, 'Buyers will pay more for a property if the seller will help finance it. What can you do to help with the financing?'" said Mary Gast, president of Doris Brown Realtors in Chicago.

You can turn the buyer's paranoia about high interest rates to your advantage. A Grand Rapids, Michigan, seller, for example, planned to reduce the price on his house to $47,000 from $50,000 in an attempt to attract buyers. But Westdales' Better Homes & Gardens Inc., a realty firm, advised him to cut the interest rate on the seller-financing contract he was offering to 9% from 14% instead. "With people so brainwashed that interest rates are too high, it's more effective to drop the rate rather than the price," said Leonard L. Westdale, Jr., the firm's executive vice president. "People think they're getting a real steal."

Advertising Your Home

Once you have your papers and financing information lined up, you're ready to get down to the business of selling your home. What you want to do now is let the world know that your home is for sale. The best way to do that is to advertise. Here is what you do:

- Get a For Sale sign and put it up in your yard. Don't stick up a piece of cardboard or plywood with "For Sale" scribbled on it with a crayon. You are in business now, so be professional. If you want the cheapest sign, go to the hardware store and buy one. Better yet, have a simple sign made for you. It should say:

> **For Sale—By Owner**
> **Phone: (your number)**
> **By Appointment Only**

The part about making an appointment is important. It discourages people who are just curious about what your house looks like from dropping in unexpectedly at all hours. A serious buyer will be glad to make an appointment. But first, take time to write an appealing ad.

- Start writing a classified advertisement for the newspapers. According to real-estate professionals, newspaper advertising is the single most effective medium for selling homes. A study of 2,500 families by the Newspaper Advertising Bureau, a newspaper-industry group based in New York City, revealed that 77% of all home buyers checked newspaper ads before they bought.

- Think about what buyers you want to reach. Make a list of the characteristics of the potential buyer of your home. What kind of people would like your house? Would they be young or older? What parts of your house would appeal to them? What appealed to you? By considering who your audience is, you can write a better advertisement.

- Think of a "grabber" headline. The headline is the most important element of a home-sales ad, representing 75% of the total value of the ad, according to the Newspaper Advertising Bureau. Thus, if the headline doesn't grab your reader's attention, you may have wasted your money.

There aren't any magic headlines that are sure-fire attention-getters. The best advice is to try to be imaginative and different. Just to get your creative juices flowing, here are some sample "grabber" headlines offered by professional realtors. "A Great Buy for Newlyweds"; "No Need for Two Cars"; "Has a Built-in Workshop"; "The Kids Can Walk to School"; "Looking for Something Different?" and "A Country Setting with City Convenience."

When writing headlines or the text of ads, remember what most people want in a house. According to the National Association of Realtors, "People buy because of schools, a quieter or more peaceful neighborhood, more space, more privacy, transportation, shopping, recreation facilities, unique features of the property or home, or maybe just because the house is easier to take care of. So tell your buyer about the spiral staircase, cathedral ceiling, double fireplace, wet bar, wooded lot and stockade fence." Oh yes. When you are selling it yourself, be sure part of the headline says, "By Owner." That will attract buyers who hope to share in the savings on the lack of a commission.

- Keep your ad short and factual. Avoid real-estate abbreviations; they only confuse people. Use bright, cheery words that make your home sound appealing. According to the newspaper-advertising survey, 82% of all real-estate ad readers look first for an indication of the neighborhood in which the home is located. Cost was the second most-looked-for factor. Then readers wanted to know things like number of bedrooms, whether the kitchen is large and modern, condition of the home and lot, type of styling and the presence of fireplaces.

· Include the price of the house, or at least a general indication, such as "Upper 50's." Nothing drives house-lookers crazy faster than spotting something that sounds appealing in the paper and then not knowing whether it's in their price range or not. By including the price, you automatically screen people who can't afford your home. And you save yourself the trouble of answering phone calls from people who just want to know the price. One caution: never say in an ad that your price is an "asking" price; that's just inviting buyers to make you a lower offer.

· Don't forget to include your phone number. If you are advertising an open house, include the address and accurate directions. Indicate some kind of nearby land-mark that will help people find you.

· Above all, make sure your ad is truthful. Exaggerations may win you lookers but will lose you buyers.

· Consider direct-mail advertising. As an individual sell-er, you don't want to get into mass mailing of advertis-ing for your home. But it might be a good idea to draw up what's called a "listing sheet" for your home and have a couple of dozen copies made. First, take a picture of your home—a Polaroid shot will do fine—and glue the photo on a sheet of paper. On the bottom, list all the features of your home, the sizes of the rooms, the taxes and the price. You can give copies to person-nel people at local offices of corporations or military bases, and you can mail copies to prospective buyers in other cities. Your listing just may fall into the hands of people who are moving to your town or looking for a new place near where they already live.

Don't overlook bulletin boards at local stores, churches, community centers, and offices. Post your listing sheet at such locations.

Handling Phone Inquiries

Once your ad runs, the phone should start ringing. You should handle phone inquiries something like this:

- Be friendly and factual. Answer questions about price, but don't haggle over the phone. Try to avoid long questioning. Tell them in a diplomatic fashion, "You really must come out and see the house."

- Thank them for their interest and arrange to show the house at a precise date and hour. Don't just say, "Why don't you drop in some time tomorrow?"

- Be sure to get the caller's name and phone number. If he is reluctant to give that information, tell him it is important in case something happens and you have to cancel the appointment.

- If you can't be at the telephone, make sure that somebody else is. If you aren't home, instruct the person who answers to say: "This is Mr. Smith. Mr. Brown will be in at 6 p.m., and he will be glad to call you then." Don't let your substitute salesperson discuss price or other details. Make sure he or she gets the names and telephone numbers of all callers.

- Sometimes a caller will want to see a house right away. If he sounds like a good prospect, and it can't be avoided, let him come over. You can whip the house in shape quickly if you have to. When one Maryland couple got unexpected lookers, they immediately yelled "Red Alert" and the whole family began cleaning up the house and tossing odds and ends behind chairs and under beds. And any veteran of the home-selling wars will tell you that as often as not the person who drops in when the house is a mess ends up buying.

If the prospective buyers are a couple, try to get them to see the house together. You must sell them both. Wives frequently make the final decision—so don't be too sure that you have sold the house if the husband comes alone and says, "I like the house. I'd like to buy it. Let me bring my wife by tomorrow."

Showing Your Home

One of the best ways to attract prospects is to hold an open house. You advertise in the newspaper that your home will be open from, say, noon to 6 p.m.—Sunday is usually the biggest house-hunting day. Then you sit back and wait—and hope that buyers will flock to your doorstep.

But first, you have to get ready. In addition to the steps we mentioned before, here is what to do:

- Put up some signs to mark the way to your house. These are called "Stake Outs," and you should put up several near main roads leading to your house. These are the signs you see that say "Open House" with an arrow pointing in the proper direction.

- Have your home sparkling inside and out. Give the lawn a fresh mowing if the grass is still growing. Shovel the snow off the sidewalk if it has been snowing.

- Let the sun shine in. Open the curtains and drapes. Turn on the lights. You want the place to look bright and cheery. If it's hot, turn on the air-conditioner so people will know it works. If it's a cold winter day, have a cozy fire burning in the fireplace (if you have a fireplace).

- Give the house a welcome aroma. Some real-estate people suggest baking bread, a cake or some cookies just before showing a house so the bakery smell will be lingering when your prospective buyers arrive. Some even suggest turning down the bed in the master bedroom and draping a negligee over the bed. That may be going a bit far—unless you're trying to sell a condo unit in a "singles" project to a bachelor. And frankly, we don't know if baking bread is the sweet smell to success either. But most things that make your home more appealing are worth a try.

- Turn soft music on the radio. But don't turn your stereo full-blast with hard rock, and don't turn on the television set. Remember, you must be able to communicate with your prospects, and loud sounds are distracting.

- Send the kids up the street to play. Get your dogs and cats out of the house. Some people are allergic to pets. And children can be distracting, too.

- Look your best. Don't try to be a comedian. Be conservative in dress, behavior and discussion.

- When the prospects arrive, be polite and friendly, but don't force the conversation. This isn't a social call, so you don't have to worry about making small talk. The cardinal rule is Silence is Golden. When Mike Sumichrast worked for a home builder in Columbus, Ohio, the builder had a salesman who resembled Abraham Lincoln. The salesman didn't have a beard, but he was skinny, tall and slightly stooped. He was the company's best salesman. His greatest strength was that he hardly said anything. He always listened, nodded his head, and smiled a lot. He was very smart, he understood people, and they admired him. They also bought houses from him.

- Answer questions honestly. If you don't know the answer, don't make one up. Just tell the prospective buyer you don't know, but that you will be happy to find out and let him know.

- Don't hover around people while they're looking through the house. They want to make their own inspection and make up their own minds. Feel free, however, to guide them to what you consider to be the strong points of the home.

- Don't apologize for your home. It's your home, you live in it, and you know it's a good home. If you believe in your home and your ability to sell it, it will be easier to convince a buyer to like it too.

- Sell the benefits of the home. Don't just say you have a big family room; describe how it is the center of activity for your family and what you get out of it. If you are close to transportation, talk about how easy it is to commute downtown. In other words, sell a way of life.

- Get the names and phone numbers of everybody who calls. Professional salesmen usually don't sell prospects the first time they see them. A good agent follows up and calls the prospects later when they have had time to think about the houses they looked at. You should, too. Perhaps all that buyer who stopped by may need is one more bit of encouragement.

- Speaking of professional sales people, your lookers probably will include real-estate agents who simply cherish the idea of knocking on the doors of FISBOs and charming the seller behind the "For

Sale by Owner" sign into their own signs. Hold your ground, but consider reasonable offers to share a "commission" on a sale. When an agent from one broker brings a buyer to a house listed by a second, the two brokers split the commission (actually, the listing broker gets a shade more), so you can consider doing the same. Just be sure that you get a price which, after deducting, say, 3%, for a commission to the other agent, will leave you at or close to the minimum price you want if you sell yourself.

If an agent claims to have a buyer for your home and wants you to sign a listing contract, consider this: Agree to sign a contract limited only to the specific prospect by name. If there is in fact a buyer and he purchases your home, you would pay the agent his commission. If the prospect doesn't buy, you have no further obligation to the agent. Again, consider the selling price before making such an arrangement.

How to Tell the Buyers from the Lookers

Don't be deceived by appearance. A man driving a Cadillac may not have enough money to pay for the car, much less enough to make a down payment on your home. But the guy who drives up in a 1968 Ford pickup truck may be a hot prospect.

So the first rule is to treat everyone, no matter how he looks, as a potential buyer. But at the same time, you must be on the alert for tips that indicate you don't have a serious buyer on your hands. According to the National Association of Realtors, the lookers often fall into the following categories:

- The Idle-Hour Lookaround: This shopper hasn't any intention of buying, but just wants to kill time and maybe pick up a few decorating ideas.
- The Disappearing Drive-By: He makes a date to see your house but doesn't show. At the appointed time, a car creeps slowly past the house and then speeds out of sight.

- The Tight-fisted Bargain Bluff: He wants to buy for chickenfeed. He thinks the commission "savings" of an owner-seller should be passed on to him.
- The Under-Financed Fledgling: He would love to buy the house, but he doesn't know how big a loan he can qualify for or even where to find it.

You can add to these a couple of other types: one is the Be-Backs. These are the prospects who promise they'll be back tomorrow, and you never see them again.

Another is the buyer with the impossible demands. Joan Thomas, a real-estate agent in Westfield, New Jersey, had a house hunter with this inflexible demand: The basement had to be no smaller than 40 feet by 23½ feet. The man was building his own airplane and needed at least that much space to work on it. He eventually bought a house in another town.

Even the professionals have a hard time separating the buyers from the lookers, but there are tell-tale signs.

For instance, you shouldn't get upset if a looker criticizes your home. That's a good sign. "When they start finding fault with a house, that's when you know they are ready to buy," said Mrs. Thomas, the Westfield real-estate agent. "On the other hand, when they say a house is 'so nice,' that means they aren't interested."

- Remember that many houses are bought on an emotional urge. When people walk in the door, they say to themselves, "This is it." Look for that light in their eyes and make sure that feeling is reinforced. First, of course, you've got to get the customer inside your door. One house hunter refused to enter a house he had been driven by five times because he didn't like the exterior. After listening to what the man wanted, the saleswoman insisted that he at least take a walk through the house. He did, and later bought the house.
- People moving from out of town aren't just looking; they must find a house. So find out something about your "lookers" and why they are looking.
- Serious buyers usually look more than once before buying. If a looker calls and wants to look again, he's serious, so treat him accordingly.

· Before you decide whether or not a looker is worth spending time with, get as much information as you can about him on a piece of paper. Take the "analysis of home-ownership costs" sheets we have shown in this chapter and sit down with the prospect and figure out exactly what he would have to pay if he bought your home. Get out your financing figures and try to determine if he will qualify for a mortgage. He may be reluctant to confide his income to you at this point, but show him what kind of payments you are talking about. It should be clear from his reaction whether he is over his head or whether he looks like a solid prospect.

Once you've picked up a "live" prospect, the goal is to wrap up a sale.

Closing the Sale

There have been whole books written on the subject of closing the sale. As we noted earlier in the book, there is an entire psychology of closing designed to carry the buyer along in a state of euphoria to a signed contract. The reason for all this attention is obvious: All of the selling work so far is for nothing unless you get a valid, signed contract.

Buying a home can be one of life's most traumatic experiences, so we would advise you to avoid high pressure tactics. Chances are, you'll only frighten a potentially good buyer away. What a buyer needs at this point is reassurance that he's making the right decision. If you're convinced you have a qualified buyer on your hands, you can help nudge him to making up his mind.

· Go over the financial figures again. Show him what he can expect to pay and what his tax savings will be. Try to answer, positively, any nagging doubts. If he wants to sleep on it, do what some home builders do: assuming the prospect lives in the area, ask if it would be all right if you drop by his own home to discuss the sale. Many people are more comfortable talking about their personal finances in their own homes.

· Never promise to hold a house for anyone. Another buyer may come along, or your first prospect may decide against buying, and you'll be left holding the bag—and your unsold home.

· Get all offers in writing. Don't haggle over price. If your home is priced at $55,000 and somebody asks, "Will you take $50,000?" tell him to make an offer in writing. Have him fill out and sign a contract stating what he will pay and tell him you'll give him a "yes" or "no" answer within 24 hours.

· Bargain hard, but don't be unreasonable. Decide on a minimum price you'll accept, but, naturally, don't tell anyone. If a contract offer is too low, make a counter-offer. Again do this in writing, with a signed contract (instead of writing a whole new contract, just cross out the offer in the first contract and write in your counter-offer and initial it). Your buyer may be willing to compromise, or he may make a third offer—again with a contract.

Remember to consider the current charges for "points." If you sell with a VA or FHA loan, write into the contract the maximum number of points you will pay. This will protect you if points rise sharply before the sale.

If you reach agreement, write up a final contract, sign it, and have your buyer sign it. Remember, when pondering whether to accept a contract offer, rather than lose a deal, consider the buyer. Sometimes it's better to accept a bit less if the buyer is highly-qualified and the deal seems sure-fire.

· Get a deposit. When you accept a signed contract, the buyer should give you a sizable deposit. This is called "earnest money," because it is evidence that the buyer is earnest about going through with the sale. The deposit is counted towards the buyer's down payment and usually is specified in the contract. If the contract is rejected, the money is immediately refunded. It also is refunded if the buyer can't obtain financing—this, too, is stipulated in the contract with a limit on how long the buyer has to obtain financing. If the buyer otherwise reneges on the deal, he loses his deposit and you get it.

This deposit should be put in escrow with a third party. Indeed, the buyer no doubt will insist on it. If you have a lawyer, he'll take care of this matter. Or you can arrange to have a title company or lender set up an account to hold the money.

Don't Get Stuck With Two Houses

It's not always easy to coordinate smoothly the sale of your old house with the purchase of your new one—as one author of this book discovered. But there are ways to limit the risks of winding up—and making payments on—two houses at the same time.

- Sell first, buy later: The safest precaution is simply to sell your house before you buy another. That way you will get rid of one mortgage before you take on another. And since you will have the money in hand when you go house-shopping, you will be in a strong position to negotiate a better deal than a buyer who has to sell a house first. If you can't wait, don't agree to buy a house regardless of whether your old one is sold first. You can always find another house to buy.

- Try not to have contingencies. A contingency is a condition of sale. Often, home buyers have to sell their homes first before they will have the money to buy another one. So they will buy a home contingent on selling their own home. This is perfectly acceptable, but you run the risk of the deal falling through if the buyer can't sell his own home. One thing you can do is go ahead and accept the contract, but include what is called a "kick-out" clause. This clause states that if you get another contract without a home-sale contingency, the first buyer has 48 hours to sign a firm contract—without a contingency—or the home can be sold to the second buyer.

- Consider getting a back-up contract. Your sale is subject to a buyer getting financing and, in some cases, selling his own home. Meanwhile, your home is off the market. If the deal falls through, you lose weeks of selling time and you have to start over. To protect yourself, you can accept a second contract with the provision that it is valid only if the first contract falls through.

· Check interim financing: If you must purchase a new home before the sale of your old home is completed, you can get a short-term financing arrangement to get most or all of the equity out of your previous home. Generally, you won't have to repay the loan until you get the money from your old house. Of course, you will have to pay interest on the loan. Some realtors offer such arrangements for buyers. Or, if you have sold your home, you can get a temporary "bridge loan" from a lender.

Keeping Track of Your Buyer

After you get a signed contract, the best thing to do is to turn the deal over to your lawyer to arrange the settlement. Settlement, or closing, is simply the time you will get your money from the sale and turn over the deed to your house to the buyer.

But do what you can to speed the final sale. Offer to provide the buyer with a loan application that he can fill out and take to one of the lending institutions that you have checked into. If he wants to arrange his own loan, make sure that he does so within the time stipulated in the contract.

Your lawyer can handle the paperwork for the settlement and work with the title company or title attorney that will handle the actual closing. You should call the title attorney's office a few days before closing to make sure all the papers are ready.

Before you know it, the papers will all be signed and the sale will be completed, and you will have done it yourself. That will give you a good feeling in the pocketbook.

What if your home doesn't sell? Be patient; it often takes months to sell a house, even salable ones. If several weeks go by without many nibbles, you might want to drop the price to attract more buyers. Remember, unless your home is way overpriced, eventually you will sell it.

If selling your home yourself seems a bit too complex to take on, you can turn elsewhere.

Selling Your Home with Some Help—Flat-Fee Agencies

Even if you aren't quite ready to plunge ahead all by yourself, you can still be a FISBO. Around the country, a growing number of a new type of real-estate broker, for a fee, are helping do-it-yourselfers sell their homes.

How do they help sellers?

By advising them on how to price a house; by offering tips on showing it to shoppers; by putting up signs and advertising the sale; and by helping them prepare the sales contract. In short, by doing all the things real-estate agents do other than actually "sitting" in the house and showing it to prospective buyers.

All of these services are lumped together for a flat fee that averages $600 to $800, as opposed to the 6% or 7% commissions of a full-service real-estate broker. On a $50,000 house, the do-it-yourselfers can save as much as $2,200 to $2,900.

The flat-fee system isn't the only bargain rate approach in the real-estate industry. Some brokers have cut commissions to as low as 3% or 4%, and many will negotiate a 1% or 2% discount. But industry-wide, the 6% and 7% fee is standard.

There's nothing new about FISBOs. For years homeowners have been tacking up crudely lettered signs and taking their chances. Sometimes it worked and sometimes it ended in frustration and disappointment. Many sellers are intimidated by the technical maze surrounding property contracts and financing.

What is new is the appearance of a relatively new breed of real-estate specialists to analyze and develop package deals of assistance at a moderate fee. United Services Homeowner Association of Baileys Crossroads, Virginia, is generally considered the pioneer. Now many aggressive real-estate professionals are entering the field, and the idea is mushrooming through franchise operations. A National Association of Real-Estate Service Agencies was organized in 1974 and is growing fast.

Here's how an assisted sale-by-owner works:

The homeowner signs a contract with the service company for a given sales period, usually 90 days to 120 days, but sometimes for as little as 30 days. Some refundable "up front" money usually is required; $75 is typical. In Tucson, Arizona, For Sale By Owners, Inc., has a unique pricing system charging either $300 as an advance, nonrefundable fee, or $110 in advance and an additional $500 after a sale.

The real-estate company helps the owner set an asking price in line with the local market. Then a For-Sale-By-Owner sign goes up in the yard, carrying the agent's name and phone number. The house sometimes is advertised in the local newspaper, and a picture and house description are displayed at the real-estate office.

It is the owner's responsibility to make appointments for showing the house and to negotiate the sale. "A well-maintained and attractive house, which is reasonably priced, should sell within six showings," Virginia Homeowners, Inc., in Springfield, Virginia, tells clients.

Once a buyer is found, the real-estate company gets into the act by providing financial information, writing the sales contract and carrying the deal through closing. If for any reason the owner decides to abandon the do-it-yourself project, many of the assisting companies are equipped to steer the sales through normal commission channels, either in their own offices or with other brokers.

"The average house we handle sells in 57 days," said John McMahon, head of Virginia Homeowners, Inc.

In Houston, the Ron Smiths sold their house at the asking price with an owner-assisted sale. Mrs. Smith attributed it in part to the fact that their house was quite marketable. "If a house is going to be hard to market," she said, "I don't know that I would recommend that owners do it this way."

For information on flat-fee companies in your area, write the National Association of Real-Estate Service Agencies, 6220 Old Keene Mill Ct., Springfield, Va. 22152[17]

Ralph Nader's Housing Research Group has urged the federal government to encourage the use of flat-fee sellers as a way for consumers to save money when they sell their homes. But the Nader group cautions that such concerns should be checked out before you sign up for their services.

Some companies may advertise low fees to sellers in order to sell them other services or to attract them in the first place and then switch to the same company's full-service and full-price real-estate contracts. Check with your local consumer protection agency.

Selling with a Real-Estate Agent

Selling your own home isn't for everyone. "There's nothing magic about selling a house," said Mr. McMahon of Homeowners, Inc. "But some people just don't dare face other people and do business."

Other people just don't have the time or don't go to the trouble of selling their houses themselves. If you are one of them—or if you have tried to sell your house without success—you can hire a professional, a real-estate agent, to do it for you. You won't be alone. After all, 9 out of 10 homes are sold by real-estate agents.

You can still save some money. For example, there are a growing number of discount-brokers who charge differing amounts for different services. For instance, the 4-3-2-1 Realty Company of Fairfax, Virginia, charges 4% for multiple services, 3% for showing a house and bringing in prospects, 2% if you show your own house, and only 1% if you bring in the buyer. But the company pays for the advertising of your home.

Other discount brokers in other areas have different arrangements, so you can check the ones in your town.

The commissions charged by full-service real-estate brokers also are increasingly discounted. One reason is a series of price-fixing suits brought against brokers by the federal government; in 1978, six major companies in the Washington, D.C., area and their presidents were convicted on felony charges of illegally fixing commissions at 7%.

The result is more price competition among real-estate brokers. In the Philadelphia region, for instance, a few brokers openly advertise rates lower than the generally accepted 7%, while others quietly accept reduced fees. Many scale their commissions downward for higher-priced houses, a more common practice. Emlen & Co., a suburban Philadelphia firm that charges 6%, angered real-estate agents by advertising: "If you're paying 7%, you're paying too much."

The fact is that a good real-estate agent can be worth his or her fee. And a real-estate company can offer a seller many advantages. They include:

- Multiple Listing Service. This is a computerized service that provides an immediate contact between most brokers and thousands of real-estate agents. With this service, a picture and description of your home is distributed to just about every real-estate company and every agent in your area. As a result, the number of potential buyers for your home is greatly multiplied.

- Access to buying prospects. Most agencies have lists of potential buyers who are seeking homes. Many companies who transfer employees work through real-estate brokers, who naturally direct the out-of-town clients to homes that are listed with that broker.

- Advertising. Real-estate companies regularly run advertisements of their clients' homes in local newspapers. They write the ads and pay for the advertising.

- Professional sales people. You will sign a contract with a specific agent that you choose. A good agent can be worth his or her weight in gold. Top agents put in long hours, many of them on weekends or at odd hours, tracking down prospective buyers. They know how to deal with buyers and to sell them.

An agent also can act as an important go-between with your buyer in some transactions. "If I let them (the buyer and seller) talk directly to each other, they may cut their throats," said Marika Sumichrast, who is a licensed real-estate agent. "So I have to bounce back and forth. Sometimes I think Carter had an easier job talking to the Israelis and the Arabs than I have talking to buyers."

- Financing arrangements. An agent will help your buyer obtain financing. The agent will arrange several financing packages with different lenders that a potential buyer can use. Many have connections with local lenders and often can come up with financing even when money is tight. By necessity, many have become experts in arranging "creative financing."

· Preparation of paperwork. The agent will handle the paper work from the time the house is sold until the settlement. When a prospect makes an offer, the agent calls you to tell you he has a contract and to arrange a meeting with you to discuss it. If you decide to make a counter-offer, the agent will make it for you—you won't have to talk to the potential buyer.

If you reach agreement on a contract, the agent will keep track of the buyer up to closing to make sure the deal isn't going sour. The agent will handle most of the paperwork connected with the closing.

· Guaranteed sales plan. Some agencies have special plans by which they promise to sell your home or else they will buy it from you. Or they may offer to loan you the down payment for your next home if your old one hasn't sold yet. The advantage to you is that you can avoid the expense of owning two houses simultaneously and being stuck with two mortgage payments—or not having the cash to put down on your next home. The disadvantage can be that the broker will buy your home at a much lower price than if it is sold on the open market.

Some plans offer buyers a fair price if the broker has to buy the home and, thus, can aid a buyer who needs the cash from his old house to move into a new one before his old one is sold. To protect yourself, find out how much you would have to pay for such a transaction.

Lloyd Kuehn, of the 750,000-member National Association of Realtors, sums up the advantages of a realtor this way:

"A Realtor knows the values in the area he is servicing. He will try to get the seller top dollar. In addition, the Realtor has a pre-screened list of prospective buyers, a familiarity with the local mortgage market and housing codes, and all the answers to the questions a prospective buyer might ask. A Realtor also has referrals from other Realtors. The Realtors of this country earn their commissions."

Working with a Real-Estate Agent

Just because you hire an agent to sell your home for you doesn't mean your responsibility ends. It's up to you to get the most out of your agent so that he or she can get the most out of your home.

Here are some points to remember:

- Choose your agent carefully. A good agent is the key to a successful home sale using a real-estate agency. Standards for becoming a real-estate agent are minimal in some states, so you can't take a chance on hiring just anyone. Top agents are dedicated, hard-working professionals who put in long hours finding buyers for their sellers. So make sure you get an agent with a proven track record for sales. Your best bet is to talk to people who have sold homes recently and ask them about agents they dealt with.

Good agents frequently are members of professional associations. Such groups have certain training and ethical standards for members, companies and agents. Realtors and realtor-associates, for instance, are members of the National Association of Realtors. Members of the National Association of Real-Estate Brokers are known as Realtists.

Don't automatically sign with an agent who promises to sell your home at an exceptionally high price. The agent who talks about a realistic price may be a better choice. And for the sake of future relationships, your best friend or relative who is working in real estate may be the wrong person to sell your home.

- Big and small real-estate companies offer different advantages. The big companies usually have more visibility, they usually advertise heavily, and, thus, they may attract more potential buyers than a smaller company. They also have bigger staffs of agents; when they list your home, they can bring in 50 or 100 sales people to look at your home, and they will all be interested in selling it.

Small companies, on the other hand, may give you more personalized service because they have fewer clients. And for the same reason, they may work harder to sell your home. Again, check with friends and others who have sold homes using agents, to find out who gave them good (or bad) service.

· Negotiate a fee. Whatever broker and agent you choose, don't just sign a contract on the dotted line. Contracts are negotiable, especially the commission. The agent may write a 7% commission into the contract, but you may be able to get 6%—if not from that company then from a competitor.

· Know what kind of contract you are signing. There are three basic kinds:

1. Open listing: This means that you simply contact local real-estate companies and tell them that you will pay a commission to any company that brings a buyer "ready, willing and able" to purchase your home. If you find a buyer yourself, you pay no commission.

2. Exclusive agency listing: This means you give a specified agency the exclusive right to sell your home. However, you reserve the right to sell your home yourself—without paying a commission—if you find a buyer.

3. Exclusive right to sell: With this kind of contract you are committed to pay a commission to the agent if your home is sold while the contract is in force. Even if you find a buyer yourself, you still pay a commission. This is the kind of contract that real-estate agencies naturally prefer. If you sign such a contract, be sure to exclude by name any potential buyer you may already be negotiating with.

· Don't lock yourself into too long a contract. Most listings are for anywhere from 30 days to 120 days. Give your agent time to sell your home—at least 60 days but usually not more than 90 days initially, so that you can switch agencies without a hassle should you decide things aren't working out.

· Make sure your contract is for multiple listing. As we explained, this means that your home will be flashed over a computerized system to other brokers in the area. Thus, your potential audience of buyers will be greatly expanded.

- Be sure you ask a reasonable price. Your agent will help you set a price on your home, but the final decision is still up to you. Listen to your agent's suggestions, because he or she should have good information on what prices comparable homes are selling for in your area. But agents can be wrong. In some areas where prices are rising rapidly, they can underestimate the market. You still may want to consider getting an independent appraisal.

- Make sure your home is being marketed aggressively. Check to see if the broker is running advertisements for your home in the local newspapers. Your agent should bring a steady stream of potential buyers to your home. Agents from other companies should call frequently, too. Your agent should work with other agents even though he would have to split his commission if the competing agent came up with a buyer. Cooperate with your agent. If people phone or stop by and ask to see your home, politely ask them to contact your agent.

- Make sure your agent holds frequent open houses. A good agent is willing to "sit" with your house and hold it open for prospective buyers to inspect. But again, you have to do your part. Get your home in tiptop shape. On the days of the open house, either leave or stay in the background. Let your agent talk to prospects and do the sales work that you hired him or her to do.

- Get the contract you want. Listen to your agent's advice on whether an offer is a "good" contract or not. But don't accept an offer only because your agent wants you to. Remember, it's your home and it's up to you to decide what price you will accept. If the offer isn't high enough, have your agent take a counter-offer to the potential buyer.

If the agent encourages you to accept a lower price in order to sell your home, urge the agent to accept a lower commission if you agree to do so. Also, make sure that you set a limit on how many "points" you will pay if you sell VA or FHA.

- Make sure your agent follows the sale through completion. A good agent keeps tabs on the buyer to make

sure his financing is arranged and that no last-minute
hitches develop. He or she also checks the house
before settlement. "You don't want the buyer coming to
the settlement with a list as long as your arm of things
wrong with the house," said Marika Sumichrast. "If
there is such a list, it should be taken care of before
settlement so there are no last-minute surprises," she
said.

· Don't be afraid to switch agencies if you aren't satisfied.
Benny Kass, a Washington, D.C., lawyer, stresses that
you can cancel a contract at any time if the agency
hasn't produced a prospect "ready, willing and able to
buy" as required by the contract.

If your contract expires without your home being sold,
think twice before signing up again with the same company.
If you feel your agent has been doing a good job and only
needs more time, go ahead and give the agent another
chance. But sometimes it's better to get a fresh start with a
new agency with a new burst of enthusiasm about selling
your home. The choice is yours.

· Finally, be patient and don't get discouraged. Sometimes even a good agent will need a few months to sell
a good home. Indeed, your patience may pay off in a
better price.

After all, most places aren't like Beverly Hills, California,
where knowledgeable brokers can peddle a home almost
overnight simply because it once was owned by a movie star.
Brokers refer to certain houses as "The Sonny and Cher
House" or "The Paul Newman House" long after the stars
have left them. As one observer there put it: "If you could
hire Charlton Heston for six weeks and have him live in six
different houses, you'd have a whole series of quick sales."

TWELVE

Where Will Our Children Live? The Future of Housing

"The first law of forecasting is
that forecasting is very difficult—
especially if it is about the future."

—Edgar Fiedler,
Conference Board Vice-President

Today my wife Marika and I live in a home we could only dream of when we hit New York City, penniless, on a cold morning in March of 1953. When I look around and see young people in their twenties looking at—and buying— houses that cost over $100,000, I can see that what we dreamed about, young people today expect.

One reason that the dream home of tomorrow will be harder to obtain is that the dream has grown. The millions of GIs returning home from World War II stood in line for a chance to buy a Levitt subdivision house—three bedrooms and one bath—for $8,500, take it or leave it. Today young people want much more—even to start with.

I tell my three sons that for what they expect they will have to work as hard as, or harder than, we did. The prices of homes will go up. I am convinced they will have to hustle to keep up with all of the things they now take for granted.

For that reason, we insisted that the age of 18 is a ripe age to buy a house. Of course, you can't expect an 18-year-old to have enough money or a good-enough job to qualify for a mortgage. But we will help them buy a small, starter house. By the time they are in their mid-twenties, they will have acquired a nice chunk of equity to help them start moving up the housing ladder.

—Mike Sumichrast

To many homeowners—and especially home buyers—today's spiraling home prices are unbelievable. "Can prices possibly continue to rise?" they ask.

The answer, according to most experts, is that they can and they will. Barring such cataclysmic developments as a depression or a war—or an end to inflation—here is the outlook:

- The rapid rise in housing prices will slow in the early 1980s and then pick up steam again, increasing steadily through the rest of the decade.

- The median price of a new home could reach $164,600 nationwide sometime in the mid-1980's, up from $63,750 in 1980. The median price of existing homes also could reach $100,000 by the mid-1980s, up from the 1980 median price of $62,000.

- Mortgage rates will stay high, between 10% to 15% for most of the decade. But rates may dip below 10% once more late in the 1980s when housing sales are expected to reach record highs.

- New housing starts will average close to 2 million units per year, a feat never before accomplished. In the 1980s, a record 19.3 million new homes are expected to be built in the U.S., up 10% from 17.6 million in the 1970s. Of the 1980s total, a record 14.8 million, or 77%, will be family houses. Production of condominiums and townhouses also will increase sharply.

- Sales of existing homes will rise to record levels in the 1980s. By 1989, annual sales will hit 7.2 million, nearly double the record 3.8 million sales of 1979.

The Facts behind the Figures

The basic factors that sent home prices soaring in the 1970s will accelerate in the 1980s. It clearly will be a decade of homeownership, for the following reasons:

- Booming demand: The millions of people who were born in the post–World War II baby boom are coming of home-buying age. They will continue to buy homes as they upgrade their living standards. Thus, they can be expected to boost housing demand until well into the 1990s.

Other demographic factors will fuel the demand as well. One of the most important findings of housing researchers is that the U.S. Bureau of Census grossly underestimated the number of new households that are going to be formed through the 1980s, because they underestimated the number of single individuals who will be forming households.

All of a sudden we have discovered there are a bunch of single individuals acting as households, and, as we have shown, more and more of them are buying homes. This swelling singles group includes young people who increasingly are marrying at an older age, divorced people, and widowed persons. And a new blip is turning up on the household radar screen—single people of opposite sexes who are living together, a group lenders have dubbed with the contradictory name of "single-couples."

The traditional husband-wife type of household accounted for less than 30% of the increase in households between 1970 and 1975; other families and individuals accounted for the balance. In the past, it always was the other way around—married couples accounted for the increase in households.

- The attitude that housing is an investment: The gradual transformation of homeownership from a predominately shelter concept to one of investment due to escalating real-estate values adds to housing demands. So does the need to obtain tax shelters as inflation drives up incomes. Compared to renting, especially during times of high inflation, owning will look increasingly advantageous.

- Disappearing lending taboos: It is becoming easier for minorities, women, and single persons to qualify for mortgage credit. Past lending barriers are coming down, and this widens the market base. Another factor is that lenders are taking a more liberal view of a spouse's income in calculating the earning power of home buyers.

- New kinds of mortgages: Innovative mortgage instruments, such as graduated-payment mortgages, also broaden the home-buying base by reducing initial payments.
- Wider homeownership choices: The condominium concept spreads the appeal of homeownership to traditional rental circles. Condominiums, townhouses and cooperatives are especially appealing to the young and older households, the mainstay of the rental market. They permit owners to reap the benefits of home ownership without being overcome with ownership chores.

The Baby-Boom Buyers

What all this means to you is that in the coming years there will be much greater demand for housing than ever before. And that demand will help to push up prices. So the sooner you can buy the better off you'll be. The reasons are explained in further detail in the following article by William M. Bulkeley in The Wall Street Journal.

You want to buy a house, but you're holding off until the crazy price spiral abates? Maybe you'd better buy now, anyway.

One big reason: it's the housing industry's turn to be swept along on the crest of one of the major demographic waves in U.S. history—the maturing of the so-called giant generation resulting from the record number of people born during the 1947-57 baby boom. Currently pouring into the housing market in burgeoning numbers, they already are buying so many houses that they are helping keep home prices high. Moreover, economists see this pressure increasing further in years ahead.

The progression of this huge population bulge through American life is like "a watermelon passing through a boa constrictor," writes William Alonso, a demographer at Harvard University's Center for Population Studies.

Now the big part of the bulge is between 20 and 30 years of age, the usual period of household formation, and it is beginning to dominate a housing market. The baby-boom generation is credited by economists and lenders with a major role in record sales and rising prices of new and used houses. Another development: members of the giant generation who are singles or childless couples are moving into cities, where their purchases and rehabilitation of block after block of deteriorating housing are raising some officials' hopes for an urban resurgence.

Behind these developments lie some impressive figures. Stuart Davis, chairman of Great Western Savings and Loan Association, the huge S&L based in Beverly Hills, California, cites the numbers of Americans reaching the age of 30. By the end of this decade, he says, 32 million Americans will have hit that milestone, up a whopping 39% from the total during the '60s. And during the '80s, about 42 million will reach 30. So he sees no significant drop in housing demand until the '90s, when the "baby bust" generation of the '60s enters the market.

"For the housing industry, the demographic factors are the most positive they've been in a long time," said Dwight M. Jaffee, a Princeton University economics professor who studies housing trends. He expects an average of slightly more than two million housing starts a year over the next 10 years compared with an average of about 1.7 million over the past 10. "The industry is ratcheted up a whole notch," he said. "The 1980s are going to be glorious."

Kenneth Rosen, assistant professor of economics and public affairs at Princeton, estimated that current housing demand is running 25% above that of the 1960s. Professor Rosen said even high interest rates aren't likely "to kill this boom because it's demographically based."

If anything, the giant generation's impact on the housing market is even greater than its sheer weight of numbers would indicate. That's because it isn't behaving as past generations did.

Its members don't get married as early and get divorced more often. Consequently, a disproportionate number live alone; today, Americans living alone total more than 15.5 million and account for 21% of the nation's households, up from 17% in 1970. As a further result, the giant generation occupies an outsized number of housing units. Between 1970 and 1976, when the U.S. population was rising 5%, the number of households surged 15%; analysts attribute the gain largely to the giant generation's departure from campuses and their parents' homes into places of their own.

Its members also differ from their elders in their eagerness—and ability—to buy homes early in life rather than rent them. For many young people, the economics of home ownership are compelling.

For example, Stephen Burakoff, a 25-year-old computer expert who works in the electronics industry near Boston, in 1978 decided to buy half of a 110-year-old townhouse in the city's historic South End. Mr. Burakoff discovered that between income from a rental unit in the building and a tax reduction because of increased deductions, his monthly housing cost will drop to $325 from $625.

Another big reason people are still able to buy houses despite steep prices is the increasing number of families with more than one income. Moreover, families with extra income are putting it into housing rather than other items. Although most lenders used to advise spending no more than 25% of pre-tax family income on housing, they have inched up their guidelines in recent years.

Rising prices, ironically, are strengthening demand. Houses are among the few investments that have outstripped the general inflation rate, and the housing market has been bolstered by it in a kind of self-fulfilling prophecy. "Like it or not, every homeowner is a speculator," said Robert Rugo, a Boston Housing Department official.[18]

Inflation and Housing

Another factor in the housing market of tomorrow will continue to be inflation. There is little chance that the rate of inflation will drop to the 1% and 2% annual rises we had during the Truman and Eisenhower administrations. But inflation should tail off from the double-digit rates of 1979 and 1980 to as low as a 5.2% annual rate towards the end of the 1980s.

The cost of building a home is inevitably going to go up—probably to about $82 a square foot by 1990 from $42 in 1981—because all the materials that go into its construction will cost more. In fact, some home-building costs are likely to increase more than the overall inflation rate. For one reason, many of the materials used to build houses require great amounts of energy to produce, and energy costs are certain to climb sharply. In addition, local governments are constantly adding requirements that make new homes more expensive. Environmental requirements will continue to push up the prices of land, and so will efforts to curb growth in some areas. Since they aren't making any more land, land costs will continue to climb anyway.

Inflation will boost the prices of existing homes as well. And if local requirements limit new construction in some areas, that will limit the supply of homes in those areas at a time when demand is booming, thus pushing up prices for existing homes. In any case, prices of used homes in prime locations will shoot up faster than new-home prices.

Of course, we all would be better off if both inflation and home prices didn't keep going up so much so fast. Inflation, by eroding the value of our money, is a great danger to our standard of living and to our economic system. If the U.S. should succeed in slowing inflation, then income and prices should rise more slowly, including housing prices. But this is all relative. The relation between income and home prices would be about the same as it is today. What would happen would be that we would have a great deal more stability, and we would be better able to figure out what's coming than we can today.

While year-to-year price changes vary, the outlook is that home prices, on average, will continue to go up faster than the rate of inflation during most of the 1980s.

The Question of Affordability

A key factor in the housing equation, of course, is whether consumers can afford to buy increasingly costly homes. If prices and mortgage rates get out of reach for large numbers of buyers, then demand could slacken and prices would either rise at a slower pace or even drop. That could happen in some places, but don't count on it. Despite the soaring prices and record mortgage rates in the 1970s, home sales were higher than ever. That is likely to continue in the 1980s.

How can that be? For one reason, two-thirds of U.S. households already own a home, and they can use the profits from one home to buy another. In addition, average family incomes will continue to increase in the 1980s, probably at a slightly faster pace than the rate of inflation. There will continue to be more two-income families who can afford to make their housing dreams come true. And those baby-boom children reaching the prime home-buying age will be upwardly mobile. They can expect their incomes to rise and, with the trend toward smaller families, they will be able to spend more for housing.

While it is of little consolation to today's home buyers, incomes generally have nearly kept pace with rising home prices. Back in 1960 the median new-home price was only $16,650. But the median family income was only $5,620. By 1979, the median new-home price had jumped 278% to $62,900, the median income had gone up 250% to $19,587. Similar ratios hold true for existing homes.

In relation to income, home prices are slightly more costly than in 1960 and far cheaper than before 1940. Consider the following table:

New-Home Prices and Income

Year	Median Price	Median Family Income	Price-to-Income Ratio
1900	$ 4,881	$ 490	9.9
1940	6,588	1,300	5.0
1960	16,652	5,620	2.9
1979	62,900	19,684	3.2

Sources: National Association of Home Builders and U.S. Census Bureau

If incomes continue to rise as expected, this will be enough to make housing at projected prices attractive. But rising homeownership costs, mortgage rates, energy costs and other expenses will squeeze family budgets even more in the 1980s. The question is whether people's disposable income—what is left after taxes—will be sufficient to offset these sharp increases. Even if we assume that gross incomes will be able to keep up with the prices of goods and services, the more fundamental question is whether "real" incomes, adjusted for inflation, will.

For the U.S., the 1980s will be a decade of austere reexamination of many of the values and needs of a maturing industrial society. This will be the result of several major factors: One is the lack of long-term capital investment in the past 20 years to rejuvenate our productive industrial capacity;

the second is the need to redirect our national resources to alternative energy programs.

Gasoline costs are expected to rise to $3 to $4 a gallon. At such levels, we will clearly have a sacrifice many things that we now take for granted and shift our resources to pay for heating, cooling, electricity and transportation.

That re-assessment will include home buying. Yet despite difficulties, especially for first-time buyers, the outlook for homeownership in the U.S. remains bright.

The Housing Crystal Ball

Looking into the housing crystal ball, here is how the future of housing looks:

- Homeownership will continue to increase. The authors strongly believe that the desire to own a home will not fade. By 1990, about 69% of all U.S. households will own their homes, up from about 65% in 1980.

- Single-family houses will continue to appreciate in value at a faster clip than other types of housing. It is quite possible that current spread between the prices of new and existing homes will narrow in some areas—currently, existing homes are, on average, about 20% cheaper than new homes. But if construction is restrained by cost, environmental or political reasons, used-home prices will move closer to new-home prices.

- Tomorrow's houses won't be much different from today's in materials and styling. They will probably be slightly smaller; we have about reached the peak size for median living area. With the trend to smaller families, more space won't be needed.

- Homes located close to major cities will be in growing demand because of the increasing costs for fuel and energy for transportation, plus the desire to live close to work and urban entertainment.

- Condominiums and townhouses will become an increasingly important part of the housing market. They will provide an affordable housing alternative for many of the surging numbers of young people entering the housing market. They also will benefit from a move to denser housing to save energy. Production is projected to add 175,000 to 200,000 units annually in the 1980s, of which about 35% will be conversions from rental units.

· Mobile homes will grow in popularity. By the late 1980s annual production should be rolling at around 350,000 units. The main attraction, of course, will be low prices. The trend toward price appreciation on used mobile homes is expected to continue in the 1980s— making mobile homes more attractive to more people.

· Privately-built rental apartments will continue to face major problems, ranging from a lack of economic feasibility—rents aren't high enough to attract builders—to stormy landlord-tenant relations. Consequently, they will decline in actual numbers, apartments will become scarcer, and rents will go up more sharply than they did in the 1970s.

Renting will become more and more expensive as the decade advances, and the advantages of homeownership— even without considering the tax benefits—will increase. This will create a serious national problem. It also will raise the question of fairness of the tax benefits for one type of housing accommodation compared with those for other types.

· Older people will become an ever-increasing force in the housing market in the United States. Nearly 25 million people, or 11.2% of the population, are over age 65, up from 20 million, or 9.8%, at the start of the 1970s. During the 1980s, this army of older people will increase another 20% to nearly 30 million, or 12.2% of the population. They will demand new types of housing that are smaller in size to fit their needs and smaller in price to fit their pocketbooks. These needs will be discussed by the authors of this book in a forthcoming book, to be published by Dow Jones-Irwin.

· The financing of homes will be expanded to include more types of mortgages and sources of money. A variety of mortgage instruments with changeable interest rates and geared to different types of buyers will compete with the traditional fixed-rate mortgage. The traditional thrift institutions alone won't be able to supply the large increases that will be needed in mortgage money, and a bigger share of such financing funds will come from life insurance, pension, and retirement funds.

Where Our Children Will Live

Basically, our children will live in the same kinds of houses we live in. But they may have to start more modestly than many of them expect. One reason young people feel housing is being priced out of their reach is because they don't want the smaller and simpler houses that their parents bought at a comparable age, according to Anthony Downs of the Brookings Institution in Washington, D.C.

With ever-rising home prices, though, it will be harder for our children to get started on the road to home ownership. They will have to start with smaller homes than they probably expected to, and they doubtless will have to pay considerably more of their income than their parents do. They may continue to pay more as they trade up. For example, they may have to buy houses priced at three times their incomes instead of the old rule of thumb of 2½ times. Whatever rule of thumb is used, tomorrow's buyers will probably have to put a bigger share of income into housing than today's homeowner. Just how they get started will depend to an increasing extent on how much help their parents can give them.

· The children of more affluent families will move out of the family home and buy a townhouse, condominium apartment or a single-family house. Their parents will help them get started—just as they pay for clothes, braces for their teeth and college. More and more, it will be up to mom and dad to come up with that first down payment.

· The children of the less affluent will live at home longer or try to find rental units. They will have to work hard to scrape up the money for a down payment on a first, modest home. In the future, a house may well stay "in the family," being passed from generation to generation, more than is the case now.

· Lower-income families will have to depend on government housing—especially for rental units. Home own-

ership will be a difficult dream to realize. Their best
hope may be new government programs designed to
help poor and lower-middle-income people buy their
own homes. By making the first step to home ownership possible, this would be a positive type of government aid that could pay off for everybody in the long
run.

· Most of our children probably will do what their parents did—work hard and save enough to buy a small
home. They will live in the home for a while and fix it
up. Then they will sell it and move up to a better
home. Somehow, they will find a way—just as their
parents did—to climb up the ever-extending housing
ladder until their dream is fulfilled.

Footnotes

1. Robert L. Simison, "Building Up," *The Wall Street Journal*, May 24, 1977
2. G. Christian Hill, "Keeping the Lid On," *The Wall Street Journal*, Feb. 8, 1978
3. Donald Moffitt, "Your Money Matters," *The Wall Street Journal*, Sept. 26, 1977
4. G. Christian Hill, "Boom in the West," *The Wall Street Journal*, Sept. 27, 1976
5. Laurel Leff, "To Live Near the Stars," *The Wall Street Journal*, Sept. 22, 1977
6. Richard Immel, "Bursting Bubble," *The Wall Street Journal*, June 2, 1977
7. Liz Roman Gallese, "Suburban Quest," *The Wall Street Journal*, June 14, 1978
8. June Kronholz, "On Their Own," *The Wall Street Journal*, Nov. 16, 1977
9. Robert L. Simison, "Out in the Cold," *The Wall Street Journal*, Dec. 10, 1975
10. Laurel Leff, "To Live Near the Stars," *The Wall Street Journal*, Sept. 22, 1977
11. Robert L. Simison, "Building Up," *The Wall Street Journal*, May 24, 1977
12. Robert L. Simison, "Do-It-Yourselfers," *The Wall Street Journal*, Sept. 1, 1976
13. Richard James, "Rustic Revival," *The Wall Street Journal*, July 1, 1977
14. Frederick C. Klein, "Rebuilding Blocks," *The Wall Street Journal*, 1977
15. Marilyn Chase, "Creative Loans," *The Wall Street Journal*, May 1, 1980
16. Donald Moffitt, "Your Money Matters," *The Wall Street Journal*, May 15, 1978
17. Peter Keresztes, "Your Money Matters," *The Wall Street Journal*, Jan. 23, 1978

18. Ronald G. Shafer, "The Pool Peddlers," *The Wall Street Journal*, 1972
19. Paul Hood, "Your Sale," *The National Observer*, March 12, 1977
20. William M. Bulkeley, "Raising the Roof," *The Wall Street Journal*, July 27, 1978

Index

351

ABOUT THE AUTHORS

DR. MICHAEL SUMICHRAST is Chief Economist and Staff Vice President of the National Association of Home Builders in Washington, D.C. He is a widely-quoted, international authority on housing and a frequent advisor on housing issues to the U.S. Government. He holds an M.B.A. and Ph.D. from Ohio State University and has worked in various capacities for home builders in the U.S. and abroad. Dr. Sumichrast wrote a weekly housing column for the Washington Post for five years and since 1976 has written a syndicated newspaper column on housing for the *Washington Star*. He is the author of numerous housing books, such as: *Housing Markets: The Complete Guide to Analysis and Strategy for Builders, Lenders and Other Investors,* published by Dow Jones-Irwin in 1977; *Profile of the Builder and His Industry,* published by the National Housing Center Council in 1979; *Opportunities in Building Construction,* published by Universal Publishing and Distributing Corporation, in 1971 and 1976; plus various studies on housing and construction. Dr. Sumichrast lives in Potomac, Maryland with his wife, Marika, and their three children.

RONALD G. SHAFER is a features editor in the Washington bureau of *The Wall Street Journal*. As a *Journal* staff reporter since 1963 in Chicago, Detroit and Washington, he has specialized in such subjects as consumer protection and housing. He is a graduate of Ohio State University. Mr. Shafer is the co-author of *How to Get Your Car Repaired Without Getting Gypped,* published by Harper & Row, and has edited such publications as *Urban Dynamics* published by Dow Jones Books in 1976 and *The Adoption Advisor.* Ron lives in a heavily mortgaged home in McLean, VA with his wife, Barbara, and their two children, Ryan and Kathryn.

MAKE MONEY!   SAVE MONEY!

These four valuable Bantam Books can help.

THE COMING CURRENCY COLLAPSE
by Jerome F. Smith

At last in paperback, the national bestseller by Jerome Smith, a man regarded by many as the world's premier investment forecaster. Jerome Smith has amassed an astounding track record that is unique in his field—all of his recommendations have been profitable! Now he gives specific capital survival advice—including the three primary ground rules of investing during runaway inflation, the eight tests of an investment's suitability under hyperinflation and the seven critical rules for timing investments in the '80s. (#20296-0 • $3.95)

WEALTH AND POVERTY
by George Gilder

William F. Buckley calls it "as important as Galbraith's *THE AFFLUENT SOCIETY*, the only difference being that Mr. Gilder's book points us in the right direction." It's the book the President gives to senators—the brilliant and provocative bestseller that's shaping American economic policy by the controversial man who, like the President, believes in risk-taking and tax-cutting. "At once a defense and celebration of capitalism and capitalists. Its call for liberty and free men smacks of the spirit of '76."—*Barrons* (#20483-1 • $3.95)

<u>SAVE $2.00</u> ON YOUR NEXT BOOK ORDER!

BANTAM BOOKS 🐓
Shop-at-Home
Catalog

Now you can have a complete, up-to-date catalog of Bantam's inventory of over 1,600 titles—including hard-to-find books.

And, you can <u>save $2.00</u> on your next order by taking advantage of the money-saving coupon you'll find in this illustrated catalog. Choose from fiction and non-fiction titles, including mysteries, historical novels, westerns, cookbooks, romances, biographies, family living, health, and more. You'll find a description of most titles. Arranged by categories, the catalog makes it easy to find your favorite books and authors and to discover new ones.

So don't delay—send for this shop-at-home catalog and save money on your next book order.

Just send us your name and address and 50¢ to defray postage and handling costs.